The Daily Telegraph

CASTLES & ANCIENT MONUMENTS

OF SCOTLAND

The Daily Telegraph

CASTLES
& ANCIENT
MONUMENTS
OF SCOTLAND

BY DAMIEN NOONAN

WELCOME RAIN PUBLISHERS
NEW YORK

Contents

Southern Scotland

44   Edinburgh, the Lothians & Borders

60   Dumfries & Galloway

70   Glasgow and around
including Lanarkshire & Ayrshire

80   Central Scotland
including Stirling, Clackmannanshire and Fife

Northern and western Scotland

92   Argyll & Bute
including Arran and Mull

114   Skye & The Western Isles
including Lewis, Harris and North Uist

122   Highland
including Inverness and Nairn

North-eastern Scotland

134   Grampian
including Bannfshire and Aberdeenshire

152   Tayside
including Perth & Kinross, and Angus

The Northern Isles

168   Orkney
Featuring the islands of Rousay, Westray and Hoy

182   Shetland

Index and bibliography 188

Features

50   Edinburgh
52   Hillforts of the Border region
76   The Antonine Wall
95   Cup-and-ring carvings
100 The Kilmartin valley
104 Arran
108 Mull
110 Iona

111 The isle of Bute
128 The Glenelg brochs
130 Neolithic Caithness
143 Pictish carvings in Grampian
150 Recumbent stone circles
154 Earth houses of Angus
161 Pictish carvings in Tayside
166 The Romans in Tayside

Introduction

11 Neolithic houses
12 Chambered tombs
13 Stone circles
14 Brochs
16 The dun
17 Souterrains & wheelhouses
18 The crannog
19 Norse settlements

History

20 Beginnings
22 Norman & Viking Scotland
26 William Wallace
30 Robert the Bruce
34 The Stewart kings
36 Mary Queen of Scots
39 James VI and I
40 Bonnie Prince Charlie

SHETLAND

ORKNEY

SKYE & THE WESTERN ISLES

HIGHLAND

GRAMPIAN

TAYSIDE

ARGYLL

CENTRAL

GLASGOW
AND
AROUND

LOTHIAN
& BORDERS

DUMFRIES &
GALLOWAY

0 Miles   50

0 Kilometres   80

Key map to the regions of Scotland

Ownership

There are several reasons why it's useful to know who owns or operates a property. Sites in the care of the official state body, Historic Scotland are likely to be well signposted, tend to have better opening hours, and are generally good value. Incidentally, places listed in the book as Historic Scotland properties are not necessarily owned by the state: in many cases, they are simply in state care. Sites owned by local councils also give excellent value for money, while those operated by the National Trust for Scotland tend to have more eccentric opening hours. Privately owned sites can tend to be a little more expensive and are sometimes not so well presented, but they are often run by a charitable trust, so don't imagine that your entry fees are just filling the coffers of some wealthy laird.

Membership: becoming a Friend of Historic Scotland will give you free entry to all the properties run by the organisation. Similarly, members of the National Trust for Scotland get free entry to the Trust's sites. Also, by reciprocal arrangement, members of English Heritage and the Welsh heritage organisation Cadw get free entry to all Historic Scotland sites in their second year of membership (half price in the first year); and members of the English National Trust are given free admission to all properties run by the National Trust for Scotland.

Prices

Prices are changed quite frequently, so any attempt to state them exactly would simply mean that this book was quickly out of date. Instead, we have employed a simple system of pound signs (£) to indicate roughly how cheap or expensive a place is to visit.

£ – Very cheap (a pound or less)
££ – Good value
£££ – Rather expensive
££££ – Very expensive

Sites rated as ££££ are few and far between, but they are ones where the price would make you think twice about going.

Opening hours

Unfortunately, it's not practical to give the full opening hours of each property; they change so often that the book would be out of date before it was even printed, and some places have quite complicated dates and times of opening. Instead, we've simplified it by using a brief phrase to sum up access arrangements. Be warned, though, that if you want to be quite certain that a property is open on the day and at the time you are visiting, you must telephone in advance to confirm the hours. Historic Scotland's offices in Glasgow can tell you about any of their properties; otherwise, phone the property itself or the local tourist office. Opening hours are described in this book using the following phrases:

'Open access at any reasonable time' – Means that a monument stands in a field or similar open setting, so you can see it whenever you like, provided that you do not disturb anyone who lives nearby.

'Open access at reasonable times only' – The distinction shows that there are houses very close to the monument and people are particularly likely to be disturbed if you visit at a strange time.

'Usual hours' – Means that a property is open roughly during usual shop hours, including weekends. Historic Scotland's standard hours are excellent: 9.30 am to 6.30 pm seven days a week, in summer (most close earlier in winter).

'Summer only' – Many properties have good opening hours in the summer months but are closed in winter, and I have tried to indicate this by adding short notes, such as 'summer only'. Broadly speaking, all privately owned houses and most of the National Trust for Scotland's properties are open from the beginning of May to the end of September, but there are numerous variations: many places are open at Easter, for example, or at weekends in October.

'Slightly limited hours' – Watch out for minor inconveniences, like the place being closed on Sunday mornings. I've tried to indicate what the limitations are.
'Limited hours' – Not open every day of the week (perhaps just at weekends) or only open in the afternoon, for example. Again, I have tried to give an idea of the limitations.

Directions

Generally, I would hope that a road atlas and this book should get you there. In any situation where signposts can't be relied on, I have tried to give accurate directions from personal experience, but if you do come across a situation where you find these directions difficult to follow, I would be very grateful if you could let me know by writing care of the publisher.

Please note
I have done everything I can to ensure that the details given are correct at the time of going to press, but I'm afraid that we cannot accept responsibility for any loss or inconvenience caused by errors. Access to private land in particular can change, and it is not to be assumed that rights of way or rights of access exist.

Introduction, part one

Scotland's archeology

Above: the Ring of Brodgar, on the Mainland of Orkney, was a later addition to a remarkable neolithic ceremonial complex which included the great chambered tomb of Maes Howe and the Stones of Stenness.

THE STORY OF SCOTLAND BEGINS with the end of the last ice age, roughly 10,000 years ago. As the sheets of ice retreated from the Scottish hills and the climate warmed up, mesolithic people (that is, folk of the middle stone age) moved in along the coasts and river valleys where food was plentiful.

These people were hunter-gatherers, living a nomadic lifestyle in tune with the natural resources on offer throughout the changing seasons. They were equipped with spears and arrows tipped with razor-sharp fragments of flint known as 'microliths', as well as with tools like stone axes and implements of wood and leather. The only signs of their presence that remain visible today are piles of sea-shells known as 'middens', which are found on the shores of islands like Rum, Jura, Islay, Colonsay and Oronsay.

The hunter-gatherers were planting crops and shepherding herds of wild animals even before they started to settle down and farm the land, but by about 4000 BC the farming lifestyle was taking over in northern Scotland just as in the rest of Britain. The climate then was on average two or three degrees warmer than it is now, so that marginal environments such as the islands of the north were then ideal places to grow crops as well as offering a wealth of other natural resources (particularly fish and birds).

In telling the story of prehistoric Scotland from neolithic times onwards, this introductory chapter will concentrate on features and monuments that are special to Scotland.

Neolithic houses

The lack of wood from which to build must have been a great inconvenience for the neolithic people of Orkney, but it has turned out to be an extraordinary stroke of good luck for the modern archeologist, since it meant that houses were instead built from stone and have survived in remarkably good condition.

The most northerly natural woodland in Britain is a sad, straggly little collection of stunted trees sheltering between two of the highest mountains on the Orkney island of Hoy. No use to anyone. However, all round the shores of Orkney are ready sources of a kind of stone that splits easily into flat slabs, making it ideal for building with.

The result is that at *Skara Brae* on the Mainland of Orkney, buried under sand-dunes and exposed during a storm in 1850, there survived a village of eight houses built in about 2600 BC in which even the furniture – box beds, cupboards and dressers – was made of stone and has, therefore, survived. In one case, a pot still stood, intact, on the top shelf of a dresser: pottery was one of the crucial innovations of the neolithic period.

Even older – dating from about 3500 BC and said to be the oldest dwellings in north-west Europe – is a pair of houses at *Knap of Howar* on the tiny Orkney island of Papa Westray, which were also buried under sand dunes.

Again, the houses were furnished with cupboards and shelves of stone. In one house is a quernstone which was used for grinding grain, and traces of cultivated barley and wheat were found. Tools of flint, stone and bone were also dug up, and on the rubbish pile (the midden) were the bones of domesticated cattle, sheep and pigs as well as wild deer, fish and birds.

The ones to see…

Skara Brae, *Orkney (page 174)*

Knap of Howar, *Orkney (page 180)*

Above: the interior of one of the two neolithic houses at Knap of Howar, which are the oldest known dwellings in north-west Europe, dating from about 3500 BC. At the near end of the house, on the left, is a quernstone, which was used to grind grain.

Left: the neolithic village of Skara Brae consists of about eight closely packed houses linked together by low, roofed passageways. This house, at one end of the village, had lots of stone chips on its floor and is thought to have been a communal workshop in which stone tools were made.

Above: the extraordinary neolithic chambered tomb of Maes Howe is one of the finest ancient monuments in Britain, remarkable for the quality of its design and the immense care that has been put into its construction.

Below: the round cairn at Camster is one of the most enjoyable of Scotland's tombs to explore, and the neighbouring long cairn is just as interesting.

Neolithic chambered tombs

In use from about 3000 BC for more than a thousand years, chambered tombs are not a specifically Scottish phenomenon; but northern Scotland has some of the most spectacular examples in Britain. The fact that many of them are in remote areas has meant that their contents are often relatively undisturbed, and modern archeological techniques can find out masses of detailed information about them. In Orkney, previously unknown tombs are still being discovered and excavated.

It seems that chambered tombs were like the cathedrals of their age, in that they were used for rituals as well as for burials: in many cases there is evidence of fires being lit in front of or inside the tomb. It is possible that only certain prestigious individuals were buried in the tombs, since not enough bones are found to represent the whole population of an area for all the centuries that a tomb was in use, but it's hard to be certain: not all of an individual's bones were necessarily taken into a tomb in the first place, and bones were often sorted into types (skulls in one compartment of a tomb, thigh bones in another) and generally shuffled around.

Several interesting ideas have emerged from studies of the many tombs of Orkney. One is that, along with the human bones, some of the tombs on the Mainland of Orkney had a very obvious concentration of the bones of a particular kind of creature: sea eagles at one, dogs at another, red deer at a third. It has been suggested that each tomb belonged to a different tribe, each with its own totemic animal.

Another interesting observation is that tombs on the Orkney island of Rousay are positioned close to the modern farms, and it has been suggested that each tomb might have belonged to a community with its own patch of good farming land.

The ones to see...

Cuween Hill, *Orkney (page 171)*

Maes Howe, *Orkney (page 172)*

Grey Cairns of Camster, *Highland (page 130)*

Cairn Holy, *Dumfries (page 62)*

The tombs of Rousay, *Orkney (page 178)*

Stone circles

These dramatic monuments are still not well understood, and it's likely that there is a lot more to be discovered about them. In the meantime, they are difficult places to make sense of, but easy places to enjoy and appreciate.

Something that is particularly evident in Scotland's stone circles is a powerful sense of a relationship between the monument and the landscape in which it stands, which gives sites like *Machrie Moor* on *Arran* a special appeal.

It is generally accepted that stone circles were probably meeting places or ceremonial centres, and the first ones were built well before 3000 BC. The earliest feature in many, which may have been more important than the stone circle itself, is a circular enclosure defined by a bank and a ditch, known as a henge. The amount of work needed to build stone circles (just digging the ditch for the *Ring of Brodgar* in *Orkney* would have taken 80,000 man-hours) suggests that a massive communal effort was involved.

Astronomical alignments are much talked about in relation to stone circles, but are seldom very convincing. The largest circle in Scotland, the *Ring of Brodgar* in *Orkney*, is part of an atmospheric ceremonial complex that includes the great tomb of Maes Howe, which is clearly aligned towards the midwinter sunset; and it is often suggested that earlier stone circles share this interest in the sun, whereas later ones are aligned in relation to the moon.

Above: although only a few of the Stones of Stenness are still standing, their interesting shapes make this a very appealing little monument.

The ones to see...

The Ring of Brodgar and Stones of Stenness, *Orkney* (page 173)

Callanish, *Lewis* (page 118)

Machrie Moor, *Arran* (page 106)

Temple Wood in the Kilmartin valley, *Argyll and Bute* (page 101)

Loanhead of Daviot and the other 'recumbent stone circles', *Grampian* (page 150)

Left: Loanhead of Daviot is one of the 'recumbent stone' circles found only in the north-east of Scotland, with a massive reclining stone set between two of the taller upright stones in the circle. These circles show a definite interest in the position of the moon in the night sky.

Brochs

The most extraordinary of all Scotland's ancient monuments, brochs are formidable stone towers which it's hard to see as anything other than the Celtic equivalent of a medieval tower house – the defended residence of a locally powerful lord.

Brochs are unique to Scotland, and exactly when and why they developed is not at all easy to pin down (not helped by the fact that the best ones were obvious targets for the interest of Victorian antiquarians, who destroyed all the decent dating evidence). They seem to have flourished between about 200 BC and 200 AD, and it used to be thought that they were built as a response to the threat of Roman invasion, or possibly because of raids by pirates looking for slaves to sell through the Romans' efficient trade networks; but these ideas are now generally dismissed as fanciful.

It seems more likely that the towers were simply a regional fashion, copied and improved on by local warlords keen to express their personal wealth and prestige. It's possible that they developed from a smaller type of iron age fortification known as a 'dun', which in the Outer Hebrides often featured chambers in the thickness of the wall very like the ones which are such a notable feature of brochs.

Not all brochs were as tall as the superb example at *Mousa* in *Shetland* (*pictured right and described on page 184*), but they all shared a distinctive construction technique that made it possible to build daringly high dry stone walls. To make them more stable, the walls started off very wide at the base, sloping inwards as they went up (the correct architectural term is 'battened'). To make the wall lighter (so that the lower parts didn't collapse) and to reduce the amount of stone needed, the walls were made hollow, consisting of an outer wall and an inner one joined by courses of wide, flat slabs that linked the two firmly together.

This had the added advantage that the space between the two walls could have a stairway built inside it, and the linking slabs could be set so as to form the floors and ceilings of level corridors inside the wall ('intra-mural galleries') which on the lower levels, where they were wider, could be used for storage. Additionally, gaps known as 'voids' were left in the inner wall – also crossed by wide bracing slabs – to reduce the weight of stone pressing down on key points such as door lintels and to allow light into the galleries (or possibly to allow smoke out of the interior of the broch).

It is now generally accepted that brochs were roofed over and might have had several floors: certainly, nearly all brochs have a small ledge (called a 'scarcement') on the inner wall about 2m (7ft) or so up on which a wooden floor at first-floor level would have rested.

Other classic broch features include guard chambers on either side of the entrance passage (generally so low that you can hardly imagine anyone standing – or sitting – guard in them) and cells or chambers in the thickness of the wall at ground level (Mousa has three) which were presumably used for storage.

The ones to see...

Mousa, *Shetland* (*page 184*)

Dun Telve and Dun Troddan, the Glenelg brochs, *Highland* (*page 128*)

Dun Carloway, *Lewis* (*page 119*)

Above: the finest broch of them all – the only one that still stands to anything like its full height – is on the island of Mousa in Shetland. Its outer walls are 'battened' (that is, they slope inwards) giving the classic broch profile.

Left: Dun Troddan (one of the two Glenelg brochs, in the Highland region) perfectly shows, in its ruinous state, some of the classic construction features of brochs. In the foreground is the lintel of a guard chamber, built in the thickness of the wall beside the entrance passage. Beyond it can be seen the outer and inner layers of the double wall, with bracing slabs crossing the 'intra-mural gallery' between; while on the right of the picture a 'void' (vertical gap) in the interior wall is also crossed by slabs.

Left: the broch of Dun Beag on the Isle of Skye is far more ruinous, but still shows guard chambers beside its entrance passage (on the far side of the broch).

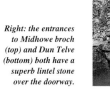

Right: the entrances to Midhowe broch (top) and Dun Telve (bottom) both have a superb lintel stone over the doorway.

The dun

The word 'dun' (pronounced with a good, deep, Scottish 'u' in the middle, similar to the 'oo' sound in 'wood' or 'good') is simply the Gaelic for 'castle', which is why so many castles in places like the Isle of Skye have 'Dun-' at the start of their names (Dunvegan, for example). It's also found in the names of brochs (such as Dun Telve and Dun Troddan) and hillforts (Dunadd and Dun Nosebridge).

In archeological terms, however, a dun is a small, thick-walled stone fortification dating from the iron age, usually small enough to have been roofed over as a fortified house (very like the brochs which probably derive from them). Duns are found more or less exclusively on the west coast of Scotland (including the islands), and they generally stand in a naturally strong position such as a rocky knoll, by the shore, with good access to the sea. Often the dun is protected by an outer wall and ditch cutting off access from the landward side.

Features of the interior of duns reminiscent of brochs include: entrance passages with door checks against which a door would have closed, and holes for drawbars to 'lock' the door with; chambers or cells in the thickness of the wall, sometimes with corbelled roofs; steps leading to the top of the wall or to an upper level; and spaces between an inner and outer wall, which suggest that the walls were sometimes built to quite a height.

An interesting variant is the island dun, built on a small, rocky island in a lochan (a small lake) and usually reached by a causeway built from heaped-up rocks.

Surprisingly often, duns were rebuilt and put back into use in later times. At *Kildonan* in Kintyre, for example, objects dating from the 800s and 1100s were found during excavations, while *Dun an Sticir* in North Uist was the refuge of a rebel clan chieftain in about 1600.

The ones to see...

Kildonan dun, Kintyre, *Argyll & Bute* (*page 98*)

Dun Ardtreck, *Skye* (*page 115*)

Dun Ringill, *Skye* (*page 116*)

Dun Aisgain, *Mull* (*page 109*)

Dun an Sticir, *North Uist* (*page 121*)

Above: the island dun of Dun an Sticir, North Uist, is reached by not just one but two causeways built of heaped-up stones, pausing along the way at another small island (from where this picture was taken).

Souterrains

These long underground passages are also found in Cornwall, where they are known by the local Celtic name of 'fogous' (pronounced 'foo-goos'). In Scotland they are often called 'earth-houses' because of a bizarre idea, popular among Victorian antiquarians, that these were the underground dwellings of the mysterious Picts. It has also been suggested that they were shelters, used when a community was under attack.

In fact, souterrains were almost certainly used for food storage: possibly for dairy products, since they would have been cool all year round, but very likely for grain. The latter suggestion is supported by the especially large examples that appeared in Angus at about the same time that the Roman army in the region would have been looking to secure regular bulk supplies of the staple food.

Souterrains are always associated with iron age villages or farms. Occasionally, examples are found that still have their roofs (such as *Grain* and *Rennibister earth houses* in *Orkney*, or the impressively large tunnel at *Culsh* in *Grampian*) and these are good fun to explore; but more often they are roofless and exposed. The roofless examples in Angus have a number of interesting features, including drains running down the middle of their stone-flagged floors,

doorposts against which wooden doors would have been set, tunnels which may have been for ventilation but could have been 'secret entrances', and houses or farm buildings built inside the curving shape of the souterrain.

The ones to see…

Culsh earth house, *Grampian* (*page 140*)

'The earth houses of Angus' (*page 154*)

Grain earth house, *Orkney* (*page 171*)

Rennibister earth house, *Orkney* (*page 175*)

Castlelaw hillfort, *Lothian* (*page 52*)

Above: Tealing earth house takes the curving theme to the extreme by completing a whole loop. A notable feature of this souterrain – which was probably used for storing grain destined for the Roman army – is a fine set of doorposts at its entrance.

Wheelhouses

These unusual round houses of the later iron age are pretty rare, but are sometimes found built in (or over) the remains of ruined or disused brochs. Their distinctive feature is a series of pillars sticking out into the middle of the house which, seen from above, look like the spokes of a wheel, giving the wheelhouse its name. Presumably the idea was that, with such substantial supports, the roof would be easier to build.

An even rarer variant on the theme is the 'aisled roundhouse', where the pillars are separate from the outside wall of the house, creating an aisle all the way round.

The ones to see…

Jarlshof, *Shetland* (*page 183*)

Kilpheder aisled roundhouse, *South Uist* (*page 117*)

Left: the interior of the second wheelhouse at Jarlshof in Shetland, which is the only really well preserved example there is. Its pillars still stand more than 2m (8ft) high.

The crannog

The distinction between an island dun and a crannog is a fairly subtle one, but essentially a crannog was a timber-framed roundhouse (rather than a thick-walled stone fort) built on an artificial island (rather than a natural one). Crannogs were found all over Ireland as well as in Scotland and were built from the bronze age right through to the iron age.

On Loch Tay, for example, traces of about 20 crannogs have been found, but it is thought that only two or three of these would have been in use at any one time: the natural resources of the area would not have supported more.

Crannogs usually started as piles driven into the silt, with brushwood and possibly stones heaped up to form an artificial island. This was often ringed by a palisade with a house built inside. The crannog was reached from the shore along a causeway of stones or on a gangway raised on piles.

Crannogs are known only from excavation, but an excellent reconstructed example can be seen on Loch Tay. This was based in great detail on the excavations at nearby Oakbank, and though many of the details are speculative – such as the steeply pitched roof, with space under it for an upper gallery floor – the overall effect is very convincing. Boats and fishing would have been of great importance to the crannog dwellers, but they were farmers too, and their animals were important: there would probably have been enough space inside the roundhouse to shelter the animals at night.

The one to see...

The Scottish Cranning Centre (a reconstruction), Loch Tay, *Tayside (page 164)*

Above: the fine reconstruction of a bronze age crannog at the Scottish Cranning Centre on Loch Tay.

Left: the approach across a gangway to the door of the reconstructed crannog house.

Viking settlements

Surprisingly, substantial remains from the early Norse era are few and far between in Britain as a whole, and the same is true of Scotland. There is one big difference, in that Norse rule carried on right into historic times in the islands of the north and west; so *Cubby Roo's Castle* on the Orkney island of Wyre, built in the early 1100s, can fairly be described as a Norse castle. That kind of thing apart, though, there is not much to be seen of the Norsemen in Scotland.

The principal exceptions are the Norse village on the *Brough of Birsay, Orkney*, which seems to have been the capital of the island earldom until the great cathedral of St Magnus was built at Kirkwall in the late 1100s; and the farmstead at *Jarlshof in Shetland*.

The most interesting buildings at the Brough of Birsay are the remains – little more than outlines on the ground – of early Norse houses built in the 800s and 900s AD. These were long, narrow 'hall houses', with a central hearth running down the middle flanked by wooden benches or platforms on either side on which people could sit or sleep (the stone settings for these can still be seen). There were no windows, but there were three doors so that you could choose which one to use according to which way the wind was blowing. Earlier Norse houses might have a barn next door (there is a good one at Brough of Birsay, with a stone-

lined drain running down the middle of it) but later the barn was incorporated into the house, creating the classic 'long house', with people living at one end and animals at the other. This arrangement is not very different from the 'black houses' that were still in use a few short decades ago in Lewis (*see page 119*).

The ones to see…

Brough of Birsay, *Orkney (page 170)*

Jarlshof, *Shetland (page 183)*

Above: a Norse barn at Brough of Birsay, Orkney, with a stone-lined drain running down its centre.

Left: one of the long, narrow 'hall-houses' built by the Norse settlers at Birsay in the 800s and 900s AD. The house would have had a long hearth in the middle, with wooden platforms or benches ranged along the walls on either side.

The Scots, Picts and Britons, 500 AD to 995 AD

Scotland's early history

Above: the hill of Dunadd, thought to have been a stronghold of the Dalriadan Scots, who arrived in the country that now bears their name as settlers from Ireland in about 500 AD.

THE SCOTS WERE NEWCOMERS to the country that would later become known as Scotland. They came from Ireland, where the native Celtic people had been christened *Scotti* by the Romans, and they arrived by sea in about 500 AD to settle on the western coasts of *Caledonia* where previously they had raided.

The settlers are said to have been led by three sons of King Erc, ruler of the Irish kingdom of Dalriada. The three sons established three small kingdoms: Fergus Mor in Kintyre; Loarn in the area around Oban (which is still known as Lorn); and Angus in the islands of Islay and Jura. Before long, Fergus's kingdom was divided between two grandsons: Comgall (who gave his name to Cowal, near Dunoon) and Gabhran, who based himself in Knapdale, and was the ancestor of the line of Scottish kings.

Already living elsewhere in Caledonia were the Picts and the Britons, both of whom were also native Celts, though they spoke a slightly different branch of the language from the Gaelic spoken by the Scots.

The Britons lived in the south, below the Forth-Clyde line which had once been fortified by the Roman frontier of the Antonine Wall. They were descendants of tribes which had been friendly to Rome, and they had three major kingdoms: one in the east, in the former territory of the Votadini; another, called Rheged, in the south-west, which stretched southward right into Cumbria; and a third, Strathclyde, to the south of the great river, with its capital on the north bank on the great rock of Dumbarton.

The Picts, meanwhile – whose name is thought to be derived from a Roman nickname meaning 'the painted people' – lived north of the River Forth. Their heartlands were in the fertile, flat land of the east coast, both in Tayside and further north, past the easternmost mountains, in the Grampian region. The Picts have a reputation as a mysterious people, but they were not greatly different from any other British kingdom of the dark ages, except that they left behind a number of remarkable carved stones, and a few inscriptions in Irish 'Ogham' script which don't make any sense when translated.

Also thrown into the melting pot were the Angles from Northumberland, whose king Edwin came to the throne in 617 and afterwards established control over much of south-eastern Scotland, right up to Edinburgh, which might be named after him.

ESSENTIALLY, THE EARLY HISTORY of Scotland is a story of constant struggles for power, influence and territory between these four peoples.

Perhaps with the help of the Irish churchman called Columba, who settled at Iona in 563, the Scottish king Aidan of the house of Gabhran became a particularly notable figure, but in 603 he was killed while taking an army south to oppose an advance on Strathclyde by the Angles. In 643, a Scottish king called Donald Braec was killed by the Britons at Strathcarron, and for perhaps a century afterwards the Scots seem to have been subjugated by the Picts.

The Picts, meanwhile, who had previously had two separate kingdoms, were unified under Brude, son of Bile, who ruled from 672 to 693 and killed Egfrith, king of the Northumbrian Angles, at Nechtansmere in 685.

In the 700s, the Angles under King Aethelfrith established supremacy in the south-west, while a Pictish army led by King Oengus rampaged across the Scottish lands, capturing the fortified towns of Dunadd and Dunollie. In 756 the Angles and the Picts joined forces to defeat the Britons at Dumbarton, but in the process the Pictish army was destroyed.

By the late 700s, the Norse and Danish raiders were causing trouble, too; but the fluctuating fortunes of the various Caledonian nations started to settle down when the thrones of Scotland and Pictland were unified more or less by accident. In 839, the Picts defeated an army of rebellious Scots led by King Alpin of the house of Gabhran, and Alpin was killed; but immediately they were attacked and wiped out by a large Norse army, and it seems that Eoghan, last king of the Picts, died with them. Bizarrely, the heir to both thrones was Kenneth, son of Alpin (Kenneth MacAlpine), probably

because his mother was of the Pictish royal family and the Picts counted descent through the female line. Kenneth pressed his claim with considerable force, and in 843 he was crowned as the first king of a unified Scotland. For some time after, the kings were called *Rex Pictorum* or *Rex Albaniae* (from the Celtic *Alba*, meaning mainland Scotland) but they were buried at the Scottish religious centre of Iona, and the kingdom was referred to as *Scotia*.

IT TOOK MANY MORE YEARS, however, before the southern lands joined the Scottish kingdom, and before then the Saxon kings of England had already started to press their own claim to supremacy over the north.

In 921, at Bakewell in Derbyshire, the sixth king of the Scots, Constantine II, swore an oath to the English king accepting him as ruler of the whole of Britain. Not long after, Constantine gave refuge to the rebellious sons of the English King Athelstan, and when an English army raided the east coast of Scotland, he made an alliance with Strathclyde and Northumbria, as well as some Danes from Ireland, and marched into Cumbria,where he was met by an English army near the Solway and was soundly beaten. Forced again to acknowledge the English king as his overlord, Constantine later resigned the throne to his cousin Malcolm (in 943) and retired to the monastery at St Andrews.

Malcolm, too, swore an oath of loyalty to an English king, but this time received in exchange the kingdom of Strathclyde, which the English had recently subdued. Similarly his successor, Kenneth II, had to demonstrate his allegiance to King Edgar in 973, but was rewarded with the gift of Lothian. As a result, the borders of the Scottish kingdom were much as they are today; but before long, Strathclyde had slipped from the grasp of the Scottish kings and was independent once more.

Below: the lower terrace and gate at Dunadd, seen from higher on the hill.

The royal house of Canmore, 1057 to 1286 (part one)

Norman Scotland

THE FIRST GREAT KING to come to the throne of Scotland was Malcolm III, known as Canmore (from the Gaelic words for 'head' and 'big', meaning 'great leader' rather than 'bighead'). He was also the last of the Celtic kings, since in his time Scotland's ruling elite was overwhelmed by the Norman influence. He himself ruled from 1057 to 1093, and his descendants ruled for nearly 200 years more.

Malcolm took the throne by force in 1057 from Macbeth, who had ruled for 17 years since killing Malcolm's father, Duncan, in a battle near Elgin. The new king had the backing of the Saxon ruler Edward the Confessor and the help of Siward, Earl of Northumberland, and he slew Macbeth in a fight near the old earth castle of Lumphanan in Aberdeenshire.

Malcolm's second wife was the Saxon princess Margaret, sister of Edward the Atheling, the only male descendant of King Alfred to survive the Norman invasion of 1066. Margaret's tastes, though, were Norman, and not just in the sophisticated piety for which she was sainted soon after her death: she liked fine clothes, feasting and dancing, and she persuaded her husband to drink wine and to give English, Biblical or classical names to their six sons. Malcolm was devoted to her, and loved to give her rich jewels, which she would pass on to whichever religious establishment she felt needed her favour at the time.

Below: the Peel Ring of Lumphanan, an old earthwork castle in Aberdeenshire near which the historical Macbeth was killed by Malcolm III in 1057.

In 1093, Malcolm travelled all the way to Gloucester to meet William Rufus, but the English king refused to see him. Enraged, he went home to Scotland, raised an army and led it on a raid into Northumberland, but at Alnwick he was killed by English treachery, and his son Edward died with him. When word was brought to the queen, she was already ill, and three days later she, too, died.

Four of the king's sons later sat on the throne of Scotland, but first his brother, Donald Bane, appeared from the Hebrides to claim the throne and drove out many of the English knights, traders and clergymen who had been attracted to Scotland in better times, along with all the former king's sons except one – Edmund – who swore loyalty to his uncle.

In 1094 Donald Bane was driven out in his turn by Malcolm's eldest son, Duncan, who had been living at the English court since he was taken prisoner many years before; but when Duncan trustingly dismissed the English troops who had helped him gain the throne, he was murdered, supposedly on Edmund's orders, and Donald Bane returned. In 1097 the king joined a rebellion against William Rufus in Northumberland and was defeated by the second son of Malcolm and Margaret, Edgar.

It was Edgar who first set up the royal household on the Castle Rock at Edinburgh, and he made peace with Henry I of England, who married Edgar's sister Matilda. Before his death in 1107, Edgar wisely divided his kingdom between two of his brothers: Alexander would rule as king, but young David would control Lothian and Strathclyde.

Alexander took it on himself to show the Celtic earls of Scotland the true meaning of Norman-style feudalism, and he became known as 'Alexander the Fierce' after he violently suppressed a rebellion by the Pictish-descended men of Moray; but he also took great pains to further the proper establishment of the church in Scotland, appointing bishops to St Andrews to help bring it closer to Rome.

On his death in 1124, however, Alexander was succeeded by his brother David, whose influence on Scotland was everything his predecessor could have hoped for.

DAVID I WAS ONE OF THE TRULY great kings of Scotland – possibly the greatest – and his influence was to last throughout the next seven centuries, not least because he had spent a great deal of time in England, and when he came to Scotland to rule, he brought many Norman friends with him, giving them lands and titles. The ancestors of the Sinclairs, Frasers, Boswells, Lindsays, Maxwells, Gordons, Crichtons and many more came north with him, along with three in particular: Bernard de Bailleul and Robert de Brus, whose fathers had fought at Hastings, and Walter FitzAlan, whom David appointed to the hereditary office of Steward and whose descendants would bear the name Stewart – or Stuart – as a result.

In imposing Norman feudal ways on the Celtic earls, David was just as fierce as his brother had been. The men of Moray rose in rebellion again, under their earls Angus and Malcolm, grandsons of Lulach, the last scion of the old Pictish royal family; David left his Constable to defeat them with superior Norman arms and armour, and then he took their lands and parcelled them out to Norman lords he wished to settle there, to keep the peace and promote the new order on his behalf. One such beneficiary was Hugo Freskin, who built the great earthwork castle at Duffus, near Elgin, and whose family became known as de Moravia after the Moray lands they now owned.

Such earth-and-timber castles, appearing first in Strathclyde and Lothian and later all up the east coast and down in the south-west, were another visible symbol of David's reign; but even more so were the abbeys and religious houses that he founded, all established on Crown land and endowed from the royal purse. David settled the Augustinians at Jedburgh and Holyrood, Benedictines at Dunfermline, Tironesians at Kelso and Cistercians at Newbattle, Kinross and Melrose.

His least successful venture was an invasion of England in 1138, following the death of King Henry, when he dared to carry the banner of his mother's royal house of Wessex as a claim to the English throne. His uneasy lords, most of whom still held lands in England, were uncomfortable when faced with an army raised by the archbishop of York, and withdrew; and David's Scotsmen were narrowly defeated. A peace negotiated at Carlisle, however, brought him Cumbria and Northumberland.

David died in 1153, outliving his own son, Earl Henry, by a year; and later, Robert the Bruce named his own son in David's honour.

The great earthwork castle at Duffus near Elgin consisted of a massive raised bailey and a high motte, both of which were entirely artificial. Only later was stonework added to fortify the castle.

The royal house of Canmore, 1057 to 1286 (part two)

The Norse influence

PROPERLY SPEAKING, 'VIKING' describes an activity rather than a person. The warlike young men of Norway and Denmark, just like the Saxons and Scots before them, would sail out in their longships and go raiding in the summer, hoping for fair winds and a good harvest of plunder from the Scottish coasts.

Iona was regularly raided from about 795 AD onwards; Dumbarton, the capital of the Strathclyde British, was sacked by the Danes in 870; and throughout the 860s and 870s the power games of the Scots and Picts were played out against a backdrop of constant conflict with both the Danes and the Norsemen.

Other northerners, however, sailed from Norway hoping to find some good, empty land in which to settle, and they found it first in Shetland (a crucial stopping-off point on the sea routes to Iceland and all points west) and in Orkney, where Norse settlements started to spring up from about 780 AD.

By the time of the reign of Harold Fair Hair, who ruled Norway from 863 to 933, the islands and the coastal lands of northern and western Scotland were effectively provinces of Norway. The Hebrides were ruled by Ketil Flatnose; Galloway was run from a Norse kingdom based on the Isle of Man; and the dynasty established in the Norse Earldom of Orkney by Peat Einar, earl from 891 to 894, ruled not only Orkney but also Caithness and Sutherland until 1231, when the earldom passed by marriage to the Scottish Earl of Angus.

In effect, then, the Norse earldoms and kingdoms in Scotland had been established at the same time as the Scottish kingdom itself had come into being. Surprisingly, though, the Norsemen were not too much of a threat to the Scots. Every time an earl or king died, a fresh dispute broke out over the succession, and so internal conflict effectively kept the Norsemen from looking elsewhere.

UNTIL, THAT IS, THE TIME of Magnus Bareleg, king of Norway from 1098 to 1103, who made a concerted effort to establish a western overseas empire. The Scots king of the time, Edgar, son of Malcolm Canmore, was forced to agree to give Magnus sovereignty over all the islands he could take his ship round, and it is said that by the simple ruse of having his ship dragged across the narrow neck of land at Tarbet, Magnus was able to claim the whole of the Kintyre peninsula.

Fortunately, Magnus's ascendancy was not to last for long. After establishing control over Orkney, the Hebrides and the Isle of Man, the Norwegian king was killed during an attack on Ireland. But Argyll and the isles had by now become established as almost a separate country, and it was a character which they retained for many years. In the mid-1100s, the region was dominated by Somerled, the half-Norse, half-Celtic ancestor of the Clan Donald, who was a perpetual thorn in the side of the Scottish kingdom: credit for his death near Renfrew in 1164 was given to the mystical influence of St Kentigern, intervening to protect the city of Glasgow, though the king's soldiers had something to do with it.

It was only in the late 1100s and early 1200s that the Scots started to go on the offensive against the Norsemen, and the fact that many of the earliest stone castles in Scotland were built in Argyll at about this time – Sween, Tioram, Dunstaffnage and Mingary among them – tells its own story.

Another of these early stone castles was the unusual circular enclosure at Rothesay on the Isle of Bute, arguably Scotland's only example

Below: Norse houses on the tidal island known as the Brough of Birsay, Orkney. Birsay remained the capital of Orkney until the superb cathedral of St Magnus was built at Kirkwall in the 1100s.

of a shell keep (a Norman castle design which consisted of a large, roughly circular wall). The castle was captured by a small Norse army in 1230, and held until 1231, but thereafter it was perfectly secure.

King Alexander II led expeditions to Argyll in 1222 and again in 1248, when he took a large fleet with him with the intention of trying to subdue the Outer Hebrides; but in 1249 he died on board his ship, moored off the little island of Kerrera, near Oban.

His successor, Alexander III, was only eight when his father died, but he grew into one of Scotland's wisest and most capable rulers. Alexander first made an attempt to buy the islands, but was rebuffed; and in 1262 he allowed clansmen from the mainland led by the Earl of Ross to make a brutal raid on Skye.

King Hakon of Norway, who had been amused by the envoys sent to him at Bergen offering money in exchange for the Hebrides, was now beginning to realise that they might be taken from him by force, and in 1263, in concord with the King of Man and the earls of the Hebrides, he gathered an army and a fleet which were said to be the largest ever sent out from Norway, amounting to as many as 15,000 men and 200 ships. The fleet left Orkney in July and joined with the Magnus of Man and some of the local lords at Kerrera in August,

but already the year was growing old and the seeds of failure had been sown.

Hakon raided Kintyre, ravaged Bute and sent 40 ships to be dragged overland to raid up and down Loch Lomond; but Alexander further delayed the Norwegians by sending Dominican monks to negotiate. Only in late September did Hakon's fleet sail up the Firth of Clyde, and there they were assailed by a fierce storm which drove a number of their ships ashore at Largs on the Ayrshire coast. When the Norwegians landed a few hundred men to rescue the ships, they were easily chased away by the Scots; and the so-called Battle of Largs turned out to be the only significant conflict of the campaign. The Norwegian fleet retired to Kirkwall in Orkney, where the old king died in the hall of the Bishop's Palace, listening to stories from the sagas which were read to him.

THREE YEARS LATER, BY THE Treaty of Perth, Hakon's successor signed away Man and the Western Isles to Scotland in exchange for 4000 marks of silver: and now, though nominally part of Scotland, the west was left to the rival claims of the MacDougalls and MacDonalds, descendants of Somerled.

In the 1460s, James III acquired the lands of Orkney and Shetland by marriage, and the Norse rule in Scotland was finally ended.

Castle Sween, on the banks of the loch of the same name, was one of the first stone castles built in Scotland, and it was placed there as part of the Scots' campaign in the late 1100s and early 1200s to control the lands of Argyll which in former years had fallen under the influence of the Norsemen.

The Wars of Independence, 1296–1362 (part one)

William Wallace

THE STORY OF SCOTLAND'S GREATEST hero starts with the death of a king on a cold and stormy night in March 1286. Alexander III had been in conference with his barons in Edinburgh Castle and, after a late supper during which he joked with his dining companions that they should eat well since for all they knew this might be Judgement Day, the king decided to return to his newly wed second wife, Yolande de Dreux, at their home at Dunfermline. Riding on ahead of his companions, he was thrown from his horse in the dark and was killed.

With him died the royal house of Canmore, since his two sons by his previous marriage to Princess Margaret of England were both already in the grave. His only daughter had been married to the king of Norway and had died in childbirth: now, her three-year-old daughter, Margaret, the Maid of Norway, was ruler of Scotland.

The Scottish lords selected a group of six guardians to rule the country in her minority and in her absence – three for the country north of the Forth, sometimes referred to as Albany, and three for the south – including two churchmen and two members of the Comyn family plus Duncan MacDuff, Earl of Fife, and James the High Steward.

One man whose name was not included and who had a particular interest in the succession was Robert Bruce, Earl of Annandale, an old

man who had been nominated as an heir to King Alexander II as long ago as 1238 and who was known as 'the Competitor' on account of his continual pressing of his claim. Bruce now started stirring up trouble in Galloway which amounted to a small-scale civil war.

AT THIS POINT, KING EDWARD I of England enters the story. Edward, the most competent, warlike, efficient and fearsome of all the medieval kings of England, had recently completed a campaign of castle-building and conquest which had subdued North Wales, and eventually he would attempt to do the same in Scotland, earning himself the nickname 'Hammer of the Scots'. Just now, however, he was quick to see a legitimate opportunity for himself in the Scottish situation.

Edward offered to marry his son and heir, also named Edward, to the Maid of Norway, and it was an idea the Scottish nobles saw no reason to reject. In March 1290, the four surviving guardians wrote to the king accepting the offer, and in July the Treaty of Birgham-on-Tweed set out formal terms for the marriage.

It's possible that, had the marriage gone ahead, Scotland and England would have been peacefully unified and several centuries of bloody conflict would have been avoided. However, in September 1290 the little Queen died in Orkney, supposedly from sea-sickness, on her way to Scotland. She never actually set foot in the country which nominally she ruled.

All of a sudden, the succession to the throne had been thrown wide open, with at least six candidates, all of whom were descended from King David I via his son, Earl Henry, pressing their claims. The two strongest claimants were John Balliol (whose mother, Devorguilla of Galloway, was the child of a granddaughter of Earl Henry) and Robert Bruce the Competitor (who was the son of another granddaughter of Earl Henry).

Determined to avoid civil war, the Scottish nobles took the reasonably obvious step of appealing to King Edward of England to help decide between the rival claims. This he agreed to do: but at a meeting at Norham, on the south bank of the River Tweed, on 10 May 1291,

Below: Norham Castle, on the south bank of the Tweed, where in November 1292 a court of arbitration, led by King Edward I of England, chose John Balliol as the new King of Scotland.

Edward also made it clear that he must be acknowledged as, in effect, the feudal overlord of Scotland.

On 17 November 1292, at Berwick, the matter was finally decided in favour of John Balliol. Scotland's First Interregnum was over, and the nation had its new king.

THAT JOHN'S REIGN WAS A DISASTER was only to be expected. The Scots later gave him the name 'Toom Tabard', 'the empty coat', and history has judged him as a weak and foolish man; but to be fair, he was in an impossible position. From the first, Edward treated him not only like a feudal subject, but also with contempt that almost seemed designed to provoke a reaction. Frequently John was summoned to appear in London to witness judgements on matters which he had every right to deal with himself in Scotland. On one occasion, he was brought to England to answer a charge of failing to pay Alexander III's wine bills.

The worm finally turned, however. In 1294, he was told to supply men and money for the wars in France, but the Scots nobles would not stand for it. They formed a council of four bishops, four earls and four barons, who now decided Scottish policy, and in October 1295 Scotland's first treaty with France was signed, foreshadowing the 'Auld Alliance' between the two nations.

Liberated by the fact that his decision had now been made for him, John declared that his acknowledgements of Edward had been made under duress and were invalid. When Edward seized the Scottish king's lands in England, John responded by ejecting all English lords from Scotland. Among those forced out were the Bruces of Annandale, who were still far more Norman than Scottish: the old Competitor had recently died, but his son and grandson, both also named Robert, now offered their swords to the English king.

By the beginning of 1296, trouble was brewing all along the border. English merchants were murdered in the streets of the royal burghs (trading towns) of Roxburgh and Berwick, and the Bruces were besieged by their enemies the Comyns at Carlisle. In March, Edward brought an army up to Berwick and took the town in an afternoon: the slaughter is said to have stopped only when the king looked down at a child clinging to the bloody skirts of its mother and said 'Enough'. It was the start of a war in which Edward effectively conquered Scotland.

Edward stayed to fortify Berwick, while his chief lieutenant, John de Warenne, took the English army on to Dunbar. Here they met and destroyed a Scottish army, capturing its commander, John Comyn, with three other earls and a hundred barons. The town of Dunbar opened its gates and surrendered, followed quickly by Roxburgh (abandoned to its fate by James the Steward) and most of the other cities of the lowlands. In June, Edward watched his siege engines pound the walls of Edinburgh

Above: Barnard Castle in County Durham was the home of the Balliol family. John de Balliol married into the Scottish royal house when he took the hand of Devorguilla of Galloway, a great granddaughter of David I, and their son John became King of the Scots.

The 16th-century bridge across the River Forth at Stirling, on the site of the bridge where William Wallace won his famous victory over the English in 1298.

Castle for eight days before it capitulated; then Linlithgow, Stirling and Perth gave up without a fight.

In July, John Balliol turned himself in to the Bishop of Durham at Brechin Castle. The embroidered arms of his country were ripped from his tunic, giving rise to his nickname, before he was taken to London and imprisoned. Later, he was allowed to retire to his Norman family's estates in France.

During the summer Edward rampaged as far as Elgin, and then on his way south again he took with him various treasures including the Stone of Destiny from Scone, a portion of the True Cross that had belonged to St Margaret from Holyrood Abbey, and large parts of the Scottish national records. He also made two thousand prominent citizens swear allegiance to him and sign a contract to say that they had done so. And then he went home, with a contemptuous comment about how good it was to get the stink of ordure out of his nostrils, leaving Scotland to be ruled by a council similar to the one he had set up in Wales, with John de Warenne as Governor and the corrupt churchman Hugh de Cressingham as Treasurer.

Resistance to the new order was immediate and widespread, but on a small scale and local, until it started to coalesce around two inspirational individuals: Andrew de Moray in the north, and William Wallace in the south.

VERY LITTLE IS KNOWN ABOUT the early life of William Wallace of Elderslie, and much of his legend was written in the 1470s by a poet called Blind Harry. All that is certain is that he was the son of a small landowner near Paisley. He was possibly of Norman descent, or possibly of Celtic ancestry (the name Wallace, sometimes spelt 'Walys', was the usual English term for a man of Welsh or Celtic descent).

There is a court record from the early days of the English occupation which refers to a thief called 'William le Walys' who escaped after stealing beer from a tavern in Perth, but there is no good reason to think this is the same man.

The 'Lanercost Chronicle' said that Wallace had been a leader of brigands, and Blind Harry claims that he was an outlaw seeking revenge for the killing of his wife; but whatever his background, Wallace came suddenly to prominence in May 1297 when he killed the English Sheriff of Clydesdale. It was as if the Scots of Strathclyde were immediately inspired by the example of someone standing up to defy the English, and quickly Wallace became the focus of an uprising in the area.

By this stage, a group of nobles including Bishop Wishart of Glasgow, James the Steward, Robert the Bruce and Sir William Douglas was gathering in Galloway to organise a resistance, but this rapidly fell apart – probably more because of squabbles among the leaders than anything else – when Hugh de Cressingham brought an English army to face them at Irvine on the Ayrshire coast.

Wallace, meanwhile, who now found himself at the head of a small army, decided to head north into the mountains, from where his freedom fighters soon made a raid on Scone. Not far away, Andrew de Moray had become the leader of a similar group of rebels in the north east, and he captured many of the castles of the region and destroyed them so that they could no longer be held by the English – a successful tactic which Robert the Bruce would himself later adopt.

Before long, most of Scotland north of the Tay had been liberated. Wallace's army was besieging Dundee when De Moray's men marched triumphantly down through Aberdeenshire, and at Perth the two leaders finally met and were elected by their followers as joint leaders of the army of the Kingdom of Scotland, fighting in the name of the rightful king, John Balliol.

By this time, an English army under John de Warenne, Earl of Surrey, was marching north to face the Scots. Most of the Scottish nobles, many of whom were of Norman descent, either remained neutral or joined Surrey. The army of the Scots was made up of the ordinary people of the land, from the Gaels of the south-west to the Picts of the north, led by small-time local knights and chieftains, and Wallace had done his best to drill them in an effective way of fighting based on a loose oval formation of men armed with spears, known as a 'schiltron'.

On 11 September 1297, the two armies gathered on the plains in front of Stirling Castle and faced each other across the deep, wide, fast-flowing River Forth, which was crossed only by a narrow wooden bridge. The rout of the English that followed could be put down to astute tactics by the Scots in taking advantage of the terrain, but essentially it seems that a major factor was rashness and over-confidence on the part of the English. Rather than waiting for support troops to be sent round by a ford further up the river, the vanguard of English knights, led by Hugh de Cressingham, dashed over the bridge and were trapped, with no room to manoeuvre or retreat. In the space of an hour, most of them were cut down. Surrey fled, leaving Stirling to surrender. The Scots chased the remnant of the English army down into Northumberland and beyond, where they rampaged through the fertile country until at the end of October an army raised by the Bishop of Durham blocked their passage across the River Tyne, and they decided to go back to their liberated homeland.

Andrew de Moray died of wounds he had received at the Battle of Stirling Bridge, but not before he and Wallace had written to the trading towns of Germany announcing that 'the kingdom of Scotland, thanks be to God, has been recovered by war from the power of the English'.

AT THE BEGINNING OF 1298, Edward of England made peace with France and came home to England to deal with the Scots. He moved his administration to York and in July he crossed the River Tweed with an army of more than 12,000 foot-soldiers and 2,000 cavalry.

The English army moved up the east coast, taking castles and towns, until its supply lines started to give out and Edward was obliged to fall back to Edinburgh. At this time, word came that Wallace's army was gathered in the forest near Falkirk, and the king eagerly took the chance to bring the Scots to battle.

On 22 July 1298 the armies met, and this time the might of the English was overpowering and the Scots had no advantageous terrain that they could exploit. The impetuous young knights of the English vanguard drove off Wallace's cavalry and wiped out his few archers, leaving the Scots schiltrons to be cut to pieces by English arrows. The defeated Wallace was lucky to escape, and fled north before making his way to France, where for several years he continued to try to raise support for Balliol.

The English, however, had won nothing. Most of the country was wasted, and Stirling was a ruin. Edward burned St Andrews then withdrew to Edinburgh before going home to England, muttering dark threats about what would happen when he came back; but he didn't return until the spring of 1300.

The tragic final chapter in Wallace's story was written in August 1305, when he returned from abroad to join the continuing resistance against the English. He was captured near Glasgow and taken to London, where he was paraded through the streets then brutally executed as a traitor, and his head was stuck on a pike and displayed on London Bridge.

Left: Caerlaverock Castle in Dumfries & Galloway was taken by siege in 1300, when Edward I of England came back to Scotland to finish off the business he had left uncompleted in 1299.

The Wars of Independence, 1296–1362 (part two)

Robert the Bruce

WE WILL NEVER KNOW whether Robert the Bruce really did sit in a cave in Arran, his fortunes at their lowest ebb, and watch with growing inspiration as a spider tried and tried again to finish its web; but the spirit of the legend is undoubtedly true. Bruce came determinedly back from the brink of utter failure and restored the independence of the kingdom of Scotland, and his refusal to submit made him one of Scotland's two greatest heroes.

Thanks to his grandfather, who had been the principal rival to the throne of John Balliol, young Robert must always have known that he had a claim to the throne of Scotland. Just after the old man died in 1295, Robert and his father were forced by King John to flee to England, where they pledged their support to the English king and held Carlisle against the Scots.

In 1296, at the age of 22, young Robert led an English army north of the Solway to reclaim the lands of Annandale for his family.

Thereafter, Robert seems to have swapped sides whenever it seemed wise. He was briefly involved in a resistance plot against the English in 1297, but he didn't join William Wallace (though some say that he fought on the Scottish side at Falkirk). In 1298, the Scots nobles made him one of three Guardians of Scotland; but in August 1299, a meeting with fellow Guardian John Comyn the Red, Earl of Badenoch, in Selkirk Forest ended in a serious argument and a scuffle; and the following year, another major disagreement with Comyn led to Robert resigning as Guardian.

In 1300 Edward of England was content just to besiege and take Caerlaverock Castle, but in 1301 he came to Scotland again and this time stayed for the winter, pressing his campaign rather more urgently. In 1302, Robert submitted to Edward and swore fealty, perhaps hoping that the English king would help him with his claim to the throne. After another year in which

Below: Kildrummy Castle in the Grampian region was probably built with the help of Edward I, but the English king had to capture it in 1306 to keep it from the Bruces.

occasional flashes of resistance from the Scots were responded to with increasing ferocity by Edward, in March of 1304 a Scottish parliament which met at St Andrews was forced to accept a new pair of Guardians, Bishop Wishart and Robert Bruce. A serious attempt at a political compromise was now made, with Edward enlisting the help of Wishart in drawing up a plan for Scotland to be governed by a parliament of 20 English and 10 Scots nobles. The plan was complete by late 1305, and it could have worked, had it not been overtaken by a very sudden turn of events.

ON 10 FEBRUARY 1306, Robert Bruce met with his enemy John Comyn in the church of the friary at Dumfries. Why they met is not known, though Bruce was by now involved in a new plot against the English, and may have wanted to bring Comyn in on it. As the two men stood aside from their companions and talked, a violent quarrel broke out; Robert pulled out a dagger and stabbed Comyn, who died, perhaps finished off by Bruce's companions.

It was later claimed that Comyn intended to reveal the plot to the English, and so had to be silenced; but even so, that was not sufficient justification for a murder committed in a church. Bruce was now effectively an outlaw, and the only sure way to redeem himself was to press ahead with his ultimate ambition and make himself King of Scotland.

Robert's brothers took Dumfries Castle and moved against other castles in the south west, while Bruce rode to Glasgow and asked for absolution from Bishop Wishart, who saw which way the wind was blowing and gave it. Within five weeks, Robert had been crowned king in the traditional way at Scone. 'It seems to me,' said his wife Elizabeth, 'that we are but a summer king and queen whom the children crown in their sport'.

King Edward was hunting in the New Forest when he heard the news, and he didn't take it terribly well. Immediately he returned to London – carried on a litter, since he was ill – and there he started issuing orders. Messengers were sent to Aymer de Valence, Earl of Pembroke, who had recently been made Guardian of Scotland and who was married to the sister of the murdered Comyn. Levies were raised in the north of England and border lords like the Percies and the Cliffords took them north to meet up with De Valence. Back in London, meanwhile, Edward created 300 new knights at the feast of Pentecost, and swore an oath on two swans clad in gold (the symbolism of

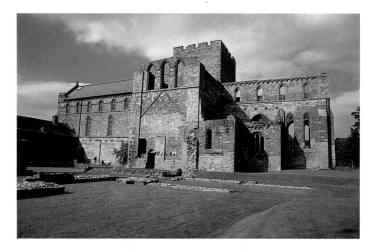

Lanercost Priory in the north of Cumbria, built of stones taken from Hadrian's Wall, was where the ailing King Edward of England stayed in 1306, making the priory a base from which he could conduct his operations against Robert the Bruce.

which is no longer obvious) that he would not rest until the Lord brought him victory over 'the crowned traitor and perjured nation'. And then he headed north.

King Robert, meanwhile, had been fighting scattered fires lit by the Comyns, as well as dealing with an uprising in Galloway by the MacDowalls, but he now retreated to Perth with a small army. Support from the Scottish lords was leaking away, with many either sympathetic to the Comyns or afraid of Edward's might.

Robert and his men abandoned Perth and then tried to return there, but were surprised and routed by the army of De Valence near Methven. The king narrowly escaped after fighting for a while dressed in only a shirt. Next he headed for Argyll, even though the MacDougalls of Lorn had already started to gather to oppose him. After a skirmish near Dalry in early August, his small army was reduced to tattered shreds.

Robert sent his wife Elizabeth and a daughter from his first marriage, Marjorie, north with his brother Nigel to seek the safety of Kildrummy, but De Valence and the Pembrokes came up and took the castle, and the women fled further north to Tain, where before long they were captured by a local earl. The king himself, meanwhile, fled to the islands of the west via the Kintyre peninsula, seeking the help of Angus Og and the men of Clan Donald, who were great rivals of the MacDougalls.

ALL THE STUFF ABOUT SPIDERS is legend rather than historic fact (though you can visit a cave on the west coast of Arran which is said to be King Robert's refuge – it's signposted on the A841 south of Blackwaterfoot). But certainly Robert was in desperate straits that winter, and

Why 'Robert *the* Bruce'?

As head of the Bruce family, Robert could traditionally be referred to as just 'the Bruce', and for some reason that form of his name has stuck. It may owe something to the fact that the old Norman form of the family name was 'de Brus'.

Robert's full title before he became King Robert I was Robert Bruce, Earl of Cattrick, so he could also be called simply 'Cattrick'.

These days, 'Robert Bruce' is the more usual form.

in sore need of inspiration. Edward, meanwhile, who was by now severely ill, had settled in at the priory of Lanercost in the north of Cumbria, and from there he was directing operations which principally involved taking bitter revenge on all those people dear to Robert who had fallen into English hands.

Robert's brother Nigel was given a traitor's execution along with several other prominent supporters; his wife was imprisoned in an English manor; his daughter was sent to the Tower of London and then to a nunnery; and his sister Mary and Isabel, Countess of Buchan, who had crowned him at Scone, were both imprisoned and put on show in specially built iron cages at Roxburgh and Berwick.

In February 1307, Robert emerged in Kintyre at the head of a small army of Islesmen and Irishmen. He split his forces in two: one half he and his captain James Douglas brought by sea to his own lands of Carrick, while the other half sailed further south to Loch Ryan on the Galloway coast, led by his brothers Alexander and Thomas. These were captured by a local chieftain and taken to Lanercost, where they were hanged, though not before Thomas had been dragged behind a horse through the streets of Carlisle.

Showing the resolution exemplified by the legendary spider, Robert fought on. He first defeated a force under Henry Percy which was occupying his childhood home at Turnberry Castle, then began a determined guerilla action from the hills and woods of what is now the National Park of Glentrool Forest. He knew this country like the back of his hand, and from here he could harass the English forces to the south, west and north and occasionally break out into Ayrshire or Lanarkshire to gather not just supplies and weapons, but also more troops.

On 10 May 1307, he had gathered enough men to fight and win a small battle against De Valence at Loudon Hill near Kilmarnock, making the most of the higher ground which his troops occupied. Perhaps provoked by this defeat, Edward of England now decided it was time for him to go into action in person. He climbed onto his horse and dragged his

Below: Robert the Bruce as depicted by a statue which stands in front of the gate of Stirling Castle.

ailing body just seven miles towards Scotland before he had to be lifted from the saddle and taken to nearby Burgh-on-Sands, where he died at the age of 68.

His dying wish was that his heart should be taken to the Holy Land by 100 knights, and his bones should be carried through Scotland as his work was completed. Instead, his son and heir, Edward II, buried him at Westminster.

WITH THEIR WARLIKE OLD KING dead, the English now withdrew from Scotland, and Robert's campaign changed in character. His task now was to start taking back the towns and the castles that controlled his country; but he could gather his men and march them freely up to the Moray Firth to face the Earl of Ross, who was soon won over to the king's cause without even a hint of a fight.

In the autumn, laid low by sickness, Robert sheltered at Inverurie, but at Christmas he rose from his sickbed to defeat John Comyn of Buchan, who fled to England. Robert's men then rampaged through the Buchan lands in the north-east, looting and burning, until by early summer all the castles of the region but Banff were in the king's hands. In July, they marched against the MacDougalls, who met them near Loch Awe; the enemy planned an ambush, but the king's loyal lieutenant, James Douglas, took his men over the summit of Cruachan and attacked them from the rear, routing them.

In the south-west, meanwhile, Edward Bruce had the Galloway lords pinned down in their castles. By the spring of 1309, Robert felt sufficiently confident to muster his supporters for a parliament at St Andrews, and not long afterwards the church gave him its backing.

Later that year, Edward II of England sent a small army to the border, but its leaders were reluctant to act as long as the unstable political situation at home caused by the barons' mistrust of Edward's favourite, Piers Gaveston, was continuing. In the autumn of 1310 Edward came himself, but as he led his army up as far as Linlithgow, Robert simply withdrew, burning the land so that it could not support the English. Before long Edward returned to England and political turmoil, while Bruce raided across the border and was bought off for £2000 by the lords and merchants of Northumberland.

This paid-for truce lasted only until February 1312, when Edward Bruce and James Douglas came raiding, burning the towns and driving off the cattle. English attention was focused on Scarborough, where Piers Gaveston had his head removed by the English nobles.

As 1313 began, Robert was busy taking Perth by the simple ruse of wading, chin-deep, through the town's moat. By the end of the year he had taken nearly all the castles and towns that the English held against him, and in the summer he had secured the sporting promise of the constable of Stirling that the castle would surrender to Robert if it had not been relieved within a year.

ON MIDSUMMER'S EVE, 1314, the Scottish army gathered on the plain at Stirling to prevent an English army led by Edward II from reaching the castle. Edward had only three of his earls with him, but he had gathered one of the most powerful armies in English history.

The battle was fought in and around a small stream called Bannockburn, and over the course of two days it proved to be the Scots' most notable victory, and England's most crushing defeat. The first day went fairly well for the Scots, who had chosen their ground with care and had guarded their flanks by digging pits; but the crucial decision came when the English withdrew to regroup at the end of the day.

They camped with the river Forth on one side and the burn, with marshy ground all round it, on the other. In the morning, they were surprised to see the Scots advancing; but they soon realised that they were trapped by the terrain, with no decent ground on which to fight, the infantry caught uselessly behind the cavalry. The slaughter was appalling; Edward narrowly escaped and was refused entry to Stirling by its constable, so fled instead to Linlithgow, then escaped by ship from Dunbar.

And, as the Lanercost Chronicle recorded: 'Robert de Brus was commonly called King of Scotland by all men because he had acquired Scotland by force of arms'.

But even now, Robert could not rest. The war on the border flickered on, and the Pope still held that the Scots king was excommunicate – hence the letter of appeal which Robert's nobles sent on his behalf from Arbroath in 1320. Eventually, after the Scots raided Yorkshire in 1322 and nearly captured Edward at Rievaulx Abbey in the process, the English king sent envoys who negotiated a 13-year peace.

In 1327, young King Edward III brought an English army north again, but could not find an enemy to fight. Robert, meanwhile, raided Durham and besieged Alnwick and Norham. Eventually, in early 1328, the English agreed on a new peace treaty that acknowledged Robert as King of Scotland. In October, the Pope lifted his excommunication; but the old warrior had died the week before.

Below: Melrose Abbey, where the heart of Robert the Bruce is thought to have been buried in a lead casket.

Further tales of the Stuarts, 1460 – 1587

Mary Queen of Scots

AGAINST A BACKGROUND of religious change that was sweeping across Europe, Queen Mary played out a passionate and personal tragedy which remains one of the most fascinating stories in British history, even if it's also one of the most bizarre.

The story starts with James III, crowned in 1460 at the age of nine, who was fortunate enough to gain the Earldom of Orkney and the Lordship of Shetland following his marriage to Princess Margaret of Denmark (her father could not afford to pay the promised dowry, and so he offered the lands instead). James's reign was a quiet one, but in the end his barons could not tolerate him, and he was killed by an unknown assassin in the country near Stirling in 1488.

His son, James IV, is remembered as one of the finest kings of Scotland. For much of his reign he was lucky in having a peaceful relationship with England, and he was married to Margaret Tudor, the daughter of Henry VII. Throughout his reign Scotland prospered, but in 1513 an envoy from the beleaguered French King Louis XII persuaded James to go to war against England; he led the largest and finest army Scotland had ever mustered into Northumberland, and Henry VIII sent an equally large force to meet him. On the hills at Flodden, near Norham, just on the English side of the Tweed, the Scots were wiped out, and the king was amongst those killed.

Once more, a king who was too young to rule was a mere pawn in the plots of rival noblemen; until in 1528, at the age of 16, James V escaped from captivity at Edinburgh and gathered an army to destroy his captor, his mother's second husband, the Red Douglas Earl of Angus, at his castle of Tantallon. Thereafter, the young king also imposed his order on the barons and the clans; but he did not do enough to win their support, and most would not fight for him when he tried to raise an army against the English. Following a defeat at Solway Moss in 1541, he died a broken man at the age of 31.

PERHAPS THE MOST SIGNIFICANT achievement of his short life, from history's perspective, was the king's marriage in 1538 to Mary of Guise, and just a few days before he died, he heard of the birth at the Palace of Linlithgow of his daughter, Mary. Again, the competing interests of various earls and nobles divided the nation, but this time there was a greater game afoot, because the infant Mary was an heir to the English throne as well as to the Scottish.

Henry VIII of England, with the intention of forcing the Scots to marry Mary to his son Edward, pursued a policy of raiding Scottish towns and burning their abbeys, which became known as 'the Rough Wooing'. After Henry's death in 1547, an English army led by the Duke of Somerset, who had appointed himself Protector of England to govern on behalf of the child Edward, inflicted a major defeat on the Scots at Pinkie, near Edinburgh, and occupied the region. Mary of Guise, who had taken her daughter to safety on the island of Inchmahome, appealed to the French for help; in July 1548, a large army of French, Italian and German veterans arrived; and after a treaty promising French aid to the Scots was signed, young Mary was sent to France as a future bride to the French crown prince, the Dauphin. Their cause now pointless, the English departed. In 1554, the Queen Mother, Mary of Guise, was made regent.

In 1558, Mary Queen of Scots was at last married to the Dauphin. At home, meanwhile, a religious revolution was in its first throes, and the people rioted in the streets in protest at the way the church abused its wealth and at the brutal suppression of the Protestant alternative. In 1559, after a crowd in Perth, stirred up by the leading Protestant preacher John Knox, turned on a Catholic priest who tried to say mass, the protests turned to riots and the riots turned to armed rebellion. An Army of the Congregation sacked St Andrews and then occupied the capital, Edinburgh; while the Queen Mother rallied her forces at Dunbar, and when French reinforcements joined her they took the town of Leith.

In January 1560 an English fleet arrived, sent by the recently crowned Queen Elizabeth, who now made a treaty with the Congregation forces. In April her army entered Scotland, and the French and English fought over Edinburgh until the death of the Queen Mother in June, after which a treaty was signed at Edinburgh,

Opposite: the old stone tower on an island in Loch Leven where Mary Queen of Scots was held captive for a year and forced to abdicate in favour of her son James.

agreeing that the French and English would leave, that there would be peace, and that the French King and Queen, Francis and Mary, would acknowledge Elizabeth as queen of England. In effect, it also ended 'the Auld Alliance' between Scotland and France.

IN 1561, AGED EIGHTEEN, Mary returned to Scotland a widow, her husband having died eight months before. She was tall, graceful and beautiful (pictures do not make her seem so by modern standards, but a death-mask at Lennoxlove Castle, near Haddington, shows her in a different light) and the her six-year reign was pure melodrama.

Her greatest problem was her lack of a husband; with religious divisions pulling Europe apart, both Catholic and Protestant countries were keen to find her a new husband to ensure her neutrality or allegiance. Elizabeth of England suggested her discarded favourite Robert Dudley, Earl of Leicester. In 1565, though, Mary chose a slender young man called Henry, Lord Darnley, who was the descendant of Margaret Tudor, widow of James IV, on his mother's side of his family, and of James II on his father's side. Mary found him very attractive and fell firmly in love.

Nobody else, however, was very keen on their marriage. The Earl of Moray stirred up a hasty rebellion, but it was quickly stifled when the Queen raised a small army and personally led it on a hard-riding campaign which chased Moray off to England.

Before long, however, the court was riddled with suspicions and divisions. The murder of a favourite of the queen's, a Piedmontese singer named David Riccio, in front of the queen in her own chamber at Holyrood in March 1566 was partly an act of rebellion by lords who supported Moray, and partly a betrayal by her own jealous husband, Darnley. The queen, now pregnant, fled to Dunbar, and for several days her future was in the balance, but inside a week she had received the support of a loyal army and was able to return to Edinburgh.

Mary's son James was born on 19 June 1566 and she declared publicly that he was Darnley's son, and no other man's. The arrival brought a wave of popular affection for the queen, but a reconciliation between the parents was looking unlikely. There was talk of the royal marriage being annulled, with Huntly claiming that Moray and Lethington suggested it to himself, Argyll and Bothwell at Craigmillar Castle.

In February 1567, Darnley, who was ill, was persuaded by Mary to come to Edinburgh and stay at a house called Kirk o' Field, where she visited him several times. One night, the house was ripped apart by a huge explosion: the bodies of Darnley and his manservant were found in the garden with their throats cut.

Exactly whose plot had come to fruition is not at all obvious, but Darnley's father, the Earl of Lennox, was in no doubt that Bothwell was the man to blame.

James Hepburn, Earl of Bothwell, had been exiled following a plot to kidnap the queen in 1562, but had been welcomed back at the time of Mary's campaign against Moray's rebellion and had supported her loyally when she fled to Dunbar after the murder of Riccio. He was now put on trial, with his consent, but nobody came forward to give evidence against him, and he was acquitted.

Within a few days, Bothwell proposed marriage to Mary, but she turned him down. this may have surprised Bothwell, since many people believe that they were already lovers. On 24 April 1567, as she rode from Edinburgh to Stirling, he met the queen with 800 horsemen and asked her to come with him to Dunbar, since there was a plot against her. She went, and a some stage she was, it appears, either seduced or raped. At the beginning of May, Bothwell's divorce from his previous wife was completed, and on 15 May he and the queen were married at Holyrood.

Public opinion was either outraged or numb with shock, but the marriage lasted only a miserable month. On June 15, an army of opposition faced Bothwell's and the queen's forces at Pinkie, but no battle resulted. In the evening, Bothwell fled to Dunbar and then on to Orkney, from where he eventually found himself in a Danish prison on a charge of breach of promise. The queen, meanwhile, surrendered herself to the opposition and was taken to Lochleven Castle, on an island in a loch south of Perth, and there she eventually agreed to abdicate in favour of her son.

IN MAY 1568 THE QUEEN ESCAPED from her island prison and met with a small army of Hamilton supporters and Argyll clansmen led by the Earl of Argyll. They were beaten in a surprisingly fierce confrontation at Langside, south of Glasgow; and Mary fled, with just 16 companions, across the Solway to England, where she asked to see Queen Elizabeth, but she was never received. She was imprisoned for 19 years, too dangerous to release or to kill, until in February 1587 Elizabeth finally signed the warrant for her execution.

James VI of Scotland and I of England

Union with England

FOR TEN YEARS AFTER MARY'S hasty departure, Scotland was again ruled by regents with their own selfish interest in mind, but in some ways James VI was fortunate. He had a good tutor in George Buchanan, a bad-tempered scholar whose main failing was an irrational dislike of James's mother, Mary; and in 1579, at the age of 13, he found a sort of combined father-figure and elder brother in Esmé Stuart, a distant relative of his father's who arrived from France and dazzled the boy with his gallantry, his courtly ways and his ready friendship.

This friendship, and the suspicion held by some of the Protestant lords that Esmé Stuart and the Earl of Lennox, James's closest advisors, were conspiring to influence the king in favour of the Catholic church, led to the bizarre episode of August 1582 known as the Raid of Ruthven. While hunting near Perth, James was kidnapped by the earls of Gowrie, Mar and Glencairn and taken to the nearby castle of Ruthven (now called Huntingtower). There he was held, apparently in no immediate danger, for ten months, while his kidnappers ruled Scotland with the widespread approval of the Protestant lords and clergy; but in June 1583 James escaped and was given the support of the powerful northern earls of Atholl and Huntly. The Ruthven raiders left the country.

A footnote to the incident was an episode in 1600 known as the Gowrie Conspiracy, in which Gowrie was set up by James's loyal Chancellor, the Earl of Arran, to give an excuse to hang him. His estates were forfeited to the Crown and the name of the castle of Ruthven was changed to Huntingtower.

THESE, THEN, WERE THE INFLUENCES that shaped James VI: the fine education provided by Buchanan; the friendship of Esmé Stuart; the plots of Gowrie and his confederates; and the absence of his scheming mother.

From the start, well aware of his position as heir to the throne of England, James seems to have conducted himself with a single-minded devotion to the idea of unifying the crowns. Among his first acts was an assertion of his own supremacy over the church, stressing his divine right to rule, though this was followed in 1586 by a compromise over the appointments of bishops. In early 1589 he dealt with a protest by Queen Elizabeth that some of his Catholic lords had been writing to France to offer Scotland's help against England; and later that same year he travelled to Denmark to collect his bride, Princess Anne. Much of the next 14 years was taken up in subtle negotiations with the church.

On Saturday 27 March 1603, Sir Robert Carey rode into Edinburgh with the news that Queen Elizabeth was dead, and four days later another messenger arrived with the news that James had been proclaimed king in London. Finally, all James's hopes had come to fruition. In early April he left for London: he would return to his native country only once, in 1617, and then for just 12 weeks.

He felt, however, that he could rule Scotland as well with his pen as other kings had with their swords, and thanks to able ministers running the country on his behalf, Scotland did not suffer for not seeing its king.

All the wars between England and Scotland had ended, ultimately, in a kind of victory for the Scots, thanks to the marriage of James IV to Margaret Tudor of England many years before; but that didn't mean an end to English armies campaigning in Scotland, nor to Scots armies raiding in England.

Huntingtower, near Perth, was still known as the House of Ruthven in 1582 when the young King James VI was taken there by force so that the earls who kidnapped him could rule his kingdom.

The Jacobite risings, 1715 and 1745

Bonnie Prince Charlie

WHEN CIVIL WAR BROKE OUT in England, the Scots found themselves in an incongruous position. Their leading party, the Covenanters, had been established to free the Protestant Church of Scotland, and so was opposed to the Catholic interests which the king represented; and yet it was also sworn to protect the king. Refusing to abandon this latter obligation, they found themselves at war with Cromwell and his English Parliamentarians following the execution of Charles I in 1649. In the summer of that year, Cromwell led his army to a decisive victory near Dunbar.

Scotland rejoiced at the restoration of the monarchy in the person of Charles II in 1660, but the country was governed insensitively by a series of commissioners appointed by the king. Things only got worse for them after the death of Charles II in 1685, when his brother, the Catholic-sympathising James II of Great Britain, came to the throne and started repealing laws against Popery and appointing Catholics in place of Protestants. The birth in 1688 of his son, James Francis Edward, brought the possibility of a Catholic dynasty which the English now decided they could not tolerate; and William of Orange was invited to take the English throne, which he accepted jointly with his wife, Mary, while James fled to France.

The Scots Convention (the parliament) met to weigh up the rival cases, hearing letters from both William and James, and voted to accept William as President of the Convention. The supporters of James – the Jacobites – most prominent among whom was the Graham of Claverhouse, recently made Viscount Dundee, prudently withdrew.

In May, the Regalia of Scotland (the nation's crown jewels) were taken to London for William to be crowned, but by this time Viscount Dundee had already assembled an army from among the Highland clans. In the Pass of Killiecrankie, not far from Dunkeld, the 2000 Jacobites met and defeated an army twice that size led by Hugh Mackay, but Dundee was killed in the action, and there was no other able leader to take his place. They were repulsed from the walls of Dunkeld and made their dispirited way home.

An uneasy peace was maintained by a standing army in northern Scotland until 1691, when the English king offered a pardon to all opponents among the Highland clans who would swear an oath to him by the new year. The clans sent to King James in France, asking if they could be relieved of their oaths to him; but his answer – that they should do whatever kept them safe – was slow in arriving, and only a few were able to get to a sheriff and officially swear the oath before the deadline. An example was made of the MacDonalds of Glencoe, whose laird, Alasdair MacDonald, could not get in to make his oath until 6 January, by which time the order to exterminate his clan had already been approved by the king. The bloody massacre that followed was later declared to be 'murder under trust' by a Commission of Enquiry, and the man responsible resigned, but it also had the desired effect on the clan leaders.

In 1702, the king died, and the queen ruled on alone. In 1707, following a major financial crisis, the Scots parliament agreed to be unified with the English and based at Westminster; and the scene was set for the most remarkable events of 1715.

BY THE TIME THAT GEORGE I came to the throne in 1714, a combination of discontent with the Union with England and affection for the old royal line of the Stuarts, as represented by

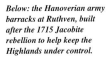

Below: the Hanoverian army barracks at Ruthven, built after the 1715 Jacobite rebellion to help keep the Highlands under control.

James Francis Edward Stuart, was enough to brew trouble in the Highlands. In September 1715, the Stuart standard was raised by the Earl of Mar and the men of the north came flocking to it, even though the Earl was an unappealing character whose motive was discontent at losing the job of Secretary of State for Scotland which he had held under Queen Anne.

The Jacobites occupied Perth and Inverness but made little effort to do anything more decisive until a force of 2000 men was led south under William Mackintosh of Borlum. He took his men as far as Kelso and Jedburgh without loss and met up with a force of Borderers led by Viscount Kenmure and the Earl of Nithsdale. They decided to march on England and ended up at Preston in Lancashire, where they eventually surrendered to a large army of the Hanoverian government, while up near Dunblane the Earl of Mar was soundly beaten by the Duke of Argyll's men.

By the time that James Francis Edward Stuart, the Old Pretender, arrived at Peterhead in late December, the cause was more than lost. At the beginning of February, the Old Pretender went back to France, never to return.

FOR THIRTY YEARS, the Jacobite faithful held on to their hopes while the Hanoverian army built roads and forts to keep them quiet. Eventually,

in July 1745, Prince Charles Edward Stuart, son of the Old Pretender, landed at Arisaig intending to start a rebellion that he hoped would bring him to the British throne.

The core of the Jacobite army that now gathered was made up of Highland clans opposed to the Campbell Earl of Argyll. They came to Stirling in September, defeated a government army at Prestonpans and marched on Edinburgh, where they celebrated for five weeks. In November they came via Carlisle and Preston to Manchester, and then on to Derby, where at the beginning of December they heard that Wade's and Cumberland's armies were approaching. The decision was taken to head for home. In January they beat a British army at Falkirk, but by February they had been chased back to Inverness.

On Wednesday April 6th, at Culloden moor, the Jacobite forces were wiped out in a morning. The noble tragedy of the battle was the heroic resistance of the clans, fighting to the death for a lost cause which was not even their own, and today the battlefield remains a touching tribute to their losses.

The Highlands were now subjected to a brutal campaign of repression, while Bonnie Prince Charlie fled to the islands of the west, from where he eventually boarded a ship and sailed back to France.

The battlefield of Culloden, where in 1746 the Highland clans were slaughtered for the hopeless cause of Bonnie Prince Charlie.

41

Castles
& ancient
monuments
of Scotland

Blackness Castle, Lothian.

Edinburgh, Lothian & Borders

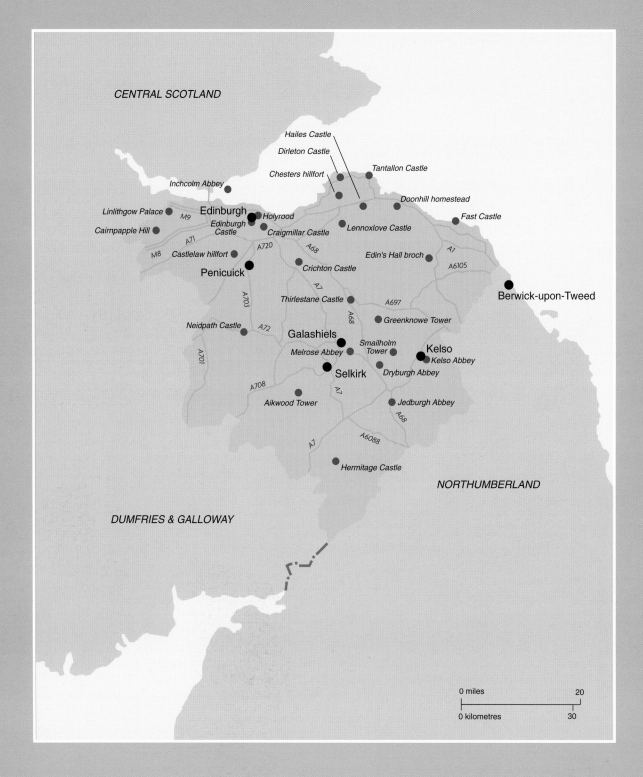

CENTRAL SCOTLAND

Hailes Castle

Dirleton Castle

Chesters hillfort

Tantallon Castle

Inchcolm Abbey

Doonhill homestead

Linlithgow Palace

M9

Edinburgh

Holyrood

Fast Castle

Cairnpapple Hill

Edinburgh
Castle

Craigmillar Castle

Lennoxlove Castle

A71

M8

Castlelaw hillfort

A720

A68

Edin's Hall broch

A1

A6105

Crichton Castle

Penicuick

A7

Berwick-upon-Tweed

A703

Thirlestane Castle

A697

A68

Neidpath Castle

A72

Greenknowe Tower

Galashiels

Smailholm
Tower

Kelso

A701

Melrose Abbey

Kelso Abbey

Selkirk

Dryburgh Abbey

A708

A7

Aikwood Tower

Jedburgh Abbey

A68

A7

A6088

Hermitage Castle

NORTHUMBERLAND

DUMFRIES & GALLOWAY

| 0 miles | | 20 |
| 0 kilometres | | 30 |

Cairnpapple Hill

Historic Scotland • ££ • Usual hours

This is a fascinating ancient monument, but it's also one of those rare places where an air of sanctity seems to linger – though frankly that could just be because it's a pleasant place to visit in a smashing rural setting. From the hilltop site, it is said that you can see both the west coast and the east coast of Scotland – the rivers Forth and Clyde – on a clear day, and the larks singing in early summer are a joy to behold.

So this was an excellent place to build a significant monument, and in fact a series of different kinds of monument were constructed here over a period of several thousand years. The first, built in

The older burial monument at the centre of the later cairn is covered by a modern concrete mound.

about 3000 BC, was a henge, consisting of a roughly oval area enclosed by a bank and ditch with two gaps on opposite sides for entrances. Inside the henge was an oval setting of upright posts, and the positions of the post-holes found during excavations are now marked by patches of red gravel.

Round about 2000 BC, an individual burial was made in a grave marked by a standing stone and covered by a small cairn of heaped stones, defined by a kerb of larger stones. This was clearly an important individual burial, but it is thought that, by this time, the site no longer had the same ritual importance that it had in earlier times.

After excavation, this earliest burial cairn was covered with a concrete dome which now, grassed over, blends in well. It's nice to have something underground to explore, too, even if it is via a modern hatchway and ladder.

Also protected under the mound are two cist burials from later in the bronze age, which were covered by a cairn the size of the modern mound (but not as high). The larger of these graves incorporated a cup-marked stone, and its occupant was buried with a wooden mask.

Later still, a larger cairn was built, and it had two burials near its edge.

Signposted on minor roads near Torphichen.

These pits near the edge of the last, largest cairn contained cremated remains buried in urns.

Left: inside the concrete mound, the cist burials and the earliest kerbed cairn can be seen.

■ *See also… Aikwood Tower*

Privately owned, ££, limited hours (open three afternoons a week in summer). On the B7009 south-west of Selkirk.

Prominent politician Lord David Steel kindly opens his home to paying visitors, but the historical interest is minimal: rather, Aikwood is a fine example of how a small border tower can be sensitively converted into a cosy home. Visitors are pretty much restricted to the hall on the first floor, however; the bedrooms at the top of the tower and the basement kitchen are out of bounds. Worthwhile if you're a political groupie or into country house interiors.

Below: at Craigmillar, an earlier tower house was surrounded by a strong but graceful curtain wall.

Craigmillar Castle

Historic Scotland • ££• Usual hours

Photographs of this interesting castle often make it look like a dramatic tower in the middle of the mountains; but in fact it's on the outskirts of Edinburgh, and the old tower house in the middle is not even its most striking feature (though it is probably the most enjoyable part of the castle to explore).

The land at Craigmillar was given by King Robert II to Sir Simon Preston in 1374, and the original thick-walled tower house was built not long afterwards. It's a pretty basic design, essentially consisting of two large spaces, each roofed by a barrel vault, stacked one on top of the other. Each level was divided horizontally by a timber floor: the two lower floors were both used for storage; above was the hall; and on the top floor was a private chamber. Higher still, the small spiral stair leads out onto the roof, from where there are excellent views on a clear day.

Back down in the hall, meanwhile, there are several fine details to look out for, including an enormous and grandly ornamented fireplace. Next door is a small room which was originally the kitchen but was later converted into a bedroom, and this is where Mary, Queen of Scots is said to have stayed during her visits to the castle in 1563 and 1566.

In fact, Mary's association with Craigmillar is a strong one. She stayed for a week in September 1563 and received an ambassador from Queen Elizabeth warning her to choose a husband carefully; and in November 1566 she was here for several weeks, recovering from depression following the birth of her son. At about the same time, the murder of her husband, Lord Darnley, was being plotted.

Interesting though the nooks and crannies of the tower undoubtedly are, the real beauty of the castle is that it was enhanced by the addition of lots of later walls and ranges, and most of this work is still pretty much intact.

Even the elements which aren't strictly speaking a part of the building – such as the terraced garden to the west of the castle, laid out in the late 1500s, which overlooks a fishpond in the shape of the letter 'P' (for Preston) – give the visitor a vivid sense of this place as an elegant residence of the Elizabethan era.

The most prominent feature of the later building work is the curtain wall, with a round tower at each corner, added in the mid-1400s. One of the most evocative parts of a visit to the castle is when you stroll in through the round-arched gate and emerge in the enclosed courtyard, which is shaded by the low branches of a yew tree. To the right is an ornate doorway leading to the West Range, the last part of the castle to be built, which dates from 1661.

South-east of central Edinburgh, signposted from the A7 and from Holyrood Park.

Crichton Castle

Historic Scotland • ££• Usual hours

One of the two very pleasing things about this castle is its unspoiled setting in open farming country. It is approached on foot: you park your car near the old church (itself an interesting medieval building, founded in 1449 by William Crichton, eighth Earl of Douglas) and you walk along the valley until, as you turn the bend, the castle suddenly comes into view.

The immediate impression it gives is of being pretty much intact, but appearances can be deceptive; on the inside, there is not as much of the castle left as you would hope, which makes it less interesting to explore than you might imagine. Still, it does have one feature that's so striking, it's worth going out of your way to see, and that's the remarkable diamond-faceted facade (more like a chocolate bar than anything else) which decorates the exterior of a later hall block built in the 1580s on the north side of the courtyard. As an ostentatious display of wealth, it takes some beating, and it is matched by some equally rich details in the stonework, including several particularly tasteful rope mouldings (that is, pieces of stone carved to look like ropes).

The history of the castle is a colourful one, thanks mainly to the characters that have owned the place. The lands here

were granted by King Robert II to a chap called John de Crichton in the late 1300s, and he is thought to have built the original tower house in about 1400. Unfortunately, the interior wall of this building has collapsed, so there is no access to its rooms, though this does mean that you get a kind of cutaway view of it. Like so many of the earlier towers, it basically consisted of two spaces roofed over by stone vaults: the lower one was divided in two by a wooden floor and used for storage, while the top one was the laird's hall.

The first major upgrade to the castle was carried out in the 1440s by the same William Crichton who built the church. Appointed Chancellor by King James II in 1448, he was one of the wealthiest and most powerful men in Scotland, but the hall range which he built on the south side of the courtyard has not survived well.

Possibly the most famous of all the owners of Crichton was James, fourth Earl of Bothwell, the third husband of Mary Queen of Scots. He fled to Elgin in 1567 after Mary's defeat and the castle was without an owner for five years, until the title of earl was claimed by a distant relation, Francis Stewart, who built the ornate new range in the 1580s.

Signposted from the A68 and the B6367 near Pathhead, to the south-west of Edinburgh; it's a five-minute walk to the castle.

The oldest part of Crichton Castle is a tower house built in about 1400; it's to the right of the gate.

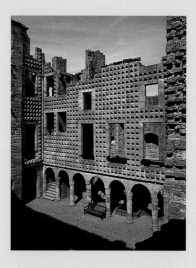

The extraordinary diamond-faceted facade of the later hall block, built for Earl Bothwell in the 1580s.

Dirleton Castle

Historic Scotland • ££ • Usual hours

Even if the castle weren't impressive – which it is – it would be worth coming here just to see the dovecot, a beehive-shaped creation of the 1500s in glowing, butter-coloured stone which has recently been restored and, on the inside, seems more like a work of modern art than a practical building. It's glorious.

The castle is, in origin at least, one of Scotland's few 'proper' medieval castles. Its oldest parts date to the 1200s and are built in the typical style of the period, characterised by thick-walled round towers. Most of the original towers have been destroyed or replaced, but the largest one, containing the lord's hall, remains, and even has its vaulted stone roof in place.

The layout of the castle was clearly always rather lopsided, so it's only when you walk to the far end of the grounds and discover the main gate – approached now, as then, by a long wooden footbridge – that you realise how big it was.

One of the things that makes it a particularly interesting place to visit is the way that the three main phases of building have very different characters. When you walk through the gate, the buildings to

The impressive facade of Dirleton Castle, with the original round tower of the 1200s on the left.

your left are an intriguing combination of the oldest part of the castle (including that original round tower) and the newest part, which is basically a spacious Renaissance house built in the courtyard in the 1500s. To your right, meanwhile, is a long hall range which was constructed in several phases in the 1300s and 1400s.

There are lots of interesting corners to explore, with some of the most impressive structures in the hall range. The kitchen on the first floor, next to the hall, has a pair of very grand fireplaces (as ever, don't forget to take a look up the chimney) while the vaulted basement below is a satisfyingly gloomy and cavernous space. And at the far end of the hall range is an intriguing two-storey prison, combining a lower pit (no light, no facilities, and very little hope for the occupant) with a more civilised upstairs level (fireplace, toilet and every chance of a fair trial).

Finally, another attraction of Dirleton is the carefully tended flower garden, which has been an important feature of the grounds since Victorian times.

Signposted on the A198 west of North Berwick.

Dryburgh Abbey

Historic Scotland • ££ • Usual hours

This is the prettiest of the region's three magnificent ruined abbeys, and it stands in the beautifully landscaped grounds of a later house, surrounded by mature trees and smooth, richly green lawns which give it the perfect backdrop.

In fact, Dryburgh was lucky enough to be adopted by one of the first antiquarians in Scotland, David Steuart Erskine, who bought the abbey in 1786 and built the nearby house, also laying out the grounds. Erskine has to be credited with preserving the abbey from further decay and making it into the romantic ruin it is today, though he did have a tendency to 'enhance' it with flourishes of his own, including some very misleading inscriptions.

The few fragments of the church that remain are, it has to be said, particularly attractive; but the thing that makes Dryburgh quite different from *Jedburgh* (*page 54*) and *Melrose* (*page 56*) is that substantial parts of the buildings around the cloister have survived.

The jewel in the crown, here, is the chapter house: not only does it still have its barrel-vaulted roof in place, but also you can make out traces – faint, but unmistakable – of the colourful paintwork with which it would have been decorated.

Equally entertaining is the floor of the dormitory above, reached by the original night stair from the church. Up here is a slender stair tower, and you can climb its steps to reach a fine vantage point from which to look down over the ruin.

The abbey was founded in 1150 by Hugh de Moreville, an Anglo-Norman lord who had become a close friend of King David I and had been given extensive lands in the area by the king.

Signposted from the B6356 and the B6404 to the south-east of Melrose.

Edin's Hall broch

Historic Scotland • Free • Open access at any reasonable time

This isn't the most spectacular site, but it's an interesting combination of a hillfort, a settlement and a broch. It's also a fine excuse for a good stretch of the legs in open country, since it is reached by a pleasant walk of half an hour or so (a mile and a half) alongside a small river.

The hillfort came first, and the huts of the settlement were built later, inside (and sometimes over) its ramparts. You can

Edin's Hall broch is a rare example of a broch in the south, and it's also very big; was it roofed, or not?

trace the outlines of a number of huts, including a large one which was clearly of special importance.

The broch represents the last phase of development at the site. Brochs this far south are something of a rarity, but this is a well-built one: the stone isn't dressed, but it is carefully chosen to give good straight lines (though straight lines were not much a part of Celtic culture).

Typically, the broch has guard chambers on either side of the entrance and side-chambers within the walls of the broch, with stairs up to a higher level. The higher levels of the walls would have been hollow, but it's anyone's guess how high they would have reached, or whether the interior was roofed over.

Clearly signposted from the A6112 north of Preston, a short way down the minor road to Abbey St Bathans. Park in the layby where the signposted path to the monument leaves the road; it's a walk of one and a half miles to the broch.

Below: lots of the domestic buildings survive at Dryburgh Abbey, and the grounds are splendid.

Edinburgh Castle from Princes Street Gardens. There is a footpath up to the castle from the gardens, but it's steep!

Edinburgh

A brief introduction to Scotland's capital city…

It's not known how Edinburgh got its name, but there's a theory that it recalls Edwin, King of the Angles of Northumbria, who controlled most of south-eastern Scotland in the 620s AD. Only in the 800s did the Anglian influence in Scotland start to wane, and there is a passing reference from about 960 AD to the capture by the Scots of a place called 'Oppidum Eden' which is thought to refer to Edinburgh (*oppidum* being the traditional Celtic word for a tribal capital).

The city came to prominence in the time of Malcolm III, who ruled Scotland between 1057 and 1093, and the oldest building in the city is the chapel built on the castle rock by his wife, St Margaret. Their son Edgar moved the royal residence from Dunfermline to Edinburgh, and his younger brother David established the town as the nation's capital.

Thanks to the road connections with England and the port at Leith, Edinburgh's importance as a trading centre grew over the centuries. By the 1500s, the layout of the city was much as it is now, with the Royal Mile running the length of the city from the castle to the abbey at Holyrood, overlooked by tall, narrow houses built by wealthy merchants.

The most important change to the city was the draining of the North Loch in the early 1800s, which allowed the new town north of Princes Street to be laid out and created the Princes Street gardens.

Edinburgh is home to the nation's most important museum, the recently opened Museum of Scotland in Chambers Street (to the south of the Royal Mile off either South Bridge or George IV Bridge), which contains Scotland's major historical and archeological treasures. It's unmissable.

Edinburgh Castle

Historic Scotland • ££££ • Usual hours

Inevitably this is one of the most popular tourist attractions in Scotland, and it does get swamped with visitors even outside the normal peak season. It's especially busy at lunchtime, when the crowds flock here to see (and hear) the firing of the famous One O'Clock Gun. If you'd like a bit of room to manoeuvre, it's better idea to come early in the morning or later in the afternoon.

Essentially the castle breaks down into two parts: a lower courtyard defended by an encircling wall, where most of the buildings are relatively modern; and a kind of citadel, known as the Upper Ward, on the highest part of the rock, which is where all the oldest and most interesting structures are to be found.

The Upper Ward is reached through a gatehouse, some parts of which date back to about 1300. Just beyond this is the oldest building in the castle, the tiny chapel founded by St Margaret in about 1100. It is charming in its simplicity, but the interior has been greatly altered.

Finally you come to Crown Square, at the heart of the castle, where a courtyard is surrounded on all four sides by the most important buildings. The palace on the east side has some splendid painted rooms, recently restored, which were decorated especially for the return to his native land of James VI of Scotland and I of England in 1617. The palace also contains a small, appropriately vault-like room where the Scottish Crown Jewels are displayed alongside the Stone of Destiny.

On the south side of Crown Square is a vast hall built in the 1500s by James IV, which has a very impressive timber roof. The ranges on the other two sides of the square are more recent.

The only other part of the castle that is of any great interest – unless you are keen on military and regimental museums, of which there are several – is the vaulted basement that supports the Crown Square buildings. Parts of these high, gloomy vaults were converted into cells to house French prisoners of war. For some reason, the massive 400-year-old cannon called Mons Meg is on display here, and very impressive it is, too.

A free audio tour is available, if you like that sort of thing, and they reckon that it contains over four hours of material. This demonstrates the great variety of things to see and do here, but to be honest, anyone who's not a military historian will find a lot of it pretty dull.

The best thing about the place by some distance is the spectacular view over the city and out across the Firth of Forth from the northern ramparts, which is far more thrilling than any of the castle's buildings.

At the top of the Royal Mile (Lawnmarket) in the centre of Edinburgh; it's best to get here on foot, but there is a (very expensive) car park in front of the castle.

The Palace of Holyrood is still owned by the reigning monarch and is used as an official residence.

Holyrood Abbey & Palace

Her Majesty the Queen • ££££ • Slightly limited hours (it's closed when the Queen needs it)

The palace was built after the Reformation of 1560, when the old abbey church went out of use, and in this democratic age it offers a rare chance to visit a working royal palace.

Basically, you get to see the state rooms on the ground floor, which are extremely grandly furnished and have some splendid paintings (including an excellent Turner). They do, however, have rather a soulless feel to them, somewhat reminiscent of the foyer of a large company's headquarters, where the main purpose of the decor is to impress visitors rather than to make anyone feel at home.

Far warmer and friendlier is the only upstairs room on view: a bedchamber which is supposed to have belonged to Mary Queen of Scots. It has its original bed and furnishings, and there is a needlework panel depicting a cat (labelled 'a catte' in case anyone was confused) which is said to have been worked by the Queen herself.

Once you've seen all the rooms of the palace that are open to the public, you emerge into the body of the ruined abbey church, which even in its ruined state is quite an inspiring piece of architecture, with some splendid details.

In the summer months, you can also wander around parts of the royal gardens and see the outside of the rest of the house before returning to the front – though you mustn't walk on the grass.

The abbey was founded by David I in gratitude and as a penance after he was nearly impaled on the antlers of a stag while hunting on a Sunday. It was named Holyrood ('holy cross') after the jewelled cross belonging to his mother, St Margaret, which he gave to the abbey.

To provide them with revenue, David also allowed the Augustinian monks who settled here to establish a trading burgh, Canongate, which attracted French and Flemish merchants. The king also settled his friends and retainers on strips of land on either side of the castle, in effect founding the city of Edinburgh.

At the opposite end of the Royal Mile to the castle, on the east side of the city centre.

Left: the interior of the abbey church at Holyrood, which has some superb architectural details.

Hillforts of the Border region

With the emphasis on beautiful hills and fine views, rather than archeology…

The massive outcrops of volcanic rock in the Edinburgh area were obvious places for ancient people to build their defended settlements and, like the castle rock at Edinburgh, both the landmark hills in the area – the cone-shaped North Berwick Law by the coast and the whaleback Traprain Law, near the A1 – had major hillforts on them.

North Berwick Law can be climbed by a signposted footpath from the town, but it's more of a viewpoint than an ancient monument, since there's not much of the hillfort left. There is, however, an arch made from a whale's jawbone.

Traprain Law is a more serious proposition. Quarrying on the hillside has recently ceased, and the hill is now a nature reserve. Again the remains are not spectacular, but this was an important site, the *oppidum* or capital of the Celtic tribe of the Votadini. It remained in use in the Roman period, so the tribe must have been on friendly terms with the invaders.

Both these hills provide a steep walk rewarded by fine views, but there's a little more on offer elsewhere…

The ramparts of Castlelaw, in the Pentland Hills, are not too spectacular – but it does have a souterrain.

Castlelaw hillfort

Historic Scotland • Free • Open access at any reasonable time

This is a good excuse for getting out into the Pentland Hills, south of Edinburgh, which is a national park with a visitor centre and lots of waymarked trails.

There are two ways to get to the fort: the easy way is to drive right up to it on the minor road to the firing range, but the more satisfying approach is to walk up from the car park at the visitor centre. The uphill parts are fairly gentle and the walk won't take more than half an hour.

The circuit of ramparts is not all that impressive, but this hillfort has one most unusual feature: a souterrain built in one of its ditches. It's a stone-lined passage about 20m (65ft) long, with an opening halfway down leading to a cell with a corbelled roof. It is thought that the passage would originally have been covered by a timber roof, but a modern

Right: inside the souterrain at Castlelaw, which has been given a modern concrete roof to protect it.

concrete one now does the job. Inside was found Roman pottery and glass dating to before 200 AD.

Signposted off the A702 south of Edinburgh. If you wish to walk to the fort, look for a sign to the Pentland Hills Visitor Centre.

Chesters hillfort

Historic Scotland • Free • Open access at any reasonable time

This is one of the few Scottish hillforts to have the flowing earthen ramparts which are commonplace in Celtic forts in England. The peculiar thing about the place, however, is that it's not on much

of a hill – and in fact, it is overlooked by a ridge that would have given attackers a huge advantage. The fort's impressive ramparts may have been more for show than for defence, though the site does offer good views over the coastal plain.

Signposted on a minor road off the B1343 or the B1377 north of Haddington.

☐ *See also…*

Eildon Hill hillfort and Roman signal station

Reached by a signposted footpath from the B6359 on the edge of Melrose.

The three hills here gave their name to the Roman fort of *Trimontium* at Melrose (explained well by a small museum in the town). The summit of the North Hill was occupied by a huge fortified Celtic town, and when the Romans arrived, life seems to have carried on pretty much as normal; the hill was still occupied by the natives even after the newcomers built a small signal station here.

Woden Law hillfort and Roman camps

From the A68 south of Camptown, take the minor road east towards Chatto and Hownam.

Here, in the bleak landscape of the Cheviot Hills, there are all kinds of ancient remains, including a Celtic hillfort and Roman siege camps.

Hailes Castle

*Historic Scotland • Free • Open access at any
reasonable time*

This is said to be among the earliest
castles in Scotland. The bottom parts of
the main tower date back to the 1200s, but
it was later modified and eventually – and
rather ignominiously – was converted into
a dovecot. Some of the nesting boxes are
carved out of single stones.

In the 1300s, a second tower was added
(it's the one at the back, on the left) and
both this and the original tower have pit
prisons, covered by modern iron grilles to
stop you from falling in.

The best bit of this modest and generally
far from thrilling castle is the range that
was built in the 1400s in between the two
towers. In its vaulted basement were the
kitchens, some details of which have
survived, and there is a postern gate
leading out to the river at the back, which
is the castle's prettiest aspect.

Signposted from the A1 at Haddington or Preston.

Hermitage Castle

Historic Scotland • ££ • Usual hours

There is no castle in the British Isles
which has a more brutal and forbidding
appearance than Hermitage. Combine this
with the bleak landscape in this remote
border region, and the effect is enough to
send shivers down your spine. It's a cold,

The main tower of Hailes Castle (on the right) was later converted so that it could be used as a dovecot.

lonely, eerie old place.

It can look like a simple enormous tower,
but in fact the castle consists of a
rectangular block (built in the late 1300s
on top of a slightly earlier tower) with four
towers of differing sizes at its corners
(three of them dating from about 1400 and
one from even later). There are very few
openings in the walls, but up near the top
there is a row of doors, just above a row
of corbels which supported a wooden
gallery or warhead from which the wall
could be defended. Bridges were built to
carry this gallery across the space between
the towers, creating the effect of high

arches that looks so dramatic today.

Inside, the castle is little more than a
shell, which is a bit disappointing, though
there are a few interesting details to be
found, particularly in the kitchens on the
basement level of the south-west tower.

Historically, Hermitage was one of the
key strategic positions in the wars
between Scotland and England, and it
changed hands repeatedly over the years.

Signposted from the A7 and B6399 in Liddesdale.

***Below: the intimidating facade of Hermitage Castle
(though admittedly from an unflattering angle).***

See also... Kelso Abbey

Historic Scotland; free, open access during usual hours only. In the town centre of Kelso.

This is the fourth of the great Border abbeys founded by King David I, and unfortunately it's not nearly so well preserved as the others: just a fragment of the west end of the church remains, crammed in to a small graveyard. However, the quality of the masonry is superb, so it's well worthwhile coming to take a look.

Below: the church at Jedburgh is in fine fettle, but the domestic buildings of the abbey are long gone.

Jedburgh Abbey

Historic Scotland • ££ • Usual hours

What marks Jedburgh out is that the abbey church is almost complete. Much of the presbytery at the east end is destroyed, as is the south transept; but the crossing of the church is still topped by a tower and, most strikingly of all, the three storeys of striding arches in the nave have survived more or less undamaged.

The reason it's so well preserved is that after the Reformation of 1560 closed the abbey down, the nave remained in use as the parish church until 1875. It's this bit of the church that really impresses, particularly since you can climb a narrow spiral stair and walk across a gallery above the door at the west end to look down on the interior of the church. It's a good spot from which to appreciate the tidy, ordered design.

The nave was built in the 1180s, more than forty years after work had begun on the eastern end of the church following the foundation of the abbey by King David and his former teacher, Bishop John of Glasgow, in 1138. The earlier work in the presbytery has a comparatively crude and heavy feel, based on weighty Romanesque rounded arches, but the later nave is a good example of an early Gothic style, where the thinner pillars and the clean, straight-up-and-down lines give the structure a soaring, weightless feel.

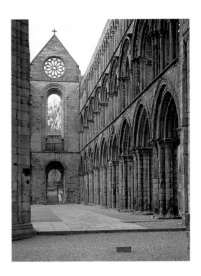

The interior of the beautifully preserved nave at Jedburgh Abbey, with its three storeys of arches.

Unfortunately, there is very little left of any of the domestic buildings of the abbey, which were built down the side of the hill overlooking the river. Only the basements of buildings like the kitchens, the refectory and the abbot's residence survive to anything more than foundation level, and none of it is hugely interesting.

Off the A68 in Jedburgh town centre.

Linlithgow Palace

Historic Scotland • £££ Usual hours

This huge fortified palace – where Mary, Queen of Scots was born in 1542 – is quite different from anything else in Scotland, and is well worth seeing. It stands on a large, grassy mound by a lake; the grounds are now a public park and a pleasant place to while away some time on a sunny day,

Linlithgow Palace was heavily fortified, and on the east side a great barbican defended the gate.

but originally the site was chosen for its defensive qualities: there was a fortified manor here from the time of King David, and a timber castle was built on the site in in 1302 by the English.

Work on the palace started in 1425 on the orders of King James I after a fire destroyed the town and, with it, the latest royal manor house. Probably the first part to be finished was the great hall, running the entire length of the east side of the building, which is still one of Linlithgow's most impressive features; but the palace as it stands today is a blend of work carried out by various kings from the mid-1400s to the early 1600s.

The result is a graceful design consisting of four ranges around a square courtyard, with a tall tower at each corner. There are plenty of details to admire, plenty of stairs to climb (you can get right to the top of two of the towers) and plenty of rooms to explore, but in the end it's the shady courtyard, overlooked by all those windows and graced by the central fountain, that is the most memorable image of the palace.

In Linlithgow, on the A803 west of Edinburgh.

Left: inside the courtyard at Linlithgow, with the ornate fountain built by King James V in 1538.

See also... Lennoxlove Castle

Privately owned, £££, limited hours (three afternoons a week in summer months). Signposted on B6368 south of Haddington.

This is a powerful L-plan tower of about 1350 which has been modernised as a country house, with extensive modifications in the early 1900s. Visits are by guided tour only; the place has a slightly stuffy atmosphere (both literally and metaphorically) but there's lots of interesting stuff to see. Some of the paintings and furniture are very fine, as is the fabric of the older parts of the building. The great hall, with its high barrel-vaulted roof, is impressive, and there's a cramped prison in the basement below, as well as two original iron yetts. Bits and pieces on display include a death mask of Mary, Queen of Scots which makes her look very beautiful. And to keep people happy who don't want to tour the castle, there are smashing gardens, and an excellent teashop.

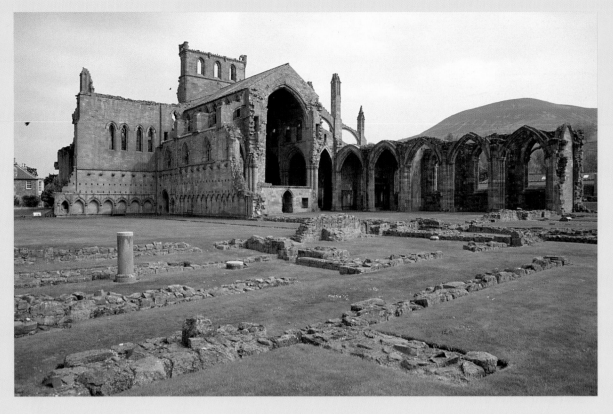

The ornately detailed church of Melrose Abbey, where the heart of Robert the Bruce was buried.

Melrose Abbey

Historic Scotland • ££ • Usual hours

Of the region's three fine ruined abbeys, *Dryburgh (page 49)* is the most beautiful and *Jedburgh (page 54)* has the best-preserved church, but Melrose just sneaks in ahead of its rivals thanks to the superb quality of the stonework in the surviving pieces of the abbey's church.

Melrose also has a long and interesting history, beginning in about 650 AD when St Aidan of Lindisfarne founded a monastery near here. (It was actually in a loop of the River Tweed which can be seen from the viewpoint known as Scott's View, signposted on the B6356 to the north of Dryburgh Abbey.) This monastery was where St Cuthbert, one of the major figures of the early English church, was brought up; he became its prior in 664.

In 1136, the site was offered by David I to the Cistercians of Rievaulx Abbey in Yorkshire, but they decided that further upstream would be a better place to build their new abbey. It soon became one of the richest and most prestigious churches in Scotland. In 1249, King Alexander II chose to be buried here.

Like the other abbeys of the Borders, however, Melrose was caught up in the wars with England, particularly in the

early 1300s. It was sacked in 1322 by the army of the English king, Edward II, and Robert the Bruce helped rebuild it; but in 1358 another English army burned the abbey to the ground, and it was decided to rebuild the church from scratch. Oddly, the work was paid for by another English king, Richard II, who firmly believed he had conquered southern Scotland, and was begun by English masons.

One upshot of this is that there is an interesting contrast in styles, obvious even to the untrained eye, between the earlier and later parts of the church. The east end (the presbytery) is in the typically English style known as 'Perpendicular', with the emphasis on straight vertical lines; this style is obvious in the large window at the far end of the church, and in the soaring vaults of the presbytery. Over on the south side of the church (round to the right when you first come into the grounds), however, a more ornate, curly, free-flowing style has been used. This is thought to have European influences, and to be the work of a French mason, John Morow.

More to the point, though, the whole of the church was richly covered in splendidly carved detail, from the likenesses of saints on the ceiling bosses to a famous gargoyle

in the shape of a pig playing the bagpipes. Add in some fine flying buttresses and some gorgeous window tracery, and it's enough to keep you busy for a while.

Outside the church, the foundations on the ground are enough to show that this was a religious community on a fairly grand scale. One building of the 1400s which was converted into a house for the commendator has survived intact and is used as a museum, filled with domestic artefacts like iron cooking pots and pottery jugs found during excavations.

One of the most striking things found in the excavations of the 1920s, however, was a conical lead casket which had been buried under the floor of the chapter house. This is said to contain the heart of Robert the Bruce, either brought here directly at the request of the dying king, or carried on crusade by a favoured knight and returned here after that knight's death in Spain. The lead casket was reburied in its original position and the spot is marked by a plaque.

After the Reformation in 1560, the middle of the church – the former monks' choir – stayed in use as the parish church until the early 1800s, and still has its roof.

In the middle of Melrose.

Neidpath Castle

*Privately owned • ££ • Slightly limited hours
(summer only)*

Romantically situated on a high bank
overlooking a bend of the wide, slow-
flowing River Tees, this is a fascinating
tower house of the late 1300s, built to a
kind of slanted L-plan design.

Privately owned castles tend to be
either spotless stately homes or slightly
eccentric semi-ruins, and this falls in the
latter category, though you have to admire
the tenacity of the owner in struggling to
keep it in repair, making it an interesting
place to visit and gradually restoring it.

In places it's a bit like a building site;
particularly in the basement, where there's
a good pit prison, and up on the top floor,
under the roof, from where there is access
to a fine wall-walk with excellent views.
In better condition are the ground floor
and first floors, which both contained
large halls.

The display of medieval and earlier
artefacts in the lower hall is interesting;
the modern tapestries on show in the
upper hall rather less so. There are several
interesting details on the 'in between'
levels, where there are small chambers in
the thickness of the wall; one contains
some pine panelling of the late 1500s.

On the A72 just west of Peebles.

Smailholm Tower

Historic Scotland • ££ • Usual hours

Again, the setting contributes hugely to
the appeal of this nice little tower, which
stands on a small, rocky ridge in an
upland area of high moorland. It still looks
much as it did when Turner painted it in
the early 1800s. The large pond in front of
it is a mill pond; its water used to drive a
mill-wheel down by the farm.

The tower is a pretty building, but not
packed with interest; the best part is that
you can get out on the roof. Smailholm is
famous for its association with the writer
Sir Walter Scott, who as a child was sent
to stay with his aunt at the nearby farm,
and the stories he heard here inspired his
interest in local ballads and legends.

This association is reflected in a very
sad display of models inside the tower.

Signposted off the B6404 west of Kelso.

*Neidpath Castle is a fascinating example of an
early, thick-walled, primitive-looking tower house.*

*Below: Smailholm Tower is an attractive and very
simple little building of the mid-1400s.*

Tantallon Castle

There are superb views out to sea from Tantallon's majestic curtain wall, with Bass Rock just off the coast.

Historic Scotland • ££ • Usual hours

Headlands and promontories have long been popular places to put fortifications – since the iron age, if not before – because they're such easy places to defend. All you have to do is throw a single rampart across the width of the headland and, if the cliffs are high enough, the natural defences of the site do the rest. Tantallon is one of the most modern and most remarkable examples of this philosophy in action.

Built in about 1350, the castle basically consists of nothing more than a single dirty great wall which cuts off the approach to a headland. Behind the wall is a flat, grassy courtyard, around the perimeter of which the cliffs are so sheer that no further walls are needed. The only other buildings are a hall block on the north side of the yard, and traces of a sea gate at the top of a path which led down the cliffs to the rocky shore.

One thing that makes this a particularly enjoyable place to visit is the castle's clifftop setting, with extensive views along the coast and out to sea. Inevitably, the bit of scenery that really catches the eye (as long as visibility isn't spoiled by fog or rain) is the astonishing little island

known as Bass Rock, a 'plug' or core of hard rock from the middle of a volcano which rises sheer out of the sea. In spring, the sides of the rock appear white because they are covered with breeding seabirds, particularly gannets: it's worth putting 20p in the telescope to get a better look.

But the thing that really makes this a memorable place to visit is, of course, that huge curtain wall. As with all the best medieval castles, it's the monumental scale of the structure that impresses, especially when you climb up on top of it and peer cautiously over the edge. Mere statistics – the wall is more than 3.5m (12ft) thick and 15m (50ft) high – don't do it justice.

On either side of the central gate tower (known as the Mid Tower), stairs lead up inside the thickness of the wall. The stairs start as a straight flight, roofed by a series of arches, like the ribs of a vast alien beast; then, halfway up, the straight flight ends and a spiral stair takes you the rest of the way up to the wall-walk. Up here you can properly appreciate the size of the wall you're standing on and the simplicity of the castle's design, but you also have superb views inland, vividly illustrating the advantages that being this high up

gave the castle's defenders. It feels as if you can see as far as Edinburgh. Prominent in the view are two more striking volcanic outcrops: to the right, the pointy North Berwick Law, and over to the left, the whale-like Traprain Law.

The towers at either end of the wall were pounded to rubble by Cromwell's artillery in 1650, and the Mid Tower has no floors, so there's not a lot else to see; but from up on the wall you get a good view of the top part of the Mid Tower, where a high bridge between the two projecting round towers helped defenders cover the approach to the gate.

The castle had a very colourful history, well worth reading up on in the guidebook. It was probably built not long after 1346 by William Douglas, whose son George, first Earl of Angus, was the founder of the branch of the Douglas family known as the Red Douglases. Their constant feuds with the other side of the family and their habit of conspiring with the kings of England meant that Tantallon was frequently besieged, but it wasn't taken by force until Cromwell's arrival.

Signposted from the A1, free car park on site.

See also...

Coldingham Priory

Church of Scotland, free, limited hours (open Wednesday afternoons in summer). In the middle of the village of Coldingham.

An early Christian community was founded here by Ebba, sister of King Oswald of Northumbria (who founded Lindisfarne in 635). St Cuthbert is said to have waded in the sea here and had his feet dried by two helpful otters. The present parish church is built from what was left of the choir belonging to a medieval priory church: one side is over-restored, but the other is quite original in appearance.

Doonhill homestead

Historic Scotland; free, open access at any reasonable time. Signposted from the A1 to the south of Dunbar.

It's not much to look at, but this was the hall of an Anglian chief, spotted on aerial photographs and excavated in the 1960s. The timber buildings left little trace: their outlines are marked on the ground. The large Anglian hall of the 500s was replaced by a smaller, newer Saxon one in the 600s. It's worth seeing just to get a glimpse of life in this little-known period of the dark ages.

Edrom church

Historic Scotland; free, open access at any time. In the village of Edrom off the A6105, in the grounds of the present parish church.

All that's left of the Norman church here is one elaborate chancel arch, dating from about 1100, with a later shed-like structure tacked on the back as a mausoleum. The remnant is important evidence of the Normanisation of this region in the early 1100s.

Fast Castle

On headland north of St Abbs Head. From the A1117 north of Coldingham, follow a minor road to the coast (signposted Dowlaw). Unless you have a rugged vehicle, park at the side of the road before the farm. On foot, follow hand-painted signs through the farm, then pass through a rickety gate and on to the coastal path that leads to the castle.

There's very little left of this stone castle perched on a precarious promontory – just a few lumps of incongruous wall that look as though you could push them over. It's a memorable location, but even the coastal views aren't that great, though this is a splendid place to watch seabirds. The walk takes about 20 minutes getting there and, because it's steeply uphill, twice as long coming back.

Greenknowe Tower

Historic Scotland; free, open access at any reasonable time. Beside the A6105 west of Gordon.

This is a superb little L-plan tower built in 1581, complete with is original iron 'yett', or gate, and with some interesting decoration over the door. There's a vaulted basement containing a kitchen, with a hall on the first floor above. From here up, all the floors are missing, but the stair still goes all the way to the top of the building.

Right: Thirlestane Castle.

Greenknowe Tower.

Inchcolm Abbey

Historic Scotland; free access to the island, but the boat trip is expensive (££££, boat sails once a day in summer months from the pier at South Queensferry).

This ruined abbey stands on an island in the Firth of Forth (and is strictly speaking in Fife, though the boat leaves from this side of the river). The abbey is in remarkably good condition and is worth seeing, but the boat fare might put you off. More of a nice day trip than a heritage experience.

Thirlestane Castle

Privately owned, £££, usual hours (summer only). Signposted on the A68 just south of Lauder.

An appealingly grand and baronial creation trimmed with pink stone. The original tower is from 1590, but the castle was rebuilt in the 1670s and 1840s to produce one of Scotland's most splendid houses.

Torphichen preceptory

(Historic Scotland, ££, limited hours (weekends in summer only), In Torphichen, south of Linlithgow

This still-roofed remnant of a church of the Knights Hospitaller is an appealing little medieval building.

And...

Ayton Castle, *Ayton, (privately owned) –* This great red sandstone baronial pile, open to visitors on occasion, is Victorian in date.

Dreva Craig hillfort, *south of Broughton –* Another of the region's excellent hillforts (*see page 52*) consisting of two stone ramparts and defended by a *cheveaux de frise* (pointy stones were stuck in the ground to hinder attacks).

Dunbar Castle, *by the harbour in Dunbar –* The once-important castle here has more or less completely crumbled away, and the remains are unsafe, so there's no access. Worth a look if you're passing, though.

Eagle Rock, *Cramond (Historic Scotland, free, open access) –* This defaced carving of indeterminate age is said to be a Roman eagle. It's of little interest in itself, but it marks one of the Romans' major bases in Scotland.

Foulden tithe barn, *beside the A6105 Duns to Berwick-upon-Tweed road (Historic Scotland, free, open access) –* A small two-storey barn used to store tithe produce by local church. It's not a very interesting example.

Rosslyn Chapel, *near Roslin, Midlothian (privately owned by charitable trust, ££, usual hours) –* Remarkably ornate chapel of 1446 featuring lots of intriguing carvings. Odd.

Traquair, *near Innerleithen, signposted from the A72 east of Peebles (privately owned, £££, usual hours, summer only) –* This fine old mansion has a long and interesting history and a very appealing atmosphere. It also has its own brewery producing excellent bottled ales.

Trimontium, *Melrose town centre (privately owned by a charitable trust, ££, usual hours in summer only) –* A small but quite interesting local museum that specialises in telling the story of the Roman fort of Newstead and the neighbouring Celtic town of Eildon Hill North, both of which have been extensively excavated. There are lots of interesting finds.

Dumfries & Galloway

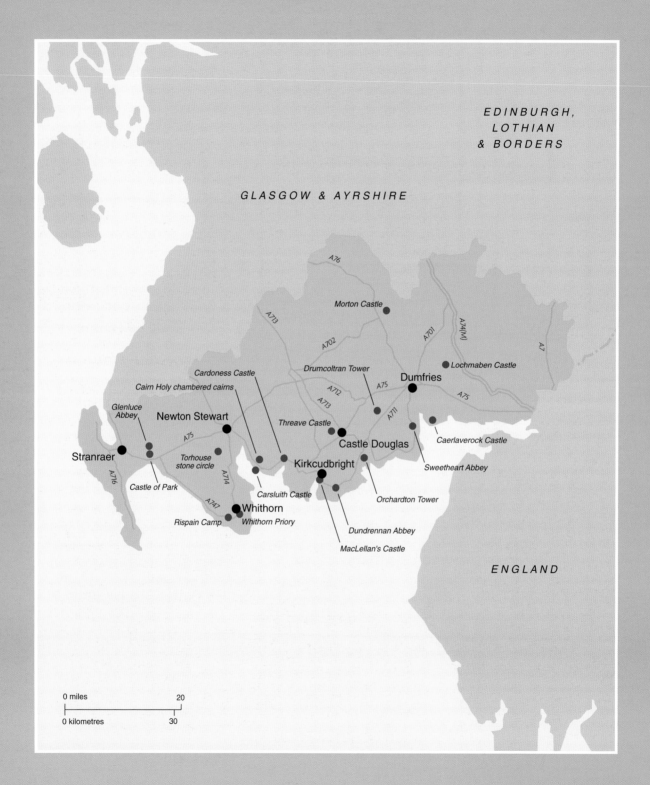

EDINBURGH, LOTHIAN & BORDERS

GLASGOW & AYRSHIRE

A76

A713

Morton Castle

A702

A701

A74(M)

A7

Drumcoltran Tower

Lochmaben Castle

Cardoness Castle

Cairn Holy chambered cairns

A75

Dumfries

Glenluce Abbey

Newton Stewart

A75

A712

A713

Threave Castle

A711

Stranraer

Torhouse stone circle

A714

Kirkcudbright

Castle Douglas

Caerlaverock Castle

A716

Castle of Park

Sweetheart Abbey

A747

Carsluith Castle

Orchardton Tower

Rispain Camp

Whithorn

Whithorn Priory

Dundrennan Abbey

MacLellan's Castle

ENGLAND

0 miles   20

0 kilometres   30

Caerlaverock Castle

With its unusual triangular plan, Caerlaverock is one of Scotland's most interesting early medieval castles.

Historic Scotland • ££ • Usual hours.

One of the best-preserved early medieval castles in Scotland, Caerlaverock was built to a most unusual triangular plan, with a tower at each of the back two corners and a double tower forming the gatehouse at the front.

These fundamental elements of the design date to before 1300, but the castle was adapted and enhanced during later phases of reconstruction which added several grand accommodation ranges to the interior of the castle.

The last phase of building was carried out by the then owner of the castle, the Earl of Nithsdale, as recently as 1634. Just six years later the earl, who was a staunch supporter of the king, was obliged to surrender the castle to an army of Covenanters, who tore parts of it down, and it fell into decay. The result is that the whole rearward wall has vanished, along with most of the accommodation range that ran along it, giving a kind of cut-away diagram effect as you peer into the courtyard from the other side of the moat.

Inside, the castle is not as much fun to explore as you might hope: there's not much medieval stuff left, and the interiors of the accommodation ranges (the ones on the right are from the 1400s and 1500s,

the rest from the 1600s) are more like the rooms of a house than a castle. The most enjoyable aspect is the fine carving of the decorative stonework: look out for the date 1634 over a door.

Beyond the castle, a short but very pleasant nature trail takes in the site of the

The ornately decorated accommodation on the north-east side of the courtyard dates from 1634.

original castle, built in the early 1200s and abandoned because it was too marshy. The site was excavated in 1999.

Other little items of interest to look out for include the carved stones that are now housed in the café, including a particularly ugly gargoyle-type face, and the graffiti of no less a figure than Robert Burns, who carved his initials and the date 1776 into the wall of the gatehouse.

By far the most interesting episode in the history of the castle was a siege by the English forces of King Edward I in 1300. What makes this event so special is that a lengthy account of it was written by one of the attackers (in French and in verse, but that hardly matters).

The writer first describes the castle: "In shape it was like a shield, for it had but three sides round it, with a tower at each corner; but one of them was a double one, so high, long and wide that the gate was underneath it, well made and strong, with a drawbridge and other defences." He praises its strength and its setting, then details how Edward, with an army of 83 knights and 3000 men, camped in front of the castle before bringing up siege engines that soon persuaded it to surrender.

Signposted on the B725 south-east of Dumfries.

Thin, weathered fingers of stone form an impressive facade for the lower Cairn Holy chambered tomb.

Cairn Holy chambered cairns

Historic Scotland • Free • Open access at any reasonable time

These two ruined monuments might not be quite as dramatic as some of the neolithic tombs in the north of Scotland, where the dark, mysterious passages and chambers are intact and can be explored. But the first of the two Cairn Holy cairns, in particular, has a lot to recommend it.

The tomb's most impressive feature is its curved facade of tall, thin, weathered fingers of stone. It's the finest neolithic tomb facade in Scotland – indeed, it's hard to think of anything to rival it between here and Wayland's Smithy or the West Kennet long barrow, way down in the south-west of England.

The forecourt of the tomb would almost certainly have been used for some kind of ceremony, and excavations found traces of fires, as well as showing that the area had been scattered with small stones. Behind the facade are two well-built burial compartments, one of

them covered with a remarkable orange lichen. The acidic soil had destroyed any traces of bones, but pieces of pottery were found, along with a flint knife and a broken ceremonial axe of jadeite.

The vast long mound of stones that formed the body of the long cairn is much reduced, but you can see how impressive it would have been. The views out to sea are also pretty striking.

A short walk up the track takes you to the more jumbled ruins of the second (or upper) cairn, which is also worth seeing.

Signposted from the A75 between Kircudbright and Newton Stewart (near the castles opposite).

Right: an immense capping stone still covers the chamber of the upper Cairn Holy tomb.

62

Cardoness Castle

Historic Scotland • ££ • Usual hours

One of the finest examples of the older, more primitive style of tower house in which all the accommodation is stacked one room on top of another in a single thick-walled tower. (Compare it with a more sophisticated later design such as *Elcho Castle, Tayside*, where the lord's private chamber is next to the hall on the first floor, and a wide, elegant staircase is located in a side-tower.)

The half-ruined interior certainly looks pretty primitive, but it's full of interesting details. Behind the door is a short entrance passage with a murder hole above, through which defenders could drop spiky things on anyone who was forcing an entry – though as the guidebook points out, it was also useful as a hatch through which bulky items could be hoisted up to the upper storage floor.

The basement level, with a barrel-vaulted ceiling, was split into two floors for storage. On both levels there is also a cramped prison cell in the thickness of the wall. Further up the narrow spiral stair, on the first floor proper, is the hall, which has a huge fireplace (note the salt-box, where the all-important salt cellar was kept dry) and finely carved cupboards.

The second floor accommodation was originally one big room, but was later divided by a large wall which hangs above the hall on a flat arch. Recently, half this level has been given a new wooden floor (wide gaps between the timbers make it feel a little precarious, mind) so that you can examine the rooms. There were two more floors above this one, too.

Right beside the A75 between Kircudbright and Newton Stewart

Carsluith Castle

Historic Scotland • Free • Open access during reasonable hours only

Follow the main road along the coast from *Cardoness Castle* (*above*) and you soon come to this small but interesting tower, which stands between the barn and house of a farm. Like most castles in the region, it's by the shore, with good sea access.

It's a thoroughly pleasant little building, based on a structure of the late 1400s but extensively renovated in 1568, when the addition of a stair-tower in imitation of a modern L-plan design made it possible to organise the rooms in a much more civilised way.

The ground floor is just cellars, with a vaulted stone roof (the kitchens were presumably in a separate building). On the

Left: Carsluith Castle is a small, very appealing tower house that was brought up to date in 1568.

The excellent Cardoness Castle is a superb example of the earlier, more basic style of tower house.

first floor is the hall, which has a number of interesting details, including a salt-box at the side of the grand fireplace, and wall-cupboards in which the family silver could be displayed.

The most unusual feature of the house, though, was a balcony, of which the only surviving traces are the holes that held the beams on which it rested. An old window was converted into a door to give access to it from the second floor, which was divided by a wooden partition wall into two rooms, the lord's bedchamber and drawing room, each with its own fireplace.

On the southern side of the A75 midway between Kirkcudbright and Newton Stewart, a couple of miles south-east of Creetown and north-west of the turning to Cairn Holy. It's a difficult turning, so take great care.

Drumcoltran Tower

Historic Scotland • Free • Open access during reasonable hours only

Just like *Carsluith Castle (previous page)*, this modest but well-preserved tower stands among farm buildings. It's quite a nice one to look round: a stair takes you all the way up to the rooftop, where a walkway leads right round the parapet.

Built in the mid-1500s, it's a very simple variation on the L-plan design, consisting of a three-storey tower with an adjoining stair tower. The stair brings you out in the hall on the first floor, with the kitchens and cellars below. At the top of the stair, at roof level, is a cap house containing a little guard room with its own window and fireplace, which is rather charming.

Signposted on a minor road just off the A711 between Dumfries and Dalbeattie. Parking in a layby on the road by the farm..

Drumcoltran Tower, standing among the buildings of a working farm, is an enjoyable place to visit.

Dundrennan Abbey

Historic Scotland • ££ • Usual hours

Since it was the principal offshoot in Scotland of the great Cistercian abbey of Rievaulx, in Yorkshire, you might expect Dundrennan to be a grand affair, and clearly it was. Today, the sheer size of the ruined abbey church is still very impressive: it takes a while before you realise that the main surviving piece is the two transepts of the church, and therefore represents just the width of the building, rather than its full length.

Having said which, it's not the most fascinating ruin to visit: there's just not enough of it left. Once you've appreciated the size of the chapter house (obviously very grand in its day, but only parts of one wall still stand), explored the foundation-level remains of the cloisters and admired the architecture of the surviving bit of church, with its soaring 'bundle of shafts' pillars, there is not a lot else to do.

The abbey was founded in 1142 at the personal invitation of King David I, who was probably Scotland's greatest founder of religious houses: he established other Cistercian abbeys at Newbattle, Kinloss and Melrose, gave the Augustinians land at Jedburgh, settled Tironesian monks at Kelso and founded Holyrood.

Here at Dundrennan, Mary Queen of Scots spent her last night on Scottish soil on May 15th, 1568, before fleeing to England to appeal for the assistance of her sister in regaining her throne.

Signposted in the middle of Dundrennan village, on the A711 south-east of Kirkcudbright.

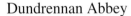

Below: the size and grandeur of Dundrennan Abbey in its heyday is merely hinted at by its remains.

Glenluce Abbey

Historic Scotland • ££ • Usual hours (all year)

The guidebook isn't quite right when it says that all too little of the abbey survives, 'but hints of its former grandeur may be seen in the south transept of the church and in the chapter house'. All too little of it survives, certainly, but 'grandeur' is hardly the right word for what was clearly a modest establishment.

It's a very pleasant little place to visit, however, in the pretty setting of a sheltered river valley, and it's not without its points of interest. The church is more or less completely destroyed: even the surviving piece of the south transept has none of its decorative stonework left. The main thing to look out for is a doorway at first-floor level where the night stairs led up to the monks' dormitory.

The best bit, though, is the cloister, where the chapter house is still complete. It's quite small and plain by comparison with chapter houses at many other abbeys, but it has a nice vaulted ceiling and some elegant carving around the door, and part of the original tiled floor survives.

Just outside the chapter house, a small part of the cloister arcade has been rebuilt, which gives a useful taste of what the cloister would have looked like. Nearby is an exposed section of the abbey's clever system of drains, and in the museum you can see some of the ingenious clay sewage pipes which were found here.

Founded in 1190, Glenluce is thought to have been an offshoot of the Cistercian abbey at *Dundrennan* (*opposite*), though there's a theory that its mother house may

Glenluce Abbey is a modest but thoroughly pleasant ruin, with a small but well-preserved chapter house.

have been *Melrose Abbey* (*page 56*), whose cellarer, Brother William, was appointed abbot at Glenluce in 1214.

Signposted from the A75 at Glenluce village.

Lochmaben Castle

Historic Scotland • Free • Open access at any reasonable time

There's not much left of this large and important castle, which was once the seat of the Bruce family; but it's still worth taking a look at. The ruin now stands on a small promontory in the loch (originally, this was an island) and has been quarried of its facing stone, which has led to the collapse of most of the walls, though the few surviving fragments are impressively heavy and solid-looking.

The most complete part of the castle – and the most interesting – is the front wall, with the main gateway right in the middle. The water-filled moat was crossed by a drawbridge, and you can still see the stone footings on which the machinery rested.

On either side of the gate, at right angles to the front wall of the castle, are two massive flanking walls which cross the moat on wide arches. It's a most unusual arrangement, and one that leaves you trying to puzzle out what the idea of it could have been. Perhaps the walls sheltered an outer bailey where supplies could be landed from rowing boats that were brought in along the moat.

Some local romantics maintain that Lochmaben Castle was the birthplace of Robert the Bruce, but Turnberry in Ayrshire is a more likely candidate for that honour. Robert's father was for a time allied to Edward I, but presumably that was no longer the case by 1298, when the English king captured the timber castle which stood here at the time. The stonework dates from not long afterwards.

Signposted off the B7020 south of the small town of Lochmaben (west of Lockerbie).

Left : the front of Lochmaben Castle, with the gate on the left, and one of the unusual flanking walls.

An elegant later tower house, MacLellan's Castle was built by a wealthy local laird in the late 1500s.

MacLellan's Castle

Historic Scotland • ££ • Usual hours (summer only)

This is a good example of a smart and spacious later tower house, the only slight drawback being that it's not terrifically interesting to look round.

The castle was built in the middle of the small but flourishing harbour town of Kircudbright by Sir Thomas MacLellan of Bombie, a local bigwig who distinguished himself in 1547 by freeing the town from a siege by a small English army. From this time on his fortunes were on the up and up, and from 1576 to his death in 1597 he served as Provost of the burgh. With the money from local customs duties, added to his income from land and trade, he was a pretty wealthy man.

Below: Morton is an unusual and surprisingly ancient type of castle in a fine pastoral setting.

In 1569, Sir Thomas acquired the land and buildings of the disused Greyfriars church, and here he started to build himself a grand new residence using the stone of the old buildings. It seems that it was never actually finished, though it was lived in. Sir Thomas's son and heir later moved to Ireland and frittered away the family's wealth.

It's a large building, shaped like an L-plan with an extra tower on the corner opposite the leg of the 'L'. The most interesting bit to explore is the dark and gloomy ground floor level, where there are lots of cellars and a kitchen. Upstairs is a large hall with a private chamber beyond, and there would have been rooms on two higher storeys, but none of the floors has survived.

Right in the middle of Kirkcudbright.

Morton Castle

Historic Scotland • Free • Open access at any reasonable time

The beautiful setting, on a promontory high above a loch, is very well groomed (it's on the estate of the Duke of Buccleuch) but it's a long way off the beaten track.

The castle dates from the late 1200s (old for a Scottish castle) and is basically a grand version of a hall-house – an early equivalent of the tower house in which the main rooms were a hall on the first floor and a basement below. In this case, though, the layout is more ambitious, with kitchens on the ground floor, an elaborate gate tower and a side-tower with private rooms.

The castle was the seat of the Earls of Morton, a branch of the Douglas family, and was occupied into the early 1700s.

Orchardton Tower is small and pretty, and is the only example of a round tower house.

It's not entirely without interest, but the surviving shell of the building is not too exciting to explore. The best reason to come here is for the scenery, and it would be a fine spot for a picnic.

From the A702 north of Carronbridge, turn right down the first minor road, towards East Morton, then straight on at the crossroads. On entering the estate, take the track on the right, signposted to the castle. A short way along, where another track leaves to the right, park and follow the footpath to the castle (on the left of the track).

Orchardton Tower

Historic Scotland • Free • Open access at any reasonable time

This exceedingly cute little building is the only round tower house in Scotland. It was built in about 1450 for a man by the name of John Carnys (or Cairns), who was a figure of some standing locally but presumably was not the wealthiest of individuals.

A door at ground level leads only to a cellar with a vaulted roof; to get to the rest of the tower, you climb an external stair to the first floor. This level seems to have been used as a chapel, at least in the castle's later days; the lord's hall, which you might expect to find here, was in one of the ruined neighbouring buildings.

There are no floors inside the tower, but a tiny, narrow spiral stair in the thickness of the wall leads up to the battlements and is covered by a tiny cap-house. It's all very charming and scenic.

Signposted down a minor road off the A711 to the south of Dalbeattie.

Sweetheart Abbey

Historic Scotland • ££ • Usual hours

The highlight of this little ruined abbey is the church, which is in an unusually good state of preservation: even its tower still stands, which is not something you find very often, and it has some very nice details in its stonework. Just as importantly, though, the abbey is set in a quiet little village in a pleasant piece of countryside not too far from the only large town in the region, Dumfries, which makes it a classic destination for a nice afternoon out.

The abbey was founded in 1273 by Lady Devorgilla of Galloway in memory of her late husband, John Balliol. In an episode that some might consider to be deeply romantic but others would find slightly morbid, after his death in 1269 Devorgilla had her husband's heart embalmed and placed in a casket of ivory bound with silver. When she herself died in 1289 at the age of 80, the casket was buried with her in the abbey, which is how the place got its name.

There's a stone effigy of her clutching her husband's heart to her breast, but it was rather badly defaced at the time of the Reformation. Another of Devorgilla's memorials was her endowment of Balliol College at Oxford University in 1282, and she also paid for the lovely stone bridge over the River Nith in Dumfries.

Probably the most beautiful part of the abbey church is the nave, with its simple, striding arches in dark red sandstone, but there are plenty of attractive details to be found elsewhere, and it's worth spending some time having a careful look around.

One interesting feature is the big window in the west end of the church, which had to be altered after some kind of accident – probably a lightning strike in 1381 – and was partly filled in, with three smaller pointed arches added at the bottom and a delicate little round window, more like a wheel than a rose, at the top.

There isn't much left of the buildings around the cloister, but one unusual survival that it's worth going in search of is a large part of the precinct wall which would once have surrounded the abbey grounds.

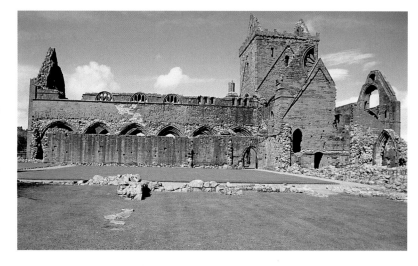

In this view, the cloister wall masks the finest feature of Sweetheart Abbey – the arches of the nave (below).

Nearby, and also in the care of Historic Scotland, is a watermill built in the late 1700s on the site of the monks' mill, which is still in working order and is operated regularly in the summer.

Signposted on the A710 south of Dumfries.

Torhouse stone circle

Historic Scotland • Free • Open access at any reasonable time

It's not terribly large, but this bronze age circle of 19 fat boulders is quite engaging. It's not actually a true circle (it measures over 21m one way and just 20m the other) and its stones show a gradation in size, with the largest ones at the south-eastern edge of the ring.

This arranging of the stones by size prompts comparison with the 'recumbent stone' circles of north-east Scotland (*see pages 150–151*), as does the setting in the middle of the circle, which has two taller stones on either side of a low one.

Where the recumbent stone circles are thought to show an interest in the position of the moon, however, the south-easterly alignment of this circle would suggest an interest in the midwinter sunrise.

In a field on the other side of the road is an alignment of three standing stones, also graded according to their height, which points to the south-west, the direction of the midwinter sunset.

Signposted beside the B733 west of Wigtown.

Left: the fat, pale boulders of Torhouse stone circle are arranged with the biggest to the south-east.

Threave Castle

*Historic Scotland • ££ • Usual hours
(summer only)*

The massive tower of Threave Castle, standing on an island in the River Dee, is a very enjoyable place to visit.

Standing on an island in the middle of the River Dee, this massive tower has a crude grandeur that you can't help but admire, but what makes it such an enjoyable place to visit is the altogether gentler appeal of its quiet countryside setting.

After a pleasant walk past fields to a small jetty, you board a small ferryboat to cross a short stretch of river to the island, which is now about three times as big as it was in the medieval period, when the level of the river was higher. Originally, boats crossed from the far bank of the river to a small dock right by the tower.

The tower is thought to have been built in about 1369 by Archibald 'The Grim', Earl of Douglas, who was given his nickname by the English because of his fierce countenance in battle. His home is one of the earliest tower houses, and when you get inside, it certainly seems ancient: it's dark, heavy and primitive.

A vast, cavern-like basement is topped by a huge barrel-vault, with a most unpleasant-looking prison in the corner. Originally, this huge space would have been divided in two horizontally by a floor, with kitchens on the higher level and cellars below.

The hall on the next floor up is less ugly, but it's still pretty plain, and what little decorative stonework it had was removed along with the timber and ironwork when the castle was dismantled in 1640.

Above the hall were two more levels of chambers, but there are no floors in place.

In front of the great tower, a wall with slot-like openings in it and a little round tower are the surviving elements of one of the earliest known artillery defences, built in 1447 and severely tested in 1455, when King James II besieged the castle as part of his campaign to destroy the Douglases. The castle held out for two months and was probably bribed into surrendering.

Signposted off the A75 west of Castle Douglas.

Left: a friendly ferryman takes you to the island, and the fare is included in the admission fee.

See also...

Castle of Park

Historic Scotland and The Landmark Trust; free, open access to exterior at reasonable times only. To the west of the minor road from Glenluce village to the abbey, near the railway viaduct; follow the track to the coal merchant's.

Recently restored, this neat little tower house is let as a holiday home, but you are permitted to drive up and take a look at the exterior, and tours are given on occasional open days.

Drumtroddan cup and ring carvings and standing stones

Historic Scotland; free, open access at any reasonable time. Signposted up a farm track off the B7085 north of Port William, just north of the junction with the B7021.

An attractive pair of tall, thin standing stones in the middle of a field are thought to have been aligned on the midwinter sunset in the south-west; the third stone in the row has fallen over. On a large outcrop of rock nearby is a really excellent set of cup-and-ring carvings of the early bronze age.

Motte of Urr

In a field next to a minor road leading west from the B794 at Haugh of Urr, north of Dalbeattie.

A huge and immensely impressive earthwork castle consisting of a large, round mound surrounded by a ditch standing within the rampart and ditch of a long, oval-shaped outer bailey. Excellent.

Rispain Camp

Historic Scotland; free, open access during usual hours only. Signposted up a farm track off the A746 west of Whithorn; from a car park by the farmyard it's a short walk through the farm to the camp.

An iron age settlement stood here, in a rectangular enclosure that was defended by a big bank and ditch. The defences were so well constructed and have survived so well that it was thought to be a Roman camp or a medieval manor house, but in fact it was a Celtic farmstead. Well worth seeing.

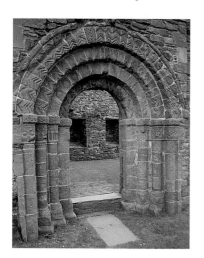

Castle of Park.

Twelve Apostles stone circle

In a field beside the minor road to Newbridge, off the B729 west of the A76 just north of Dumfries.

Said to be the fifth largest stone circle in Britain, this is an oval-shaped setting roughly 80m (260ft) across. Only five stones still stand, but there were probably 18 in the original design. A tall, fallen outlying stone to the north-east suggests that the circle was aligned with the midwinter sunset in the south-west.

Ruthwell Cross

Historic Scotland, free, key available from nearby house during usual hours only. Signposted from the B724 north of Ruthwell village, west of Annan.

This extraordinary carved cross, more than 5m (16ft) high and probably made in the early 700s, is one of the artistic masterpieces of its time, but it now stands inside a church in a crowded setting which somehow makes it seem a little sterile. As well as religious scenes on its faces and leafy tracery on either side, the cross is carved with both Latin text and Saxon runes, the latter being lines from an Old English poem called 'The Dream of the Rood'.

Whithorn Priory

Historic Scotland, ££, usual hours (summer only). In the middle of Whithorn.

The bishopric of St Ninian in the fifth century AD, this was an early Christian site of great importance, but it's not a terrifically interesting place to visit. In the churchyard of the more recent church are parts of the medieval cathedral church, which can be visited free of charge; the bits you pay to see are a few catacomb-like underground vaults and a museum containing a collection of carved stones, some of which are very, very old. They include a monument of the mid-400s AD which bears the oldest Christian inscription in Scotland.

Other early Christian sites associated with Whithorn include **St Ninian's Cave**, *on the coast at Physgill*, where there are carved crosses which date to the 800s; and **St Ninian's Chapel**, *on the island at Isle of Whithorn*, which was built in the 1200s and has been restored. **Chapel Finian**, *on the coast by the A747 south of its junction with the B7005*, was a small chapel of about 1000 AD thought to have been used by Irish pilgrims on their way to Whithorn, but only its foundations survive.

Left: Whithorn Priory.

And...

Barsalloch fort, *on a cliff above the A747 to the north of Barsalloch Point (Historic Scotland; free, open access at any reasonable time)* – This small iron age fort defended by a horseshoe-shaped ditch is not very interesting to look at, and there is no proper path by which to reach it. Don't bother.

Bruce's Stone, *off the A712 south-west of St John's Town of Dalry (National Trust for Scotland, free, open access at any time)* – A monument marks the spot where Robert the Bruce defeated the English in 1307.

Castle of St John, Stranraer, *in the town centre (Local council, £, slightly limited hours; April to September, closed on Sunday)* – A tower of the early 1500s which was once used as the town gaol, now restored and operating as the local museum.

Castle Kennedy gardens, *signposted off the A75 east of Stranraer (Privately owned, £££, usual hours, April to September only)* – Pleasant gardens surround the ruin of a tower of the early 1600s which burned down in 1716. Only the exterior can be viewed.

Druchtag motte, *just to the north of Mochrum (Historic Scotland; free, open access at any reasonable time)* – A fine steep-sided motte of the 1100s on which a timber castle stood.

Drumlanrig Castle is a very fine house of the late 1600s with a castle-like appearance.

Hoddom Castle and **Repentance Tower**, *at the junction of the B725 with the B723 north of Annan* – Hoddom Castle is an L-plan tower of 1590 with various later additions, and it stands, neglected, in the middle of a holiday park. The estate encourages walkers to visit the grounds (a leaflet is available) and one of the trails leads up the hill to the tower, which was built in the 1550s and has been restored.

Kirkmadrine, *Rhinns of Galloway, signposted off the A716 at Sandhead (Historic Scotland; free, open access at any reasonable time)* – Three of the earliest Christian memorial stones in Britain, dating from the 400s or early 500s, displayed in a restored chapel.

Laggangairn standing stones, *on the Southern Upland Way miles from anywhere, in the countryside to the north of Glenluce (Historic Scotland)* – Two stones with early Christian carvings.

Lincluden College, *signposted on the western outskirts of Dumfries (Historic Scotland; free, open access at any reasonable time)* – Ruin of a Collegiate church plus accommodation.

Mote of Mark, *by signposted footpath from the village of Rockcliffe (National Trust for Scotland)* – Interesting remains of a hillfort occupied and burned in the 700s AD and associated in local tales with the King Mark of Arthurian legend.

Glasgow and around
Including Ayrshire, Lanarkshire and Dunbartonshire

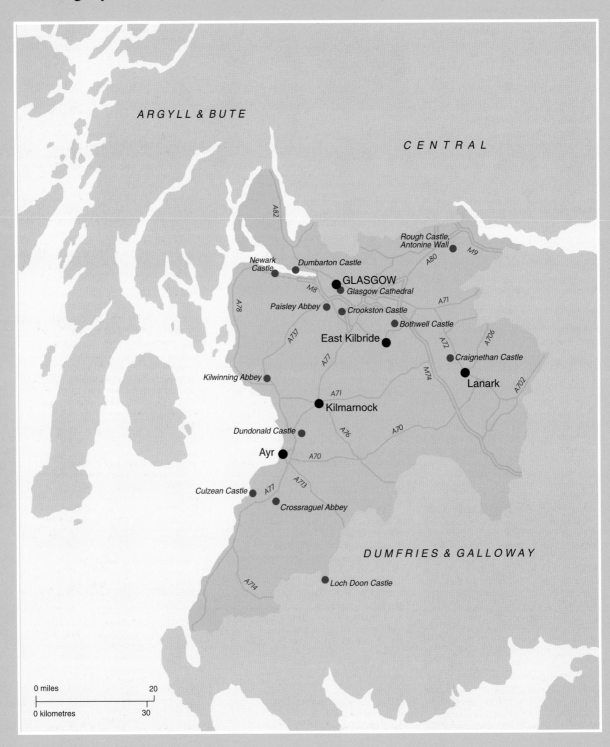

ARGYLL & BUTE

CENTRAL

A82

Rough Castle,
Antonine Wall

A80

M9

Newark
Castle

Dumbarton Castle

GLASGOW

Glasgow Cathedral

A71

M8

A78

Paisley Abbey

Crookston Castle

Bothwell Castle

A706

A737

East Kilbride

A72

Craignethan Castle

A77

Kilwinning Abbey

M74

Lanark

A702

A71

Kilmarnock

Dundonald Castle

A76

A70

Ayr

A70

A713

Culzean Castle

A77

Crossraguel Abbey

DUMFRIES & GALLOWAY

A714

Loch Doon Castle

| 0 miles | | 20 |
| 0 kilometres | | 30 |

A castle of two halves: the curtain wall and the accommodation at the east end are later work…

Bothwell Castle

Historic Scotland • ££ • Usual hours

If it had ever been finished, this would have been one of the finest medieval castles in Europe; but just as it neared completion in the late 1200s, it was caught up in the fiercest stage of the conflicts between England and Scotland.

It's some consolation that the castle was later completed to a different design which also had a certain grandeur, but there's not even enough of this work left to make it a truly inspiring place to visit.

The castle is in a superb position next to the deep, wooded valley, almost a gorge, in which the River Clyde runs. (There's a footpath by the riverbank if you fancy a stretch of the legs.) A timber castle had stood somewhere in the area – probably by the old parish church – since the 1100s, but in the late 1200s work started on the splendid new stone castle. It was probably ordered by William Moray, lord of Bothwell from 1278, whose nickname 'William the Rich' suggests he had a bob or two to spend on good masonry.

Only the great round keep and a short stretch of wall next to it leading to a narrow prison tower had been finished when the castle was first captured by the English in 1296. William Moray was captured and killed; his nephew and heir, Andrew Moray, died fighting alongside William Wallace at the Battle of Stirling Bridge the following year, but the son born after his death and named Andrew in

his honour would later play a decisive part in the castle's history.

In 1298, the Scots began a siege that lasted 14 months before eventually the castle was taken 'by famine and assault'. In 1301, Edward I brought an army of 7,000 men and a vast siege-tower and in just a month regained the castle, which then stayed in English hands until after the Scottish victory at Bannockburn in 1314.

In the midst of all this upheaval, the original plan to build a curtain wall surrounding a huge courtyard and fortified by round towers had long been forgotten, though the foundations of the towers had already been laid and can still be seen.

The final chapter in the story of the great round keep began in 1336, when it was occupied by Edward III. In early 1337 the castle was retaken by the very same Sir Andrew Moray of Bothwell mentioned above, who had already thrown the English out of the castles at Dunnottar and St Andrews, and he then threw down half the wall of the keep so that it would never be of any use to the English again.

Bizarrely, the half-keep was later walled up and used as accommodation, and both the basement and an upstairs floor of this bastard tower can be visited. Its most interesting features are all details that survive from the original keep, such as the graceful vaults and windows.

The ruin was acquired in 1362 by Archibald Douglas, called 'the Grim',

who rebuilt it as his principal residence. An immense square tower at the north-east corner of the castle, taller even than the old round tower, was the main residence, but this has now completely disappeared. It may have been abandoned in favour of a more elegant range along the south wall of the castle. On the east side of the courtyard is a great hall of the early 1400s which is the best-preserved piece (the curtain wall excepted) of the later castle.

On the east bank of the Clyde, signposted on the 'B' road from Bothwell north to Uddingston.

…while the original great round tower or 'donjon' was destroyed only a few years after it was built.

Crossraguel Abbey

The church and sacristy of the charming Crossraguel Abbey, with the eccentric gatehouse visible beyond.

Historic Scotland • ££ • Usual hours

This is one of the most enjoyable of Scotland's ruined abbeys to visit, its quiet charm more than making up for the lack of grandeur in its architecture.

It's good that so many different parts of the abbey have survived, including some unusual buildings, the most eyecatching of which is a tall gatehouse built in the early 1500s to reflect the growing prestige and, no doubt, wealth of the abbot. With its eccentric-looking stair turret topped by a tiny square room which originally gave access to a wall-walk, the restored gatehouse is a good place to start your tour of the abbey, because it offers an excellent vantage point from which to look down over the ruins.

The church is pretty unusual in that it has no transepts (the side-arms which give a church a cross-like plan) and no aisles, consisting instead of a single long building. A cross-wall built in the 1500s separates the nave (the public end of the church) from the choir (the end used by the monks). It's quite a plain church, but the choir is rather more decorative than the nave.

Distinctly more entertaining is the sacristy next door, where the clothes, books and vessels used during the mass were stored. The room is still roofed, with lots of good details in the stonework including some excellent carved bosses where the ribs of the vaulted ceiling meet.

That gatehouse in full: you can climb right to the top for an excellent view over the abbey ruin.

An enjoyable bonus is the chance to try making your mark on a lump of stone using the chisel and mallet provided.

Next to the sacristy is the equally well preserved chapter house, where the monks met every day to hear a reading from the Rule of St Benedict and to discuss the business of the community. Outside, in the middle of the cloister lawn, is an unusual well with steps leading down into it.

The land on which the abbey stands was given to Paisley Abbey in about 1214 by a local earl on the condition that it was used for a daughter monastery, but Paisley was reluctant to give up the income until a judgement by the Bishop in Glasgow in 1244 forced them to get on with it.

The abbey slowly accumulated wealth and rights until in 1404 it was made a regality by King Robert III, giving the abbot the power to judge crimes normally reserved for the Crown (murder, rape, arson and robbery). In 1530, the old abbot's house was replaced by a large, modern tower house, one side of which stands almost to its full height, but there is no access to its upper floors.

Signposted on the A77 south-west of Maybole.

Craignethan Castle

Historic Scotland • ££ • Usual hours (summer months only)

It's an unusual castle, this one, tucked away in a pretty landscape of deep valleys winding among rolling hills and set on a plateau overlooking the River Nethan, which meets the Clyde not far to the east.

There's an outer courtyard surrounded by a wall with a big gatehouse; to one side stands a house built in 1665. At the back is an inner courtyard with a squat tower house in the middle, protected by a wide ditch and some unusual artillery defences. Most of these defences are ruined, but one interesting feature that survives is a very early 'caponier' – a below-ground gun position from which the dry moat could be defended with pistol fire.

The tower has an odd layout, with the hall next to the kitchen on the ground floor. Cellars below are reached by a stair, while an upper floor had four rooms.

Craignethan was built in the 1530s and 1540s by Sir James Hamilton, a son of the Earl of Arran; the family's support for Mary, Queen of Scots led to the castle's destruction as early as 1579.

Signposted on a minor road from the A72 just north of Crossford, near Lanark.

Dundonald Castle

Historic Scotland in association with a local historical trust • ££ • Slightly limited hours (and summer months only)

Scotland's earlier tower houses tend to be massive in construction, plain in shape and primitive in appearance, and this is the biggest, plainest and most primitive-

Craignethan Castle is an odd little tower house of the early 1500s in a very pleasant countryside location.

looking of the lot. Only its size would hint at the fact that this was the home of a King of Scotland, built by Robert II just after he came to the throne in 1371.

Inside the thick walls of the ruined tower is a vast, gloomy, cavernous space roofed by an immense barrel-vault; modern steps lead to a wooden platform halfway up, at the level where a wooden floor originally divided this space between cellars in the basement and the 'low hall' occupying the entire first-floor level.

The floor above this is now open to the sky, but originally it, too, was roofed by a huge barrel-vault and contained a hall that occupied the entire floor. This was the king's Great Hall, warmed by a big fireplace (the low hall only had braziers,

standing next to open flues, more like holes in the ceiling than chimneys, which can still be seen) and its ceiling enhanced by decorative stone vault ribs. There were toilet chambers in the thickness of the north wall, and it's worth peering down the latrine chute. Talk about a long drop.

Originally, the design of the tower provided no small, private chambers at all, but a tall, narrow tower was soon added at the side of the stair tower on the south-east corner of the building. It contained a number of little rooms above a pit prison, and you can go into the latter just so long as it's not flooded at the time.

Though the sheer size of the thing is undoubtedly impressive, it takes quite an effort of the imagination to picture the place as a royal residence, as James Boswell found when he visited the castle in the company of Dr Samuel Johnson in 1773. 'It has long been unroofed; and though of considerable size, we could not, by any power of imagination, figure it as having been a suitable habitation for majesty. Doctor Johnson, to irritate my old Scottish enthusiasm, was very jocular on the homely accommodation of 'King Bob', and roared and laughed till the ruins echoed.'

The tower is built on the foundations of a gatehouse with two round-fronted towers, part of an earlier castle destroyed during the wars with England in the early 1300s. Its well survives; it's full of toads in spring.

Signposted from the A759 and the B730 at the village of Dundonald, west of Kilmarnock.

Left: the immense tower of Dundonald, home of King Robert II, has a certain primitive grandeur.

Dumbarton Castle

Historic Scotland • ££ • Usual hours

Behind the Governor's House of 1735, a path leads up between the Rock of Dumbarton's two summits.

This is a pretty spectacular place to visit, as long as you're prepared for two things: there isn't much castle (most of the surviving defences are from a fort built in the early 1700s) and you will have to climb an awful lot of steps.

The Rock of Dumbarton is a basalt 'plug', the core of a long-extinct volcano: the castles of Edinburgh and Stirling are on similar rocks. Here stood the capital of one of the early kingdoms of Scotland, the Britons of Strathclyde, who struggled for survival against the Angles from Northumbria, the Scots of Dalriada, the Picts of the north-east and Vikings from overseas until in 1018 their kingdom was simply absorbed by the Scots.

There is nothing left of the British fort, though you can see how the rock might have been made habitable. The route to the top is up a narrow defile with steps all the way up, and this path emerges in a kind of saddle between two peaks, where a community could have made the best of the limited shelter available.

There was a succession of medieval castles on the rock, but little trace of them survives: the earliest remnant is a gate of the 1300s with a pointed arch, which was once secured by a portcullis.

The other buildings are nearly all of the 1700s, starting with the Governor's House at the bottom and moving up the steps past two older structures that secure the route – the Guard House, from the late 1500s but modified later, and the aforementioned Portcullis Gate – to the saddle near the top, where a gaol was built in the 1770s to hold prisoners from the Napoleonic wars. High on the east summit are several artillery batteries and a magazine for storing gunpowder.

In the end, none of the buildings is all that interesting; but the summit of this ancient rock is one of those places where it seems like you're at the top of the world, and the views are splendid.

Signposted from the A82 and A814 on the Glasgow side of Dumbarton.

Left: the prison built to house Frenchmen captured in the Napoleonic Wars. An ancient well is nearby.

Loch Doon Castle

Historic Scotland • Free • Open access at any reasonable time

A fair trek into the wilds on a minor road along the shore of Loch Doon brings you to this odd little castle of the 1300s, which originally stood on a small island in the loch but was moved to the shore when the water level was raised for a hydroelectric scheme in the 1930s.

Originally, the water of the loch lapped at the foot of the eleven-sided curtain wall, and the gate was lower than the courtyard so that a boat could be rowed in. All the accommodation would have been built against the wall: a square tower house was added later, but its foundations were not transferred to the present site.

If you don't relish going back the way you came, for a small fee you can use the forest road, which comes out onto a minor road that runs south to Glentrool Village and north to Straiton via Tallaminnock.

Signposted off the A713 south of Dalmellington.

Newark Castle

Historic Scotland • ££ • Usual hours (summer months only)

It's not often you find a castle standing amongst the tall cranes of a shipyard, but that's not the only claim to fame of this fine little tower house. The way that the

This peculiar little eleven-sided enclosure was moved from its original site on an island in Loch Doon.

area around the castle has been tidied up is a credit to whoever did it, and being able to stand in the wee bit of park here and look out over the great River Clyde sets the tone perfectly for the visit.

The original rectangular tower house of the late 1400s was considerably upgraded in 1597–99, when a dubious character named Sir Patrick Maxwell – a man of great wealth and taste who beat his wife and murdered his neighbours – built a splendid Renaissance mansion with all the latest architectural refinements, including a superb long gallery on the top floor with extensive views over the river.

It's a hugely enjoyable place to explore, full of interesting details – not least a small bedchamber in which most of the original wooden fixtures have survived, including a drop-down bed that folds out of a cupboard.

The gallery is very nice, as is the hall, which takes up most of the first floor of the new range, with a back stair for nipping down to the wine cellar.

Signposted by the A8 in Port Glasgow.

Below: standing on the banks of the Clyde, next to the shipyards, is the elegant Newark Castle.

The Antonine Wall

The well-preserved fort of Rough Castle, seen from the northern side of the Antonine Wall.

A northerly successor, built of turf, to Hadrian's Wall.

The Emperor Hadrian was extremely keen on consolidating the existing frontiers of the Roman Empire, and the famous wall which in 122 AD he ordered to be built across the north of Britain was a concrete symbol of this idea. In 138 AD, though, Hadrian died and was succeeded by his appointed heir, a capable and respected senator called Antoninus Pius.

The policy that Antoninus followed was if anything even more cautious than that of his predecessor, and there was only one place in which he actively pursued the expansion of the Empire: northern Britain.

One of the new emperor's first acts must have been the appointment of the former governor of Lower Germany, a man by the name of Quintus Lollius Urbicus, to the same job in Britain. In 139 and 140 AD, Urbicus is recorded as having carried out building work on the fort at Corbridge in Northumberland, which was the ideal base for any northern campaign. By the end of 142, or the beginning of 143 AD, coins were minted celebrating a victory in Britain.

Urbicus had successfully pushed the frontier north to the narrowest stretch of Scotland, between the estuaries of the great rivers Forth and Clyde, and immediately work started on a new wall similar to, but more economical than, the one built by Hadrian.

There must have been some pressing reason for Antoninus to move the frontier north by force of arms, but there is not even a hint in the historical record of what it might have been. One thing that *is* clear, though, is that it was no longer considered necessary or desirable to separate the native tribes who lived on either side of Hadrian's Wall: the gates at the milecastles were removed and sections of the 'vallum' – the double bank and ditch that ran along the back of the wall – were destroyed.

The Antonine Wall was built in the same way as the hastier sections of its predecessor, from turf on a stone base some 4m (14ft) wide, fronted by a ditch 12m (40ft) across and 3m (10ft) deep. Originally it had forts at intervals of about

eight miles, with 'fortlets' (similar to the milecastles on Hadrian's Wall) at regular intervals in between. Instead of building a vallum all the way along the wall, the forts were provided with an annexe which provided an extra refuge in case of attack from the rear of the wall.

Eventually, the closely spaced fortlets were replaced by more proper forts, with the result that each fort was no more than a day's march from the next: *Rough Castle* (*opposite*) is one of these additional forts. With all these forts, and because this wall was much shorter than Hadrian's Wall, the upshot was that this was a far more heavily defended frontier, with almost twice the concentration of troops.

Even so, it didn't last long. A major military crisis in the 150s meant that more troops had to be brought from Germany, but for a while after 158 AD both walls were restored and manned. After two decades of peace, a major raid on the Antonine frontier prompted a final and permanent withdrawal to Hadrian's Wall.

Rough Castle

Historic Scotland • Free • Open access at any reasonable time

Although the turf-built Antonine Wall must have been just as substantial in its day as the longer-lasting stone of the frontier built by Hadrian, the truth is that it doesn't look like much today. The most dramatic remnant is the ditch, sections of which can be glimpsed sweeping dramatically across fields on either side of Castlecary; but this is the busiest and most densely populated part of Scotland, and even where the wall has survived, it's not always easy to find.

The only site on the Antonine Wall that is *really* worth seeing is this rather well preserved fort, where not only do you have its ramparts and its annexe to look at, but also the ditch and bank of the wall are at their best. It's a pretty spot, too.

The fort was sited next to a steep-sided gully through which a stream runs, and the Military Way crossed the stream on a timber bridge. The fort is not a large one, but the annexe doubles the space available. Excavations found buildings inside the fort and a bath-house in the annexe, but these have since been covered over again.

The north gate of the fort leads to a gap in the wall and a causeway across the ditch, and just outside this entrance is an interesting defensive system known as 'lilia' (lilies), consisting of deep pits which had sharp stakes set in them.

Signposted from the A803 near Bonnybridge, west of Falkirk, down a minor road that turns into a rough track. There's a car park when you reach the end of the track.

A system of pits containing sharp wooden stakes, known as 'lilies', defended the approach to Rough Castle.

☐ **See also...**

Bearsden bath-house

Historic Scotland; free, open access. Signposted from the A809 in Bearsden, north-west of Glasgow.

Excavated foundations of a bath-house in the annexe of a fort, in pretty good condition (though in a prosaic urban setting) and well worth seeing.

Kinneil fortlet

Historic Scotland; free, open access. In the grounds of Kinneil House, Bo'ness.

Fortlet partly restored after excavation, with a section of restored wall and a small museum of finds nearby.

☐ **And...**

Other sections and features of the wall that are in state care and can be visited include: **Bar Hill fort**; **Croy Hill fort**, where there's a decent section of wall and some beacon platforms; sections of ditch at **Dullatur, Tollpark and Garnhall**; the earthworks of a fort at **Castlecary**; a long stretch of rampart and ditch at **Seabegs Wood**; and one of the clearest sections of ditch at **Watling Lodge**.

Below: the wide ditch and rampart of the wall in one of its better stretches at Seabegs Wood.

See also...

Crookston Castle

National Trust for Scotland; free, open access during usual hours. In the middle of a housing estate in Pollock, south-west Glasgow.

A ruined tower house of the early 1400s built to an unusual design consisting of a central block with four projecting towers. Destroyed in 1489, it was later reoccupied and then abandoned again. It's very badly ruined, but modern steps lead to a viewing platform right at the top of one of the towers.

Culzean Castle

National Trust for Scotland, £££, usual hours (summer only – April to October). On the coast west of Maybole, signposted from the A77 and A719.

Not really a castle at all, but a glorious and romantic house of the Georgian era designed by Robert Adam in 1777 and famed for the splendour of its interiors. There are also extensive grounds.

Dean Castle, Kilmarnock

Local council, ££, usual hours. In a country park off Dean Road, Kilmarnock.

Nice tower house of the mid-1300s and palace from 1465 which burned down in 1745 and were rebuilt in the early 1900s. The castle now contains a local museum and the extensive grounds are a country park with facilities such as a children's zoo.

Dunure Castle

Local council; free, open access to exterior only at any time. On the coast, in the town's seaside park.

Sketchy remains of a castle of the 1200s, hardly worth visiting in itself but with a colourful history; in the 1550s, the Earl of Cassilis brought the abbot of Crossraguel Abbey here by force and roasted him on a spit in an attempt to get him to sign over the abbey's lands. The abbot lived to tell the tale and later successfully sued for damages.

Dinvin motte

Near the A714 south of Girvan; park at the start of the road to Fardenew and follow the track to the north of the main road.

Truly awesome earthwork castle, presumably of the 1100s or 1200s, consisting of a huge oval mound surrounded by two vast ditches and ramparts. It looks more like an iron age hillfort than a castle.

Glasgow Cathedral

Historic Scotland and church authorities, free, slightly limited hours (afternoons only on Sundays). In the centre of Glasgow.

The finest cathedral in Scotland, founded by David I and largely built between the 1100s and the 1300s. Unusually, it somehow managed to come through the Reformation more or less unscathed. A recently fitted lighting system has brought out some of the building's finer points.

Kelburn Castle

Privately owned; grounds – ££, usual hours (summer only, April to October); castle open by arrangement. Off the A78 south of Largs.

The very extensive, romantically wild grounds are the actual advertised attraction here, with facilities like a pet zoo and adventure playground for the kids; but you can also book a tour of the house, which is based on a tower house of 1581 and features tasteful Victorian interiors.

Paisley Abbey

Historic Scotland and church authorities, free, slightly limited hours (afternoon only on Sunday). In the centre of Paisley, south-west of Glasgow.

Only the graceful nave of the mid-1400s is original; the rest was restored in the late 1800s. On view here is the Barochan Cross, a weathered but interesting Celtic cross of the 700s.

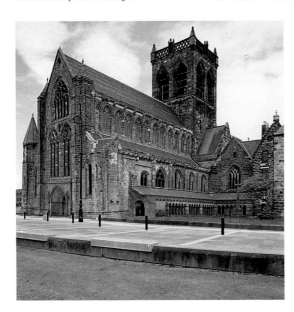

Left: Paisley Abbey.

And...

Arbory Hill hillfort, *reached by a footpath from Raggengill Burn, on the minor road from Abington village which crosses the Clyde and follows the east side of the valley* – One of the best hillforts in Scotland, with two earlier earth ramparts around a smaller, later stone enclosure. There are traces of three round houses.

Biggar gasworks, *signposted from the town centre (Historic Scotland and National Museums of Scotland, ££, usual hours)* – Typical small-town Victorian gasworks, built in 1839 and with lots of its original equipment. Great if you like industrial archeology.

Castle Semple collegiate church, *signposted down a private road off the minor road from Howood to Lochwinnoch (Historic Scotland; free, open access at any reasonable time)* – The ruin of a large, late Gothic church founded in 1504, with an unusual three-sided apse at the east end.

Coulter motte, *signposted off the A72 just south of Biggar (Historic Scotland; free, open access at any reasonable time)* – Large motte of an earthwork-and-timber castle from about 1200.

Kilbarchan Weaver's Cottage, *Kilbarchan, on the A737 south-west of Glasgow (National Trust for Scotland, ££, limited hours – afternoons only, April to September)* – Another part of the story of the region's industries is told eloquently by this little cottage with typical handlooms of the late 1700s and early 1800s. In the 1830s, there were 800 such looms in the village.

Kilwinning Abbey, *in Kilwinning town centre (Historic Scotland; free, open access at any reasonable time)* – Fragmentary but tidy remains of a Tironesian abbey.

New Lanark mills and village, *signposted south-west of Lanark (being restored by a local trust)* – The planned village that accompanied the factories on this site is one of the outstanding monuments of the industrial revolution, built between 1785 and 1825 as a model of enlightened practices by the social reformer Robert Owen. The buildings are slowly being restored, and many are now lived in or used as workplaces by craftspeople.

St Bride's Church, Douglas, *signposted for pedestrians in the town centre (Historic Scotland, free, key from nearby house during usual hours only)* – The choir, re-roofed in the mid-1800s, and part of the nave of a church of the 1300s. Apart from a cute little octagonal bell-tower added in the 1500s, the main attraction is a fine collection of ornate tombs dating from the 1300s onwards.

Skelmorlie Aisle, *signposted for pedestrians in the town centre of Largs (Historic Scotland, free, key from museum during usual hours only)* – One small surviving piece of the old parish church contains a highly decorated burial monument and a richly painted ceiling, both from the 1630s.

*Threave Castle, Kirkcudbright –
see Dumfries & Galloway, page 68.*

Central Scotland

Stirling, Clackmannanshire and the Kingdom of Fife

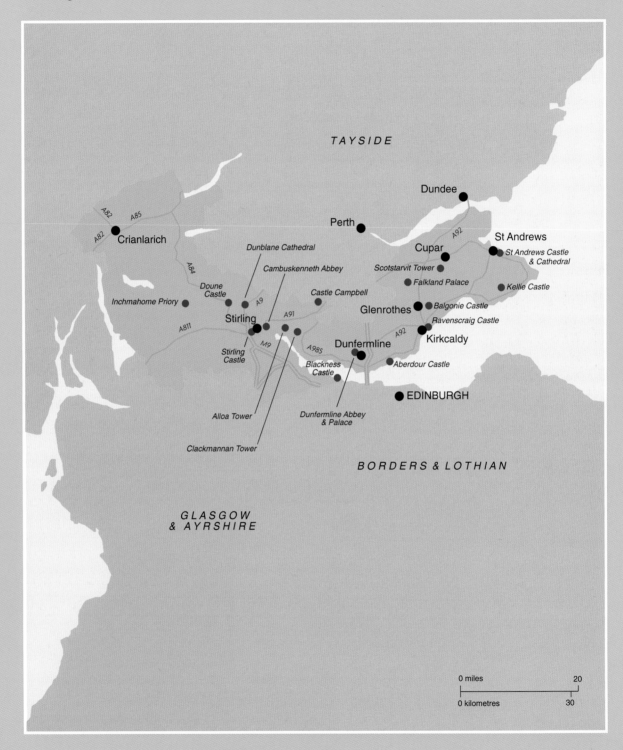

TAYSIDE

Dundee

Perth

Crianlarich

Dunblane Cathedral

Cambuskenneth Abbey

Cupar

St Andrews

St Andrews Castle
& Cathedral

Scotstarvit Tower

Doune
Castle

Inchmahome Priory

Castle Campbell

Falkland Palace

Kellie Castle

Stirling

Glenrothes

Balgonie Castle

Ravenscraig Castle

Kirkcaldy

Stirling
Castle

Dunfermline

Aberdour Castle

Blackness
Castle

EDINBURGH

Alloa Tower

Dunfermline Abbey
& Palace

Clackmannan Tower

BORDERS & LOTHIAN

GLASGOW
& AYRSHIRE

0 miles 20

0 kilometres 30

Aberdour Castle

Historic Scotland • ££ • Usual hours

There's a straggling assortment of ruins on this site, plus a few bits and bobs such as a walled garden and an old church. None of it's very exciting, but it all adds up to a reasonably nice spot to visit.

The first building here was a hall-house (a simple two-storey tower) of the 1100s, which in the early 1400s was rebuilt as a taller, more modern style of tower house. All of this part of the castle, which is easily distinguished by its thicker, cruder masonry, is very badly ruined, though there is a decent bit of gloomy basement.

Various ranges were added to the tower in later years, starting in the 1550s with a building now known as the Central Range. Originally containing a kitchen and store on the ground floor with well-appointed chambers above, this range is now pretty much a ruined shell. It was put up by James Douglas, third earl of Morton, who ruled Scotland as regent from 1572 to 1578 after the abdication of Mary Queen of Scots in favour of her infant son, James VI.

The best-preserved part of the castle is the East Range, which was built in about 1630 for William, the seventh earl, and his wife Anna, Countess of Morton, whose initials appear on a rather charming sundial. The whole of the first floor was taken up with a long gallery, recorded in 1647 as having 46 pictures on display, below which was, oddly, the stables. Most of this range is intact, but its splendour has been tarnished by later alterations. The interiors are pretty ordinary, though there's a good painted ceiling in the adjoining wing.

Aberdour Castle is a mixture of buildings of all sorts of ages; it's pretty, but not terribly exciting.

There are gardens that were laid out at the same time as both ranges: the broad terraces in 1550, which are slowly being restored but are currently unplanted, and the Walled Garden in the 1630s.

The parish church just beyond the garden wall was built in about 1140 and contains some sturdy Norman architecture. It was abandoned in 1790 but restored in the 1920s, at which time a superb stained glass window was installed – clearly the work of a major artist, but unattributed.

Signposted off the A921 in Aberdour, on the coast east of Dunfermline. There is a railway station right by the castle, which makes it a good day trip from Edinburgh across the Forth Bridge.

Alloa Tower

National Trust for Scotland • ££ • Limited hours (summer only, afternoons only)

This sizeable tower house of the 1300s was greatly modified in the early 1700s, when it was incorporated into a baroque residence built by the sixth earl of Mar. Before his house was completed, the earl had to flee into exile as a consequence of having supported the wrong side in the Jacobite uprising of 1715.

The tower was given larger windows and a new entrance, but it does retain some of its original medieval features, including a very old timber roof and some splendid stone vaults.

It has recently been restored and is now furnished, but sparingly, and with the emphasis on portrait paintings.

Signposted on the east side of Alloa town centre (off the A907 west of Stirling).

Left: the origins of Alloa Tower are in the 1300s, but it was considerably upgraded in the 1700s.

See also… Balgonie Castle

Privately owned, ££, usual hours. Signposted on the minor road from Coaltown of Balgonie to Milltown of Balgonie, near Markinch, east of Glenrothes.

You pays yer money and you takes yer choice, of course, but this mildly eccentric castle-visiting experience is said by some to be one of the most enjoyable in Scotland. Guided tours are offered on an *ad hoc* basis by the present 'laird' of the castle, the artist and craftsman Raymond Morris, who simply gives a personal guided tour to anyone who turns up and rings the doorbell.

The main event is a substantial tower house of the 1300s which was restored in the 1970s. It is surrounded by a courtyard with various ruined buildings; one accommodation range of the 1600s has three vaulted cellars, one of which was a kitchen and is now a workshop, the other two forming a chapel. The tower also has a vaulted basement, with the hall on the first floor and a chamber above. Rob Roy of the outlawed Clan MacGregor is said to have stayed here with 200 men in 1716.

Below: at Balgonie Castle, you'll be given a personal welcome by the laird and his family.

Blackness Castle

Historic Scotland • ££ • Usual hours

This fascinating castle is remarkable in a number of different ways, but probably the thing that lives longest in the memory is its severe, uncompromising appearance. In places it's quite astonishingly stark – especially in the courtyard, which is just a jagged expanse of bare rock between high stone walls.

That's not to say, however, that this is an intimidating place to visit. Far from it. The castle's setting, on a headland in the River Forth, is surprisingly scenic, with excellent views across the water and down to the famous Forth bridges. Outside the walls, on a piece of ground drained and levelled during Victorian modifications, is a wide lawn where the kids can play or the family can picnic on a sunny day.

The castle is a peculiar shape because it stands on a long, narrow outcrop of rock, the outline of which its walls are obliged to follow. The result is that it is shaped like a ship – long and narrow, with a point at one end – and it's sometimes referred to as 'the ship that never sailed'.

It was placed here to guard the bay, which is the best natural harbour for miles around and the only one within reasonable distance of the royal palace at Linlithgow.

The massively thick walls of the remarkable Blackness Castle were designed to protect it from cannonfire.

The first castle was built in the mid-1400s by Sir George Crichton, Earl of Caithness, a member of one of the most powerful families in Scotland. Essentially, its basic structure is still intact: the ship-like course of the walls and the tall tower right in the middle both date from this original phase of construction, though both have been altered in later phases.

In 1453, Blackness was acquired by King James II when he annexed the lands owned by the Crichtons. From then on, though its strategic value would have been immense, the castle's most visible role was as a state prison: Cardinal Beaton was held here for a month in 1543.

The 1530s saw a major campaign of rebuilding at Blackness under the direction of Sir James Hamilton of Finnart, who came up with innovative ideas for his own castle at *Craignethan* in Lanarkshire (*see page 73*) and who also worked at Linlithgow Palace and Stirling Castle. His brief was to make the castle safe from attack by artillery, and this was achieved simply by making the curtain walls on the south and east sides immensely thick.

At the same time, a new tower was built at the southern end of the castle to replace the older tower as the main

residential accommodation. This is a particularly confusing part of the castle to visit, because it has been rebuilt a number of times: it gives an impression of hugely thick walls containing very small rooms.

The rebuilding work went on right into the reign of Mary Queen of Scots in the 1560s, and the main addition at this time was the Spur, an outwork that defends the main gate. It turns the entrance into a narrow, dark corridor between high walls which gets your visit to the castle off on an appropriately grim and forbidding note.

You can, incidentally, walk all the way round the wall-walk at the top of the curtain walls, and you can climb right to the roof of the original central tower (often called the Prison Tower), which still has all its floors, though its interiors are fairly plain.

The final phase of the castle's long career was in the 1870s, when it became the central ammunition depot for Scotland. The whole courtyard was roofed over and lots of other modifications were made: most have now been removed, but the pier, reached across a drawbridge, has been kept and makes a fine finishing touch.

Signposted on the B903 east of Bo'ness.

Cambuskenneth Abbey

Historic Scotland • Free • Open access at any reasonable time

Standing on water meadows next to a big loop of the River Forth near the royal castle of Stirling, this was one of the most important abbeys in the land, often at the centre of events. It was founded in 1147 by King David I and was a daughter house of an Augustinian abbey at Arras in France.

After it was dissolved in 1559, most of its stone was taken away to be re-used at Stirling, and sadly there's not much left: just the outline of the church's foundations on the ground, and the bell-tower (which, incidentally, always stood on its own as it does now, and is the only major example in Scotland of a free-standing belfry in the style of an Italian campanile).

Most of what you see was restored by the Victorians, whose excavations in 1865 uncovered two coffins thought to contain the remains of King James III (died 1488) and his wife, Margaret of Denmark. They were reburied on the site of the high altar, in a tomb paid for by Queen Victoria.

Signposted from the A907 north-west of Stirling, not far from the Wallace Monument.

The restored bell-tower is the only substantial remnant of the once magnificent Cambuskenneth Abbey.

Clackmannan Tower

Historic Scotland • Free • Open access to view exterior only at any reasonable time

It would be great if this tidy little tower, which was owned by the Bruce family, could be opened to the public, but in recent years it has at least been rescued from imminent collapse, which is a start.

For the time being, we'll have to be content with looking at the exterior.

The oldest part of the building is a rectangular tower of the late 1300s. This was updated in the following century by the addition of a stair tower one storey taller than the original, turning the tower into an L-plan design. Other buildings would have stood next to the tower, and the whole thing was ringed by a moat crossed by a drawbridge.

It's a pleasant stroll up from the church at the edge of the town of Clackmannan to the gentle rise, called King's Reach Hill, on which the castle stands. You can easily see the strategic advantages of the position, which offers extensive views down to the Firth of Forth and beyond.

In the town, an oddity worth seeing is a boulder known as the Clackmannan Stone, which in 1833 was incorporated into a tall monument that stands by the Tollbooth. In Gaelic the name 'Clach Mannan' means 'stone of the Manau', who were a local tribe of the iron age, and it is thought that the stone marked a tribal meeting-place; though a similar item, the Clockmabon Stone, near Lochmaben in Dumfries, is associated with the Celtic god Maponus.

From the church, on the west side of the town of Clackmannan, it's a short walk to the castle.

See also... Balmerino Abbey

National Trust for Scotland; free, open access at any time. At Balmerino, on the south bank of the River Tay north-west of St Andrews.

This former Cistercian abbey is so badly ruined that only a few lumps of stone remain. It's not worth going out of your way for, though the scenery hereabouts is very pleasant.

Left: Clackmannan Tower is an appealing little building, but you can't get inside it.

Castle Campbell

Historic Scotland • ££ • Usual hours

Castle Campbell has arguably the most magnificent setting of any Scottish castle, at the head of a wooded glen.

It's only a shame that this gaunt tower is no longer known by its ancient name of 'Castle Gloom'. It stands between two streams called the Burn of Sorrow and the Burn of Care, at the head of Dollar Glen, which you can't help but feel should be spelled 'Dolour'. Fairytale stuff.

Names aside, though, it's the glorious location that makes this castle so special. The glen is a steep-sided, wooded ravine which climbs from the small town of Dollar up the southern slope of a range of hills called the Ochills. The castle's position near the top of the glen gives it extensive views over the flat country to the south, beyond the Forth valley to the Pentland Hills south of Edinburgh. You can see the Forth road bridge, even (but sadly not the far more beautiful rail bridge).

A more satisfying way to get here than letting your car drag you all the way up the hill is to stop at the lower car park, where there is a signposted walk through the glen alongside the cheerfully babbling Burn of Care. The walk is steep in places, but it's not very long, and shouldn't take more than 15 minutes. Even if you don't walk up, you could always stroll down after visiting the castle and have the driver

in your party pick you up, but be warned that even in the downhill direction there is a short but steep uphill section at the end, as you climb out of the ravine.

Whether you get here by car or on foot, walk back down the road a short way from the upper car park to get a fine view of the castle through the trees (it's the spot from which the picture above was taken).

As you approach the castle, the setting seems very peaceful and pleasant: far from gloomy, in fact. Beyond the simple arched gate is the castle courtyard, with the original tower house immediately to your left and a ruined hall range straight ahead; the two are linked by the later East Range, on the ground floor of which there is a most welcome tearoom.

The tower house is an old one, but is very well preserved. It was built in the mid-1400s by Colin Campbell, the first Earl of Argyll, who held many important offices of state under King James III, culminating in his appointment as Lord High Chancellor in 1483.

The family seat was at Inverary in Argyll, but the earl needed a base near to the royal castles at Edinburgh and Stirling, so he set up home here. After the death of the king in 1488, Argyll was retained as

Chancellor by James IV, and in 1490 the new king rewarded the earl with an act of parliament ordering the castle 'to be callit in tyme to cum Campbele'.

The tower still has all its floors, most of which are stone vaults, and the top is also covered over with a fireproof stone vault. There are fantastic views from the roof. The architecture is heavy and primitive, but there are hints of luxury (such as the 'buffet' niche in the hall, where the best silver would have been on show) and the odd bit of ornamentation (notably two charmingly grotesque gargoyle-like masks on the ceiling of the top-floor room which had lanterns hanging from their mouths).

Rather more splendid than the cramped rooms in the tower would have been the hall built in about 1500, which took up most of the southern side of the courtyard. This range was burned down in 1654 by Scots after the castle was garrisoned by Cromwell's English troops, and only the low, vaulted cellars survive intact.

Beyond this is a lovely terraced garden, a pleasant place to sit for a while if it's sunny, and further down the slope is the spot where John Knox preached in 1566.

Signposted from Dollar, on the A91.

84

Doune Castle

*Historic Scotland • ££ • Usual hours
(slightly limited opening in winter)*

Although it's a real gem, Doune is a quiet and unassuming little castle and attracts far fewer visitors than you'd expect it to. Essentially it, too – like *Falkland (below)* – is a royal palace, though one from an earlier and far more rough-and-ready era.

The castle was built in the late 1300s by Robert Stewart, earl of Albany, the third son of King Robert II and the brother of Robert III. He was made guardian of the realm by the lords after his father simply abdicated responsibility in 1388, and he ruled the country until 1420.

What's appealing about the castle is not only that it is much as it was when it was built, but also that it displays a crude, early medieval kind of grandeur. There are three main buildings: the huge gatehouse tower, with halls on the first and second floors; the vast Great Hall; and the appropriately named Kitchen Tower.

The sheer size of both the Great Hall and the kitchens (conveniently sited next to the hall on the first floor) suggests a deliberate display of wealth, but the fact that the hall has no fireplace or chimney – just a hearth on the floor and holes in the roof to let the smoke out – shows what a basic variety of luxury this was.

In Doune, on the A820 west of Dunblane.

The East Range and restored South Range of the ornate Falkland Palace, built in grand style by James V.

Falkland Palace

National Trust for Scotland • ££ • Usual hours

This was a royal palace, the country retreat of the Stuart kings from the late 1300s, where they hunted, played games, danced and generally got away from the business of the city.

It started life as a castle of the MacDuffs, earls of Fife, with a big round tower, traces of which can be seen in the garden; but it developed into a splendid stately home, reaching its zenith in the mid-1500s when King James V employed the best Scottish and French architects to create a spacious L-shaped mansion in a highly ornamented Renaissance style.

Unfortunately, the roofed rooms in the restored range are principally the work of the late 1800s and are a heavy, unpalatable blend of Victorian and Jacobean. There are some fine old pieces of furniture, though.

The best bits are the historic gardens (complete with a real tennis court) and the lovely old buildings of the town.

In Falkland, on the A912 north of Glenrothes.

Below: Doune is a proper medieval castle, with a certain simple, primitive grandeur.

In the foreground are the remains of the royal palace, with the rebuilt abbey church visible beyond.

The importance of Dunfermline

In 1070, just four years after the English defeat at the Battle of Hastings, a princess of the Saxon royal house named Margaret married the Scottish king Malcolm III at Dunfermline. A woman of immense piety, sainted by the Scots soon after her death, Margaret founded all sorts of religious houses, but the most notable was here at Dunfermline. It was important because, at the time, the church in Scotland had developed its own local peculiarities, out of step with the rest of Europe; Margaret brought the country its first taste of the official Benedictine rule.

The seal was set on the importance of Dunfermline with the involvement of King David I, Scotland's greatest founder of new religious houses, who in 1128 arranged for a prior of Canterbury to come here as abbot. About this time, work started on the ambitious new abbey church intended from the first to be the finest in Scotland, with experienced masons drafted in from all over England.

In the end, though, the most resonant distinction of Dunfermline was as the last resting place of Scotland's kings, just as Iona before it had been given a special importance by the royal graves on its hallowed ground. Not only were Malcolm III and Margaret buried here, but in later years Alexander I (David's older brother, who died in 1124), Malcolm IV (died 1165) and Robert the Bruce (died 1329) were also laid to rest here.

Dunfermline Abbey & Palace

Historic Scotland • Abbey nave: free access, usual hours • Royal palace: ££, usual hours

You'd be forgiven for thinking that the majestic abbey church at Dunfermline is the original, but it isn't. The present church was built between 1818 and 1821 on top of the ruined east end of the medieval abbey church, and it's not even known how much of the older building survived at the time to influence the shape of the new one.

During the course of the work, human remains thought to be the body of Robert the Bruce were discovered, and these were reburied under the new church. Probably this explains the unusual lettering around the top of the tower.

Luckily, the nave of the old medieval church was still pretty much intact and plans to modify it were abandoned in favour of simply conserving it. This is now by far the most impressive piece of the whole abbey/palace complex to visit, and it's free to get in. Built largely in the early 1100s, it's a lovely example of simple, graceful Norman architecture, its round arches and stout pillars decorated with chevrons and other patterns.

The bit you have to pay to see is much less substantial and less interesting. Basically, it consists of the undercroft of the abbey's refectory and the lower parts of a large guest house which, because the abbey was so important, was in effect a royal residence. Sandwiched in between is a tall, thin gatehouse.

In 1587, after the Reformation put the abbey out of business, the guest house was given by King James VI to his wife, Anne of Denmark, and she had it remodelled as her palace. Next to each other on one long floor were a kitchen, servery, great hall and private chamber, the last two lit by big, modern windows.

All that there is to see of this, however, can be seen perfectly well from outside. Save your energy for a wander around the park at the bottom of the hill, from where these buildings look their best.

Signposted in the centre of Dunfermline.

Inchmahome Priory

Historic Scotland • ££ • Usual hours

On a fine spring day, this is one of the finest places on earth to be. Just like *Lochleven Castle, Tayside (see page 163),* the priory stands on an island in the middle of a lake and is reached by a short ferry trip (the fare, by the way, is included in the admission price). Along the way, the ferryman points out items of interest such as the site of a crannog (a pre-Roman defended house on an artificial island).

To be honest, though, it's the boat trip and the island setting that give the place most of its appeal: the priory ruin itself is pretty modest, and it was clearly not the grandest of buildings in the first place. The main remnant is the church, of which the most attractive part is the east end, lit by five tall lancet windows which have a simple elegance that is very satisfying. The chapter house, with its plain barrel-vaulted roof, is also impressive.

The Augustinian priory was founded in 1238 by Walter Comyn, Earl of Menteith. In 1547, the four-year-old Mary Queen of Scots was sent here for safe-keeping when an English army threatened Stirling Castle following the Battle of Pinkie.

On the Lake of Menteith; the ferry leaves from near Port of Menteith, on the B8034, signposted from the A81 and A811 west of Stirling.

Below: it's a modest ruin, really, but its island setting makes Inchmahome Priory a special place to visit.

Externally, Kellie Castle still looks pretty much as it did when building work finished in the late 1500s.

Kellie Castle

National Trust for Scotland • £££ • Usual hours

A tall, roughly square tower of the 1300s, now referred to as the North-West Tower, was extensively updated in the late 1500s by the Oliphant family, who had owned the castle since 1360. The first change was the addition of the East Tower in 1573 by Lawrence, fourth Lord Oliphant; his son completed the work after 1593, adding a three-storey range that linked the towers together, and building a third tower at the south-western end to create a large, very grand T-plan house. The only drawback was that he couldn't afford it, and in 1613 he was forced to sell up.

By the 1800s the castle had fallen into disrepair and was used for storage by the neighbouring farm, but in 1878 it was leased by Professor JA Lorimer of Edinburgh University, who agreed to carry out some restoration.

The fabric of the building is well preserved and is really quite attractive, and there are some fine original features, including some remarkable plaster ceilings. On the whole, though, the interior of the castle has a slightly sad, neglected feel, not improved by the removal of some of its loaned furniture. It needs a little love and affection.

Signposted on the B9171 south of St Andrews.

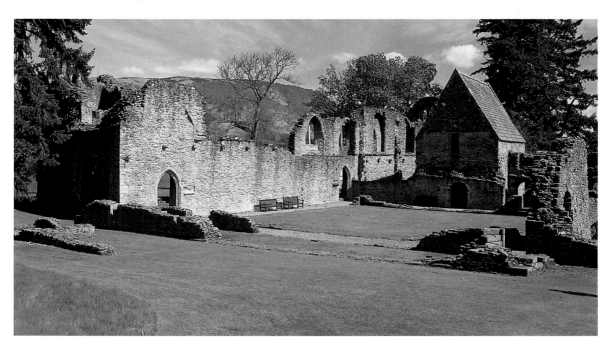

Ravenscraig Castle

Historic Scotland • Free • Open access during usual hours only

Built on the orders of James II in 1460, this is said to be the first castle in Scotland designed to be defended by, and from, guns. It's a strange construction, consisting of two towers with rounded fronts on the inland side and square fronts facing out to sea, linked by a short range which was meant to contain a hall but was never finished.

Access to the interiors of the towers is very limited, and in all it's not a terrifically entertaining place to visit. A feature of the kitchens described as a 'dough trough' sticks firmly in the memory, however, if only for its oddly unpronounceable name.

On the edge of Kirkcaldy.

Ravenscraig Castle is said to have been the first castle in Scotland designed to be safe from artillery fire.

Scotstarvit Tower

Historic Scotland • Free • Access by key during limited opening hours

There's always something thrilling about taking away a big iron key, unlocking a stout wooden door and having a whole medieval building all to yourself; but the experience somehow seems even more special at Scotstarvit, perhaps because the tower is out in the countryside. If you come all alone, it's actually a bit spooky.

The key is available from the nearby House of Tarvit, a mansion rebuilt in 1906. This is a National Trust for Scotland property, which limits the hours at which you can gain access to Scotstarvit Tower (basically, afternoons only from May to September and at weekends in October).

The tower is a tall, thin affair with a tiny stair tower on the side. It manages to pack in six floors, each with just a single room of ungenerous proportions, dimly lit by small windows.

Despite its lack of grandeur, this is an appealing little building with a genuinely romantic flavour. Well worth seeing.

Signposted on the A916 south of Cupar.

Below: tall, thin and charming, Scotstarvit Tower is like something out of a medieval romance.

St Andrews

The history of this attractive little town has been dominated (though golfers might disagree) by its importance as an ecclesiastical centre. Originally called Kilrimont, from the Gaelic meaning 'church of the king's mount', the town was home to a monastery before 800 AD, and was becoming pre-eminent in the religious affairs of Scotland by the time of Queen Margaret (*see Dunfermline Abbey, page 86*), who lavished attention on a church here and established a ferry across the Forth to encourage pilgrims (hence the name Queensferry).

The story really starts, however, with the arrival of a group of Augustinian canons in the 1120s. In 1160 they started work on a new cathedral church, but it was not finally consecrated until 1318, four years after Robert the Bruce's victory at Bannockburn, when the fact that the splendid new church was dedicated to the patron saint of Scotland must have had a particular resonance.

The ruined gatehouse is the principal remnant of St Andrews Castle, and there's not much else left.

St Andrews Castle

Historic Scotland • ££ • Usual hours

As was usually the way, the bishops of St Andrews were wealthy landowners who lived, like other nobles, in heavily fortified luxury.

They had a castle here on the headland from the late 1100s, but it played its part in the Wars of Independence of the early 1300s and was destroyed in 1336 by the Scots under Sir Andrew Moray (who also tore down the great castle at *Bothwell, near Glasgow – see page 71*).

The castle was rebuilt just before 1400 and most of the ruins you see today are basically of that period. Unfortunately, there's really not much left.

The seaside setting is probably the most appealing thing about the castle, though there are a couple of interesting details: there's a good bottle dungeon, and there are some interesting tunnels which were dug during a siege of 1546 and which, in theory, you are allowed to get inside and explore; in practice, they don't normally seem to be open.

Signposted on the north-west side of the town.

St Andrews Cathedral

Historic Scotland • ££ • Usual hours

The enormous cathedral church is pretty badly ruined, but the good news is that the grounds within which it stands can be visited free of charge. The main bits to survive are the east gable end, given a very distinctive appearance by its single arched window and two pinnacles, and one entire wall of the nave, which not only helps give an idea of how very grand the church was, but also hints at what the cloister beside it might have been like.

Paying an admission fee entitles you to visit the museum, which houses some wonderful examples of stone-carving. It also gets you a token that allows you through the turnstile at the bottom of the remarkable tower of St Rule's Church. This older church – the Augustinians' place of worship before the cathedral was built – was given its immensely tall, disproportionately thin tower in a bid to spread its fame. Today, the tower is one of the most epic step-climbing experiences on this or any other continent, but the views from the top are superb.

You might expect St Andrews to be a place of superlatives, but it's somewhat surprising to find them in a museum and up lots of steps rather than in the remains of the cathedral or castle.

On the east side of the town, near the castle.

Left: looking west in the ruined cathedral church, with the sole intact wall of the nave on the left.

Stirling Castle

Historic Scotland • £££ • Usual hours

The rock on which Stirling Castle stands is simply magnificent: it really does rise sheer out of the plain, and as well as looking superb from a distance, it also offers amazing views when you're up on top of it. Comparisons with the similarly situated *Edinburgh Castle* (*see page 50*) are unavoidable, and though the views at Edinburgh are probably a shade better by virtue of having a city to look over and the sea in the distance, the castle at Stirling is a good deal more interesting.

More to the point as far as the builders of the castle were concerned, however, was that Stirling's massive rock provided a fine defensive position. It was also next to the lowest point (that is, the nearest to the sea) at which the Forth river could be crossed, and the river crossing would play almost as important a role in Scottish history as did the castle: not least, of course, at the Battle of Stirling Bridge in 1297, where William Wallace routed the English army.

Although no evidence has been found, it's likely that the Stirling rock was home to a fortification as early as the iron age. Ancient Celtic forts have been found on a number of neighbouring hills. There's no doubt that there was a castle here in the early 1100s, when King Alexander I built a chapel here. By the time the Wars of Independence began in the late 1200s, Stirling was one of the most important fortifications in Scotland. In 1304, it was the only castle left to the Scots patriots when Edward I took it after a siege lasting 12 weeks; but by 1313, contrastingly, Stirling was one of only three castles still held by the English, and the following year an attempt to relieve its garrison led to a crushing defeat for the English at nearby Bannockburn.

Unfortunately, any traces of a castle of this period have long since been buried under later work. Today, the castle is a sprawling hotchpotch of structures dating from about 1500 onwards. It actually remained in military use, principally as a barracks, right up to the First World War, before being put into state care. Restoration work now in progress is stripping away all the alterations to (hopefully) reveal much more of the original.

The first bits you come across are the more modern Outer Defences, built between 1708 and 1714 at the time of the Jacobite unrest and showing many of the typical touches of a later artillery fort: large earth banks; stone walls and vaults; wide, dry moats crossed by drawbridges.

When you emerge at the northern end, it's a similar story; here there are more artillery fortifications, plus what used to be a magazine for storing gunpowder.

The oldest part of the castle is in the middle, on the highest part of the hill, and consists of a courtyard surrounded by a curtain wall. The wall and the gatehouse, with its twin round towers, date from about 1500, contemporary with the most impressive of the castle's buildings, the Great Hall. This vast medieval hall, built by King James IV, was greatly altered in later years but has recently been restored to something like its original condition, and its simple grandeur is very pleasing.

Nearby is another interesting building, the palace, on which work started in about 1540. It's one of the earliest examples in Britain of a classical Renaissance exterior – very different from the Great Hall even to the untrained eye, despite the fact that it's only a few decades newer. The interior has been greatly altered, and is also now being restored: the only significant detail to survive is a series of remarkable wooden medallions carved with portraits, known as the Stirling Heads, which once decorated the king's audience chamber.

In Stirling; a steep walk from the town centre.

Stirling Castle's awe-inspiring setting on a massive outcrop of volcanic rock contributes greatly to its appeal.

See also...

Bannockburn monument

National Trust for Scotland; free, open access at any reasonable time (heritage centre open during usual hours only, shorter hours in winter). Signposted from junction 9 of the M80/M9.

A large equestrian statue in a modern style depicting Robert the Bruce stands on the site of his 1314 victory over the English, and a visitor centre tells the story of the battle.

Culross Palace

Historic Scotland & National Trust for Scotland, £££, usual hours (summer only – May to September). On the A985 four miles east of Kincardine Bridge.

Small, pretty Culross is an outstanding example of a Scottish burgh (a planned town) of about 1600. The Palace is a mansion of the same age with fine restored interiors of the period.

Culross Abbey

Historic Scotland; free, open access at any reasonable time. Signposted in Culross.

The choir of a former Cistercian monastery, still in use as the parish church.

Dunblane Cathedral

Historic Scotland; free, open access during usual hours only. Signposted in the town centre.

A splendid but slightly eccentric-looking church, mostly of the 1200s and restored in the 1890s.

Below: Stirling Old Bridge.

Kinneil House, Bo'ness

Historic Scotland and local council; free, open access during usual hours only. On the south-west side of Bo'ness; signposted from the A993.

A long-abandoned stately home based on a tower house of the 1500s was being demolished in the 1940s when a series of splendid medieval painted ceilings and walls were uncovered; the painted rooms are now open to the public. The extensive grounds of the house are a public park, and an excavated Roman fortlet of the Antonine Wall (*see page 76*) was partially restored and can be visited.

Norman's Law hillfort

Near the Firth of Tay east of Newburgh; reached from the A913 with permission from the house at Denmuir.

A big hillfort consisting of an oval stone rampart, with superb views over the Firth of Tay.

The Pineapple House

National Trust for Scotland; can be viewed from the exterior only. Off the A905 near Airth.

This magnificent folly built in 1761 is, quite literally, a house shaped like a pineapple. It is now let as a holiday cottage.

Stirling Old Bridge

Historic Scotland; free, open access at any time. On the north side of the town centre.

Not the bridge where William Wallace defeated the English in 1297, because this one was only built in about 1500; but it's a very attractive structure, and worth seeing if you're in Stirling for the castle.

And...

Argyll's Lodging, Stirling

Historic Scotland; entry on same ticket as Stirling Castle. On Castle Wynd in Stirling.

Splendid house of the 1600s, recently restored. Worth a look if you're not worn out by the castle.

Dogton Stone

Historic Scotland; free, open access at any time. Off the B921 north-west of Kirkcaldy

A weathered Celtic cross. Not thrilling.

Kings Knot garden, Stirling

Historic Scotland; free, open access at any time. To the west of the castle.

Formal garden of 1628 in a field below the castle.

Mar's Wark, Stirling

Historic Scotland; free, open access to view exterior at any time. On Castle Wynd in Stirling.

Decrepit facade from a fine Renaissance house built in about 1572 for the Earl of Mar.

St Bridget's Kirk, Dalgety

Historic Scotland; free, open access at any time. By the Forth, south-west of Aberdour.

A ruined church with many 1600s alterations including a 'laird's loft'.

Westquarter Dovecot

Historic Scotland; free, open access at any time. At Westquarter, near Lauriston.

A rectangular dovecot built in 1647.

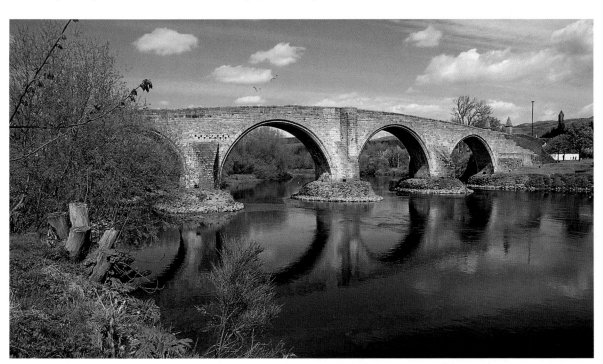

Argyll & Bute

and the 'Argyll islands' including Arran and Mull

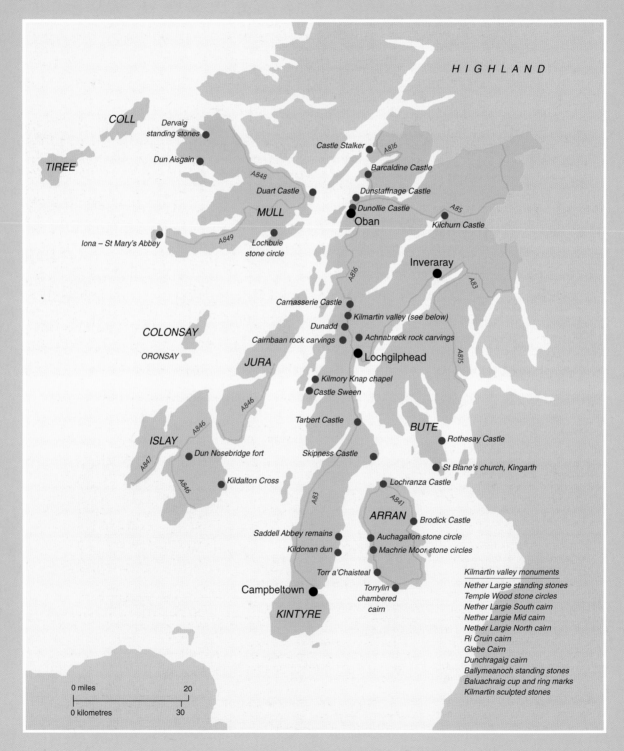

HIGHLAND

COLL

TIREE

Dervaig standing stones ●

Dun Aisgain ●

Castle Stalker ●

A816

Barcaldine Castle ●

A848

Duart Castle ●

Dunstaffnage Castle ●

MULL

Dunollie Castle ●

● **Oban**

A85

Kilchurn Castle ●

Iona – St Mary's Abbey ●

A849

Lochbuie stone circle ●

● **Inveraray**

A816

A83

Carnasserie Castle ●

A815

COLONSAY

Kilmartin valley (see below) ●

Dunadd ●

Cairnbaan rock carvings ●

Achnabreck rock carvings ●

ORONSAY

JURA

● **Lochgilphead**

Kilmory Knap chapel ●

● Castle Sween

A846

Tarbert Castle ●

BUTE

ISLAY

A846

Rothesay Castle ●

Dun Nosebridge fort ●

Skipness Castle ●

St Blane's church, Kingarth ●

A847

A846

Kildalton Cross ●

Lochranza Castle ●

A83

A841

ARRAN

Brodick Castle ●

Saddell Abbey remains ●

Auchagallon stone circle ●

Kildonan dun ●

Machrie Moor stone circles ●

Torr a'Chaisteal ●

Kilmartin valley monuments

Campbeltown ●

Torrylin chambered cairn ●

KINTYRE

Nether Largie standing stones
Temple Wood stone circles
Nether Largie South cairn
Nether Largie Mid cairn
Nether Largie North cairn
Rì Cruin cairn
Glebe Cairn
Dunchragaig cairn
Ballymeanoch standing stones
Baluachraig cup and ring marks
Kilmartin sculpted stones

0 miles   20

0 kilometres   30

Carnasserie Castle

An attractive tower house of the 1560s, Carnasserie Castle is a dignified building with many fine details.

Historic Scotland • Free • Open access at any reasonable time

Sitting on a rocky bluff at the narrowing northern end of the Kilmartin valley, this is a particularly attractive tower house of the 1560s. It was built by a high-ranking clergyman called John Carswell, who from 1567 was Bishop of the Isles. He was a great supporter of the native culture and language of the region, and his translation of John Knox's *Liturgy* (a definitive work on Presbyterian doctrine) was the first book ever to be printed in Gaelic.

Carnasserie is a well-designed and elegant building with lots of very pleasing little details in its stonework, and it survives in really quite good condition. Visitors can climb right up to the parapet of the main tower, where there are fine views down the valley. On the first floor of this tower is the lord's private chamber or withdrawing room, with a very large, elaborately carved fireplace.

At the opposite end of the castle is a smaller tower. You can climb a spiral stair up the full height of this structure, too,

although this end of the castle is rather less well preserved. In the middle, between the large and small towers, there is a range of rooms which contained the kitchens on the ground floor and the main hall on the first floor above.

One detail of the castle's layout worth noting is the way in which the hall connects directly, by a door, to the lord's chamber on the first floor of the main tower. This arrangement, with the important rooms next to each other on a single floor, is a thoroughly modern improvement on a traditional castle layout in which the rooms – hall, lord's private chamber, lord's bedchamber – were stacked on top of each other in a single, very strong tower.

The castle went out of use after it was destroyed by Royalist forces during the Monmouth Rising of 1685: a very short career for such a fine building.

Signposted on the A816 Lochgilphead to Oban road north of Kilmartin. From the car park, it's a short but fairly steep walk to the castle.

See also... Barcaldine Castle

Privately owned, £££, usual hours (end May to mid September). Signposted from the A828 at Benderloch, north of Oban.

Built by the Campbells in 1609, this tower house was abandoned in 1735 and restored in 1896 by Sir Duncan Campbell. Something of a crumbling Victorian pile, it is opened to the public by the present laird and his family. There isn't much to see, but the welcome is very warm. Tea and cakes are sold in the great hall and B&B offered in two guest bedrooms.

The ancient Castle Sween (above) is a powerful, solid-looking ruin in a very beautiful location.

Castle Sween

Historic Scotland • Free • Open access at any reasonable time

One of Scotland's earliest stone castles, its oldest walls dating from about 1200 AD, this is a satisfyingly squat and powerful ruin in a superb location near the mouth of Loch Sween, with views out to sea towards the islands of Jura and Islay. It's worth coming just for the setting, which is only *slightly* marred by the holiday camp of static caravans that surrounds the castle.

■ *See also...* **Kilmory Knap carved stones**

Historic Scotland; free, open access at reasonable times only. At Kilmory village, at the southern end of the south shore of Loch Sween; signposted from the B841 Lochgilphead-to-Crinan road.

Just a short way from Castle Sween, further down the minor road that winds along the southern shore of the loch, you come to Kilmory, where a ruined chapel has been given a modern roof and now houses a collection of the medieval carved stones that are characteristic of this part of Scotland.

In the quality and variety of its carvings, this is a very good collection – the only one worth going out of your way to see – but one of the carvings in particular is outstanding. It's a tall, round-headed cross known as Macmillan's Cross, with Jesus on the front and a lively hunting scene on the back.

Above: the amazing MacMillan's Cross at Kilmory.

The oldest part of the castle is a roughly rectangular enclosure of walls supported at the corners by fat buttresses. Inside, two ranges of wooden buildings would have provided accommodation: on the inner faces of the walls you can still see the holes that held the timbers to support the floors and roofs. Over the gate, thicker walls held up a defensive platform.

At the back, on the left, a square tower and a round tower were added within the first century and a half of the castle's life. More significantly, a large tower house – known as the MacMillan Tower – was tacked on at the back right-hand corner in the late 1400s. This contained up-to-date accommodation on the upper floors, with kitchens in the basement: take a close look at the brick-lined oven in the corner.

Little is known of the castle's history. It was apparently taken by Robert the Bruce from its owners, the MacSweens, during the Wars of Independence (1296–1314). It was eventually destroyed in 1647 by Colkitto (Alasdair MacColla Ciotach), the hero of the Highland army that fought on behalf of the deposed King Charles at the time of the English Civil War.

On the minor road that follows the southern shore of Loch Sween, signposted from the B841 Lochgilphead-to-Crinan road.

94

'Cup-and-ring' carvings

The extraordinary prehistoric art of northern Britain

The simple but evocative carvings known as cup-and-ring marks are found all over Scotland, but there's a spectacular concentration of them in the area just north of the town of Lochgilphead.

The same markings are often found on isolated stones, and sometimes these stones are incorporated into monuments, like the amazing carved slab used as a capstone at *Nether Largie North cairn* in the *Kilmartin valley* (*see page 102*). However, the carvings are at their most spectacular in large collections on broad outcrops of natural, living rock. And for this, you're in the right place.

North of Lochgilphead at *Achnabreck* is the largest collection of all, with dozens of carvings spread over several large rock-sheets. Try to see them in the evening, when the low, slanting sun picks out the carvings. Nearby at *Cairnbaan* is another fine group of carved outcrops.

The fact that both these sites have wide views over the surrounding country has prompted suggestions about the social function of the carvings. Did they mark meeting places, perhaps for exchange between tribes? Or were they sacred sites, akin to the rock faces painted by aboriginal Australians?

Equally mysterious is the significance of the designs (though a signboard at Achnabreck makes an interesting comparison with the symbolic power of the circle in native American culture).

The basic shape is a circular, fairly deep, round-bottomed hollow, known for obvious reasons as a cup. You'll find lots on a single large rock outcrop in a field at *Baluachraig* (*see page 103*). Other carvings add a ring around the cup to give the classic cup-and-ring motif.

Often, extra concentric rings are added, and frequently there's a line leading from the centre to the outside. Another typical form is a maze-like spiral, again with a line crossing its rings.

Above: just a taste of the carvings at Achnabreck, home of Britain's largest collection of rock art.

Achnabreck rock carvings

Historic Scotland, free, open access at any reasonable time. Signposted from the A816 not far north of Lochgilphead.

The biggest collection of all, with dozens of carvings on several large rock sheets. On the edge of forestry, an easy uphill walk from the car park. Good views, too.

Cairnbaan rock carvings

Historic Scotland, free, open access at any reasonable time. Signposted path from the B841 on the east side of Cairnbaan village.

An uphill walk of about 15 minutes, starting off steeply, brings you to two outcrops with an interesting variety of carvings, and there's another, smaller carved rock not far away.

See also...

There are other carved rocks, also in the care of Historic Scotland, in the Kilmartin valley not far north of Achnabreck and Cairnbaan, at **Ballygowan** (*near Poltalloch*) and at **Kilmichael Glassary** (*just off the A816*). Also, note the carved outcrop at *Baluachraig* (*page 103*) and the large marked stone used in *Nether Largie North cairn* (*page 102*).

Left: well-defined carvings on the smallest of the three rock faces at Cairnbaan.

The kingdom of Dalriada

When the Romans left Scotland in 400 AD most of the country north of the Clyde was occupied by the native Picts, but already Gaels from Ireland were raiding and settling on the western coasts, in the region of Argyll. These settlers were known as Scots, from the Roman name for the people of Ireland.

In about 500 AD, the people of *Dál Riata* from County Antrim established themselves in Argyll, founding the Scottish kingdom of Dalriada. Its capital might have been at *Dunadd* (this page), and it has been suggested – fancifully, perhaps, but resonantly – that a carved rock at Dunadd was central to the ceremonies for crowning kings, almost as if it were the original 'Stone of Destiny'.

For many years, the Scots alternately fought with the Picts and became gradually integrated with them. For a stretch, after a major defeat in about 640 AD, Dalriada may have been a client kingdom of Pictland.

Eventually, it was the arrival of Norse invaders that unified the two. In 839 AD, a Pictish army defeated Scottish rebels led by their king, Alpin, but the Picts were then surprised and wiped out by a Norse army. Kenneth the Hardy, son of Alpin, claimed the thrones of both the Scots and the Picts (the latter was passed down through the female line, so he may have had a right to it through a royal Pictish mother).

Although Kenneth MacAlpin was called King of the Picts, the unified kingdom became known simply as *Scotia*.

Right: cut deep into this rock at Dunadd are a 'sink' and a 'footprint', with a delicate, traced carving of a boar in between.

Dunadd

Historic Scotland • Free • Open access at any reasonable time

On this stout rock, rising out of the plain, stood a high-status fortress-residence of the dark ages, which may have been the capital of the kingdom of Dalriada.

It's a fantastic place for views, even if there isn't much fortress left. On the way up, you pass through a natural gateway in the rock into an area like a lower ward, with traces of its walls remaining.

Above: the hill of Dunadd was a stronghold of the Dalriadan kingdom in the 500s to 800s AD.

Further up is an upper ward, where metalworking took place; higher still is a terrace with unusual carvings in the rock (a basin, a footprint and a boar); and on the small summit at the top, walled all round, is what was some kind of citadel.

At the southern end of the Kilmartin valley, signposted from the A816 about 4 miles north of Lochgilphead. Car park at foot of hill.

96

Dunstaffnage Castle

Historic Scotland • ££ • Usual hours (all year)

With its rough stone walls rising sheer from a craggy rock, this is an appealing little castle. Its setting, too, is very pleasant: yachts ride at anchor in a sheltered bay, and there are views across the water to the mountains in the north and east and, after a walk through the trees, to Mull in the west.

The ground plan – a quadrangular shape with two corners close together, so that it's almost a triangle – follows the rock on which the castle stands. The rough, almost primitive look of the walls is indicative of the era in which the castle was built, the mid-1200s. One reason for its rounded-off corners is that three of the four corners were originally equipped with round towers; but in any case, rounded-off was the style in this part of the world.

Inside the walls, the castle isn't quite as interesting as it promises. There's a ruined range of buildings with a kitchen, dating from the 1500s, and there's a well, framed rather oddly by four large pillars. Steps lead up to a wall-walk. The main building is a tower house converted from the gate-tower (itself a conversion of the original round tower). This residence contains work dating from the late 1500s to the

The small ruined tower of Dunollie is in a fine coastal setting, just a short walk from the centre of Oban.

early 1800s. On the first floor is an exhibition, but the upstairs is the private property of the hereditary Captain of Dunstaffnage, who still owns the castle.

Built by the MacDougalls, Lords of Lorn, Dunstaffnage Castle was taken by Robert the Bruce in 1309 and remained in royal ownership until 1470, when it was given to the Campbells, Earls of Argyll.

Clearly signposted off the A85 about 4 miles north of Oban.

See also... Dunollie Castle

On private land; free, open access at any reasonable time. On the cliffs just north of Oban town centre, by the road to Ganavan.

A steep footpath leads up the hill to this ruined four-storey tower of the 1400s on the site of an ancient stronghold. You can, theoretically, get inside the tower at basement level and up the stairs to the first floor, but notices warn that stones fall off regularly, which is intimidating. Even if you don't risk your neck, the castle is well worth seeing, and the views are superb.

Below: Dunstaffnage Castle crouches on a large rocky outcrop, with impressive overhangs in places.

Kilchurn Castle

Historic Scotland • Free • Open access at any reasonable time

On the right day, and especially if you get it all to yourself, this is a magical place. The castle isn't signposted or advertised, so you have to 'discover' it, diving off the main road down a dirt track, then going – slightly daringly – on foot across a railway. In actual fact the ruin is well maintained and has been equipped with signboards to tell you about its history, but it still feels unspoiled and romantic, like a relic from before the days of state care.

This is also Scotland's most famous picture-postcard castle. From a layby on the A819 (just before it joins the A85), a stile over the wall allows access to the wooded eastern shore of the loch, and from here you can recreate those postcard views in your own photographs.

The oldest part of the castle is the four-storey tower, which was built in about 1450 by Colin Campbell, first Lord of Glenorchy (the Glenorchy Campbells were a branch of the family of the Earls of Argyll who owned *Dunstaffnage Castle – previous page*). The entrance to the castle is into a dark cellar on the ground floor of this tower, and there's an even darker

Above: Kilchurn Castle on Loch Awe, seen from the tip of the peninsula on which it stands.

pit-like prison lurking in the corner: bring a torch if you want to get a good look down into it.

From the courtyard beyond, where there's a rather fine piece of upside-down turret that fell off during a storm, you can climb to the first floor of the tower, site of the castle's great hall. A narrow stair leads up to a high viewpoint.

Other accommodation ranges inside the courtyard have not survived well, but on the north-west side is a vast barrack block built in about 1690 to house 200 troops, said to be the oldest barracks in Britain. The castle was struck by lightning in the 1760s and was not restored afterwards.

At the north end of Loch Awe, on a peninsula jutting out into the loch. Access is from the A85 Crianlarich-to-Oban road, just west of its junction with the A819 (to Inverary).

A small track, marked by a post with a red ring on it, drops steeply away from the verge on the south (westbound) side of the main road just before a crash barrier on a bend. Park the car and follow the path across the railway and along the marshy peninsula to the castle.

Kildonan dun

Forestry Commission land • Free • Open access at any reasonable time

From Claonaig (near *Skipness Castle – opposite page*), where in summer the ferry leaves for the Isle of Arran, a 'B' road heads down the east side of the Kintyre peninsula to Campbeltown. It's not as speedy a route as the 'A' road on the western side of the peninsula, but it's a lot more scenic, and it passes right next to this interesting ruin.

Most of the features of a typical dun can readily be discerned here, with steps to a higher level and a chamber in the thickness of the wall. The entrance still has its door jambs and holes for the bar that would have 'locked' the door.

Excavations found not only objects from the first two centuries AD, which is probably when the dun was built, but also items from the 800s and 1100s, suggesting that the ancient stronghold was re-used in medieval times: not an unusual practice in this turbulent region of the country.

By the B842 south of Ugadale. Look out for the Forestry Commission car park. The dun is on the seaward side of the road, just to the south of the car park entrance; there's a gate in the wall.

Skipness Castle

Historic Scotland • Exterior: free access during usual hours only (all year) • Interior of tower: free, usual hours (weekends in July & August)

Another attractively craggy castle, worth visiting even when the interior isn't open. Dating right back to the early 1200s, it was built in a surprisingly open setting, with just a gently sloping stretch of pasture between it and the shore and with views across the Kilbrannan Sound to Arran.

Although it seems that the design of the castle is perfectly straightforward – a tower house with a tall curtain wall around a courtyard – the sequence of construction is actually quite complicated.

The first castle here was a hall-house, thought to be one of the earliest defended manor houses in Scotland, which stood across the courtyard from a chapel. Parts of both these buildings were incorporated into the castle as it developed. In about 1300, it was rebuilt as an enclosure castle, with big ranges of buildings on the north and south sides joined by walls on the east and west. The seaward gate dates from this period.

Soon after 1502, the north-east corner had three storeys built on to form the tower-house, though this was rebuilt again about a hundred years later.

Originally a castle of the MacSweens (see *Castle Sween, page 94*), Skipness was owned by the MacDonald Lords of the Isles from 1325 until the clan was finally suppressed by the king in 1493. The castle was given to the Campbell Earls of Argyll in 1502 and survived until the late 1600s, when it was abandoned in favour of a new house nearby (itself rebuilt in 1881).

Signposted on the B8001 south of Tarbert. An easy, level walk from the free car park.

Above: the tower at Skipness Castle seems like the main building, but really it's an afterthought.

Below: Kildonan dun, with great views to Arran, is a fine example of this type of Roman-era stronghold.

See also… Saddell Abbey remains

Historic Scotland, free, open access at any reasonable time. Off the B842 at Saddell.

There's barely anything left of the abbey here, which developed from a monastery founded in the mid-1100s, possibly by Somerled, first Lord of the Isles and founder of Clan Donald. What there is, however, is a collection of interesting tombstones (*pictured above*) carved with the figures of soldiers in high relief.

Nearby is **Saddell Castle**, an attractive tower-house of about 1510, which is let as a holiday home by the Landmark Trust. You are allowed to walk in the grounds.

Above: the standing stones at Nether Largie form an unusual cross-shaped arrangement of five pillars with a cairn near the central stone.

Visiting the Kilmartin valley
– getting your bearings

There are two distinct groups of monuments in the Kilmartin valley, each conveniently provided with its own car park.

The main group is strung out along the valley just south of the village of **Kilmartin**. Here you'll find an unusual stone circle and three fine chambered tombs, plus an intriguing arrangement of standing stones.

A couple of miles further south, where the valley widens out, you'll find the second group of monuments centred on **Dunchragaig** cairn. Nearby are two rows of tall standing stones, a small stone circle and an interesting cup-and-ring-marked rock. Access here has improved hugely in the last couple of years thanks to a new arrangement with the landowner.

The Kilmartin valley

Historic Scotland and local landowner • Free
• Open access at any reasonable time

South of the village of Kilmartin, scattered along a shallow, pretty valley, is a series of quietly impressive ancient monuments which together make up one of the finest ritual landscapes in Britain. Individually none of the monuments is all that dramatic, but with so many of them gathered together in a small area, this is a very rewarding place to visit.

In fact, on a sunny morning, the stroll along the valley is unquestionably one of the most pleasant activities this area of Scotland has to offer (though you'd have to say that it's thirsty work on a really hot summer afternoon).

It might take only 15 minutes to stomp directly from the car park to the most distant of the chambered cairns, but you would be wise to allow yourself a couple of hours to wander along the valley and visit all the monuments.

The village of Kilmartin is at the far end of the walk and offers facilities such as toilets and refreshments, as well as an interesting visitor centre with a good bookshop and café. As an additional point of interest, housed in a small building in

the village churchyard is a fairly decent collection of the medieval carved stone slabs peculiar to this part of the west coast of Scotland.

One reason the valley boasts such a concentration of monuments is that the area was buried under peat and uncovered again only when the land was cleared and drained for agricultural use in the 1800s.

Unfortunately, this doesn't mean that we now have a perfectly preserved ancient ritual landscape to wonder at. Since they were exposed, the monuments have been used as a ready source of stone for roads, field walls and drains. One even had a lime kiln built into it. In any case, archeological investigations suggest that the peat formed from about 900 AD, so the original monumental landscape is scarcely likely to have survived intact until then. Consequently, it's not easy to draw firm conclusions about how the monuments would originally have looked.

By the B8025, clearly signposted off the A816 Oban-to-Lochgilphead road just south of Kilmartin village. Park in the official car park at Lady Glassary Wood: the footpath starts just over the road, crossing a bridge over a stream to the Nether Largie stones. There's also a car park at the visitor centre in Kilmartin village.

Nether Largie standing stones

This 'X'-shaped arrangement of five tall standing stones – two at either end, and one in the middle – certainly seems as if it may have had a practical function, though what that might have been is anybody's guess. There are also the remains of a cairn next to the central stone.

It has been suggested that the stones formed a lunar observatory in conjunction with the nearby stone circle and a 'notch' in the skyline to the west.

Temple Wood stone circles

The main circle at Temple Wood is the most significant monument in the valley. It's a circle of 22 upright stones: but the space inside the circle has been filled with boulders to transform the monument into a huge cairn. Stone cists containing burials were later inserted into the cairn.

Careful archeological exploration in the 1970s revealed a profusion of detail about the phases of its construction (all summed up neatly in explanatory signboards at the site) but offered no simple explanation of how old the monument is or how it might have been used. It's an odd one, basically, and it doesn't slot easily into any of the standard categories.

Its most singular feature is a double-spiral carving on one of the stones; there is a spiral on each of two adjoining faces,

linked by lines across the corner of the stone. The carving can be seen quite clearly when the sun is high.

Equally intriguing is a smaller circle that was only discovered quite recently. This started life as a rough circle of timber uprights which were replaced in stone before 3000 BC, making it one of the oldest circles in Scotland. It seems that a scheme to rebuild it in a more elaborate fashion was abandoned when the builders moved on to the larger circle instead.

Visitors whose mobility is restricted may park a car in the layby right next to Temple Wood.

Above: one of five remarkable cairns in a row, Nether Largie Mid cairn (see over the page) has been robbed of much of its stone.

Below: the most impressive of the Kilmartin valley monuments is this extremely unusual stone circle at Temple Wood.

Above: inside the chamber of Nether Largie South cairn. Divided into four by cross-slabs, it's a typical 'Clyde type' of tomb.

Above: a neolithic chambered tomb, rather than a bronze age barrow, Nether Largie South is the oldest of the Kilmartin cairns.

Bottom left: Ri Cruin cairn is remarkable for the axe-head carvings on a stone slab.

Bottom right: hidden under a modern mound at Nether Largie North cairn, you'll find an extraordinary cup-and-ring-marked stone.

☐ *See also… The other Kilmartin cairns*

Ri Cruin cairn

About 5 minutes' walk from Temple Wood; walk south down the road, turn first left, and look for the path to the cairn on the right.

Very heavily disrupted by stone-robbing and by having a lime kiln built into it, but well worth seeing: it has three large cists, one of which has a stone slab with about seven faint but remarkable axe-heads carved on it.

Glebe Cairn

Just north of Kilmartin village, visible from the visitor centre.

Rather dull, because it's now just a big pile of rocks. Excavated many years ago, it had two cists which may have contained burials.

Leaving Temple Wood by the gate near the smaller circle and walking up the road towards Kilmartin village, you come almost immediately to the first of the three Nether Largie cairns.

Nether Largie South cairn

The oldest of the cairns, this is basically a neolithic chambered tomb rather than a bronze age cairn (specifically, it's a good example of the 'Clyde type' of tomb that is found throughout Argyll). Originally it may have had a 'facade' of tall stones at the end of the chamber.

Its outstanding feature is the long burial chamber, which you can climb down into, covered by immense stone slabs (now propped up by modern iron bars) and divided into four by cross-slabs.

Nether Largie Mid cairn

The least interesting of the three cairns, because a lot of its stone has been robbed. It originally had a 'kerb' of larger stones running all the way round. There are two cists which would have contained burials.

Nether Largie North cairn

The most fun of the lot. You enter the modern mound through a large, sliding hatch. Inside, a large slab of stone which once covered the cist is now propped up to show the cup-and-ring carvings that cover its surface.

From here, you can carry on up the track, which leads to the village, or retrace your steps.

The Dunchragaig group of monuments

Historic Scotland and local landowner •
Free • Open access at any reasonable time

This smaller collection doesn't give the same impression of being part of a large, integrated ceremonial landscape, the way the Kilmartin monuments do. And to be honest, none of the individual monuments is quite as interesting either. But all the same, with three very different kinds of monument in three neighbouring fields, there is more than enough material here to make for an intriguing visit.

A convenient car park for visitors has been provided just over the road from Dunchragaig cairn. From the cairn, it's a very short walk to the carved rocks, and only a slightly longer stroll to the field in which the standing stones are located.

Close as the monuments are to each other, you shouldn't underestimate the amount of time you will need to visit all three sites: just a quick look around could take a good half-hour.

By the A816 Oban-to-Lochgilphead road 4 miles south of Kilmartin. Signposted to the car park; cross the road to reach the monuments.

Dunchragaig cairn

Set in a thoroughly pleasant patch of woodland, this particularly large cairn of the bronze age – it was originally 30m (95ft) across, and it still stands almost 2m (7ft) high – has been excavated several times, and is a little untidy as a result. Three cists were uncovered, containing burials, cremations, pottery, a flint knife and a stone axe. One of the cists is covered by a huge capstone.

The standing stones of Ballymeanoch: a pair of stones and a row of four make up a most unusual alignment.

Ballymeanoch standing stones

Until recently, you could only peer at these stones from afar, but an improved access arrangement means you can now walk right by them – though you are requested to keep to the edge of the field.

It's a peculiar arrangement of stones (though reminiscent of the *Nether Largie standing stones*). There's one row of four stones, two of which have weathered cup-and-ring markings, plus a second row of just two stones nearby.

A short way across the field is a small henge – a circular bank and ditch, with two entrances – inside which are the remains of a circular cairn with two cists.

Above: pleasingly simple cup-and-ring markings on a rock surface at Baluachraig.

Baluachraig cup-and-ring marks

A broad stone surface here is marked with lots of very simple cup-and-ring carvings, quite different from the far more elaborate carvings at *Achnabreck* (*see page 95*) and therefore thought to be earlier.

☐ *See also…*

Kilmartin sculpted stones

Historic Scotland; free entry during usual hours only. In the grounds of the church, Kilmartin village.

A set of early medieval grave slabs carved in the local West Highland style is now kept in a disused mausoleum in the churchyard. These aren't the best examples of the art form, though (*see also Kilmory Knap on page 94*).

Left: the main feature of Dunchragaig cairn is a cist covered by a huge stone some 4m (13ft) long.

Above: Lochranza Castle started life as an early type of fortified residence known as a 'hall-house'.

Arran

The island's slogan, 'Scotland in miniature', is inspired by the fact that Arran is divided into two different kinds of landscape, in just the same way that Scotland as a whole is. The northern end is all mountainous highland, while the southern half is gently rolling lowland.

Ferries from Ardrossan on the Ayrshire coast (one hour) or from Claonaig on the Kintyre peninsula (30 minutes) make it easy to get here. Arran's only main road completes a 55-mile circuit of the whole coast, so it's not difficult to tour the whole island in a day; but if you do come for a day trip, you'll almost certainly leave wanting to return again and explore a little further.

In particular, though, the 'ritual landscape' of *Machrie Moor* (*over the page*) is, on its own, a good enough reason for making the trip.

Lochranza Castle

Historic Scotland • Free • Open access at any reasonable time

Its attractive setting on the shore of a bay overlooked by Arran's highest mountains is a good enough reason to visit this modest, pleasant ruin, but it also has a particular claim to fame. Although it was rebuilt as a tower house in the 1500s, it started life in the late 1200s as a basic type of defensive residence known as a hall-house, of which it is one of the best surviving examples.

The hall-house was a simple two-storey building with access by a ladder or a wooden stair directly to the lord's hall on the first floor. The ground floor would have been used only for storage.

Restoration work at Lochranza has revealed features of the original hall-house such as the original doorway on the first floor and arrow slits in the walls of the lower level.

At Lochranza, at the north end of the island, a short walk from the ferry terminal for Kintyre.

See also... Brodick Castle

National Trust of Scotland, £££, usual hours (open April to October). Signposted from the main road on the north side of Brodick Bay, two miles north of the town of Brodick.

Immortalised in a fine engraving on the back of the Royal Bank of Scotland's £20 note, Brodick Castle (*pictured right*) is basically a Victorian stately home, rebuilt after 1844 in the Scots Baronial style by the noted architect James Gillespie Graham, though it's based around a tower of the late 1500s with bits added by Cromwellian troops in the 1650s.

Splendid furnishings will please fans of lavish Victorian interiors, as will a connection with the great English eccentric William Beckford, but it's the excellent gardens and grounds (open all year) that are the outstanding feature of the place.

Torr a'Chaisteal dun

Historic Scotland • Free • Open access at any reasonable time

There's not much left of the walls of this circular iron age fortification, though the stonework does stand two courses high in places; but what's really nice about this little dun is its absolutely typical setting, on an odd-looking hill, with easy access to the sea but surrounded by good farmland. As a bonus, there are splendid views across to Kintyre. Although car-parking is not too easy, this is otherwise a very accessible site that is well worth seeing.

A signposted footpath leaves by a stile from the A841 west of Corriecravie; it's a walk of about 5 minutes downhill to the fort.

Torrylin chambered cairn

Historic Scotland • Free • Open access at any reasonable time

The mound of this neolithic chambered cairn has been severely robbed of its stone, leaving its original shape uncertain, so the point of interest here is the partly ruined burial chamber. Divided by cross-slabs into four separate compartments, it is typical of local 'Clyde type' monuments.

   Frankly it's not tremendously thrilling, but it's a good excuse for a pleasant little stroll that ends up on a clifftop path with excellent views over to the large, pointy island of Ailsa Craig.

Signposted footpath from the A841 by the shop at Lagg; it's an easy, fairly level walk of about 10 minutes to the monument.

Top: at Torr a'Chaisteall, there are very few traces of the iron age dun which stood on the knoll.

Above: the ruinous Torrylin chambered cairn is near the clifftop, with excellent sea views.

Below: Auchagallon stone circle.

■ **See also… Elsewhere on Arran**

Arran has a wealth of archeological sites to keep interested parties happily occupied – though in most cases, the scenery is a better reason for visiting than the monument itself.

Auchagallon stone circle

Historic Scotland, free, open access at any reasonable time. Reached by a very short walk up a farm track, from the minor road that leaves the A841 coast road at Auchagallon.

Although it's not much to look at, this monument is an interesting oddity. It's not, in fact, a stone circle: it's a cairn of the late neolithic or early bronze age, surrounded by a circle of 15 upright stones. It's been suggested that the design is influenced by the 'recumbent stone circles' of north-eastern Scotland.

Carn Ban chambered tomb

Historic Scotland, free, open access at any reasonable time. Access on foot only via signposted forest trail (a round trip of about 6.5 miles or 12km) starting from the A841 east of Kilmory.

One of the region's finest neolithic long cairns, quite well-preserved, with parts of a curved facade still intact (though its four-compartment burial chamber is filled in). It's in a splendid location but it can only be reached by a pretty long walk. It's said to be a great spot for a picnic on a clear day.

Kilpatrick 'dun'

Historic Scotland, free, open access at any reasonable time. There's a signposted parking place by the A841 at Kilpatrick; it's a rough uphill walk of about 15 mins to the dun, and the path is not terribly easy to follow – look out for the striped posts.

The remains of a circular dry stone structure of uncertain date, so ruinous as to be little more than a few rocks scattered in a field. It might be a dun, or perhaps a bronze age cairn. Disappointing to visit, but the views are good.

Above: next to the abandoned Moss Farm is the first of the Machrie Moor circles, a double circle which had a burial cist at its centre.

Right: this remarkable monolith is the sole survivor from a circle of nine or ten stones.

Below: the sixth and last of the stone circles is the smallest of the lot, and was discovered in 1978.

Machrie Moor
stone circles

Historic Scotland • Free • Open access at any reasonable time

An extraordinary and beautiful place, this is a 'ritual landscape' similar in many ways to the *Kilmartin valley (pages 100–102)*. It's a series of fairly small stone circles, none of which is remarkable individually, but which collectively make this a very evocative place. As is often the case with stone circles, particularly in Scotland, it is the relationship between the monuments

Above: the tallest of the Machrie Moor standing stones is as high as three tall men.

and the surrounding landscape that is so effective, with the mountains of northern Arran seeming like a crucial part of the 'architecture' of the site.

The path from the main road leads across two fields to Moss Farm Road stone circle, which is actually an unusual type of burial cairn ringed round with large upright boulders. From there, the track passes near two significant standing stones on the top of the ridge and heads to the derelict Moss Farm, cutting across a badly ruined chambered cairn on the way.

By the farm is the first of six circles, a double ring of small, fat boulders which

had a burial cist in the middle. Over the stile and a little to the right is a four-stone arrangement which may have had more stones originally but might be what they call a 'four-poster'.

Off to the left, a single tall pillar is the survivor of a nine-stone circle that was probably broken up to provide building material for the farm. Further down the slope is the most impressive monument: three tall stones, one a massive 5.5m (18ft) high, are all that's left from a circle of seven or eight. A failed attempt to shape a millstone from one of the fallen stones is evident nearby.

Next to last is a circle of small, carefully chosen stones in which grey granite boulders alternate with red sandstone slabs. Finally, at the end is a tiny circle found in the last 30 years: excavations showed that a ring of timber posts once stood here too.

Just south of where the main road crosses a stream called Machrie Water, there's a signpost marking the footpath and (on the opposite side of the road) a small parking place. It's a walk of about half an hour to the furthest monument.

107

Above: Duart Castle, rebuilt from a ruin in 1910, has a splendid setting on a small cliff by the sea.

Below: the stone circle at Lochbuie seems to have a definite relationship with the mountain behind.

Mull

A good deal larger than many of the other western islands, Mull has some of the most astonishing geology and spectacular scenery in Scotland. The only place really on the tourist trail is Iona, an island off the south-western tip of Mull, and the long road to reach it can be busy. The pretty town of Tobermory should not be missed.

Duart Castle

Privately owned • £££ • Usual hours

The view of this castle from the Oban ferry is probably one of the most inspiring sights in Scotland. It's in a superb setting by the sea, controlling the Sound of Mull and the entrance to Loch Linnhe.

It isn't quite all it seems, however, since Duart was rebuilt between 1910 and 1912 from a ruin, and therefore is directly comparable with *Eilean Donan* (in the *Highland* region) and Lindisfarne Castle in Northumberland, England, both of which are comfortable houses rebuilt from ruins in the early twentieth century.

The castle consists of a tower and a circuit of walls, with a range of buildings along the wall across from the tower: this part of the castle is not open to visitors. The tower contains kitchens in the basement, a hall above and bedrooms further up, but since it was all put in fairly recently, it's not terribly thrilling. Far and away the best part of a visit here is the climb up a narrow stair to the roof, from where the views are fabulous.

Historically, Duart is a great stronghold of the Macleans, who put up the earliest parts of the castle in the 1400s.

At Duart Point, about 3 miles south of the ferry terminal at Craignure, off the A849.

Dun Aisgain

On farmed moorland • Free • Open access at any reasonable time

The beauty of this fine monument is partly its glorious location, with views over the blue waters of Loch Tuath, and partly the fact that it hasn't been excavated, restored or tidied up: it's just there, waiting for you to come across it.

Details can be tricky to pick out in the piles of rubble, but you can readily make out things like the door jambs in the entrance passage as well as the broch-like methods of construction used in the dun, such as the 'battened' slope of the outer wall and the 'intra-mural gallery' between the inner and outer walls (both of which made it possible to build the wall higher).

The coastal setting is typical for a dun: it has ready access to the sea, but it stands on an excellent piece of farmland, and it makes the most of the natural defensive strength of a small rocky knoll.

You usually find either that the walls of a dun exactly follow the contours of the rock it stands on, so that it needs no outer defences, or that it's defended by an extra ditch or wall. In this case, there was originally an outer wall all round the edge of the rock outcrop.

By the coast ,west of the two-house community of Burg, off the B8073 south of Calgary. You can see the dun from the south end of Burg, but to reach it, park just north of the village and walk across the moor past the ruined cottages, trying to follow the ridge and keep at the same height until you are nearly at the dun.

Lochbuie stone circle

Historic Scotland with the aid of local landowner • Free • Open access at any reasonable time

A small but very tidy circle of nine stones, with three outliers, one of which is a fine pillar 3m (10ft) high. The most striking thing about the circle is its relationship with the landscape: it stands at the head of Loch Buie in a sheltered valley beneath a mountain called Ben Buie. Worth seeing.

On a minor road near Lochbuie on the southern coast of the island. After the turning to Laggan, look out for a surprisingly straight stretch of road, then park before the bridge over the stream and follow the path to the monument.

☐ **See also… Elsewhere on Mull**

Dervaig standing stones

Historic Scotland and Forestry Commission; reached by footpath from car park off the B8073 north (up the Z-bend hill) of Dervaig.

A linear setting of three stones in a forest, reached by a walk of almost half an hour. They're not really terribly interesting, but the very first part of the walk, through a maze-like mass of trunks to a tiny stream, is worth trying.

Inchkenneth chapel

Owned by Historic Scotland; there are no formal access arrangements.

Another of those little churches with carved slabs, on an island off Mull. A simple building of distinctive West Highland type.

Incidentally, **Torosay Castle** is actually a Victorian house. The gardens are extremely pleasant for a walk, though.

Below: in a splendid clifftop setting, Dun Aisgain is one of the best-preserved duns in Scotland.

Iona

The abbey of the 1200s was restored by the Victorians in a pleasantly unassuming, domestic style.

One of the most important early Christian communities of Britain was established on this beautiful little island in 563 AD when an Irish nobleman called Columba landed here with twelve followers.

The island is now mostly owned by the National Trust for Scotland and is reached by a passenger ferry which only takes five minutes to cross the narrow stretch of water from the island of Mull.

After a long drive across Mull, it feels like you've come to the edge of the world (though to the people of medieval times, for whom the seas were highways, it would not have seemed so remote). It really is a lovely place, but it's very, very busy.

Peace and quiet can be sought by walking to the far side of the island, but they say that the only way to discover the island's ancient air of sanctity is to stay overnight.

Founded by the Benedictines in about 1200, the medieval Abbey of St Mary (*Iona Cathedral Trust, free but donations are encouraged, usual hours*) was rebuilt from a fairly intact ruin in Victorian times and is the home of a modern Christian community. The church and cloister are open to visitors and are quite pretty, but it's too busy and too extensively restored to feel ancient and venerable.

The real treasure of Iona, though, is the series of early Christian carved crosses from the late 700s and early 800s, some of which stand in front of the church, while others are housed in the Abbey Museum (behind the abbey; don't miss it).

On the way to the abbey from the ferry, you pass a ruined Augustine nunnery also dating to about 1200 (*Historic Scotland, free, open access at any time*) and the tall, elegant MacLean's Cross, which dates from the late 1400s.

Left: the ruined nunnery of the 1200s is now a flower garden where tourists rest their tired feet.

Bute

Although it calls itself 'The Unexplored Isle', the great beauty of Bute is precisely that it is so easy to explore, even on a day trip. It's the closest to civilisation of all the Scottish islands – a 30-mile drive and a 30-minute ferry ride from Glasgow – and its capital, Rothesay, is a nice blend of seaside resort and country town.

If you're journeying to the west coast of Scotland, you should seriously consider a 'Hopscotch' ferry ticket that will take you from Wemyss Bay on the mainland to Rothesay on Bute, then onwards from Rhubodach at the northern end of Bute to Colintraive, back on the mainland.

Rothesay Castle

Historic Scotland • ££ • usual hours

The walls of this pretty little castle in the centre of the island's main town date back to before 1230, little more than 60 years after the Scots first won Bute and the western islands from the Norse kingdom of Man and the Isles.

Originally the castle was built to an unusual circular plan, which might have reflected an earlier timber castle, but after Norwegian armies succeeded (briefly) in capturing the castle in 1230 and 1263, four large round towers were added, from which arrows could be shot to defend the walls, and a major gatehouse was built facing the sea.

The gatehouse was rebuilt in the late 1400s as a grand residence, and it was also the focus of restoration work in the early 1900s, roughly 200 years after the castle fell out of use, when the Marquis of Bute restored the great hall.

Pleasant though the castle is to visit, there isn't all that much to see or do once you've looked at the ruined chapel and the restored hall, and climbed to the top of the wall for a view of the town.

Signposted in the centre of Rothesay; free car parking by the harbour front.

St Blane's church, Kingarth

Historic Scotland • Free • Open access at any reasonable time

Near the southern tip of the island, within easy reach of interesting beaches, with views over to Arran and in the shadow of

Above: the attractively curvaceous Rothesay Castle has defended Bute since the Scots first won it.

a dramatic rock topped by a hillfort, lies this atmospheric remnant of the early Christian church. It's the ruin of a simple Romanesque chapel of the 1100s, on a site that seems to represent a monastery of the Celtic church.

Apart from the beautiful, peaceful setting (surprisingly sheltered, too, you'll notice if you come on a windy day) the site has many points of interest, explained by signboards. It's well worth going out of your way to make a pilgrimage here.

Near Dunagoil Bay, signposted down a minor road south from the A844. Walk of 10 mins.

See also... St Mary's Chapel, Rothesay

Historic Scotland, free, open access during usual hours only. In the churchyard of the present church on the southern side of the town of Rothesay next to the B881.

Recently given a modern roof to protect it, this ruined chapel of the 1300s is notable for two finely carved tombs with stone effigies of a knight and a lady. The whole island of Bute was originally one parish centred on *St Blane's* (*above*), but a second parish was formed in about 1300 based on St Mary's.

Left: St Blane's church is in a beautiful spot on the site of a monastery of the Celtic church.

See also... Mainland

Ardchattan Priory

Historic Scotland; free, open access at reasonable times only. On a 'C' road off the A828 north of Oban.

Some of the buildings of this dissolved priory were rebuilt as an attractive house, the gardens of which are open to the public (there's a small fee, with an honesty box for payment). Open separately, and reached by an entrance just east of the car park for the house, are the remains of the priory church, with a display of carved stone slabs. It's pretty dull.

Bonawe ironworks

Historic Scotland, ££, usual hours. Signposted from the A85 at Taynuilt.

The most complete example of a charcoal-fuelled ironworks in Britain, this is a fascinating relic of the early industrial era. Vast sheds are proof of just how much charcoal was consumed to produce very small amounts of iron, and the well-preserved furnace helps explain how the process worked.

Castle Stalker

Privately owned, £££, only open occasionally by arrangement with the owner. Near Port Appin.

This is a superb-looking restored tower house set on a small island. Visitors are taken out by rowing boat, but the castle is only open for a few weeks each year. For details, contact Tourist Information at Oban or ask at the village post office at Port Appin.

Keills Chapel

Historic Scotland, free, open access at any reasonable time. At Keillmore, right at the end of the B8025, south of Tayvallich.

Like *Kilmory Knap Chapel (see page 94)* this is a small West Highland chapel, ruined and roofless, which has been given a modern roof and houses a collection of carved stone grave slabs and crosses. It's a good collection in a beautiful, isolated setting.

Above: Castle Stalker, with Morvern beyond.

Below: Innischonnel Castle, on Loch Awe.

Bonawe ironworks.

Keills Chapel.

And...

Ardifuir dun, *on coast north of Duntrune Castle, near Kilmichael* – A fairly well-preserved iron age fortification, its circular wall still up to 3m (10ft) high.

Innischonnel Castle, *at the south-western end of Loch Awe, seen from the B840 north-east of Ford* – This powerful-looking ruin on an island a stone's throw from the shore was once the main stronghold of the Campbells. It started out in the 1200s as a rectangular enclosure like *Castle Sween (page 94)* but was greatly altered in the 1400s.

Kilberry Sculpted stones, *at Kilberry Castle, on the B8024 17 miles south of Lochgilphead (Historic Scotland, free, usual hours)* – An assortment of late medieval carved stones from around the estate.

Kilmodan sculpted stones, *Clachan of Glendaruel (Historic Scotland, free, open access at any reasonable time)* – A collection of West Highland carved grave slabs in a churchyard.

St Cormac's Chapel, Eilean Mor, *on small island off the Knapdale coast west of Kilmory* – There are no formal visiting arrangements for this small island with a holy cave and a vaulted chapel of the 1200s.

Tarbert Castle, *Tarbert (local council; free, open access at any reasonable time)* – An interesting set of ruins possibly dating back as far as the 1220s, with a tower and an enclosure from about 1502.

See also... The other islands of the region

Islay

Dun Nosebridge fort

On farmland • Free • Open access at any reasonable time

A large and unusual hilltop fort. A thick wall encloses a small, rectangular area on the top of a ridge; around it is a series of ramparts defending the hill, and on either side, more ramparts enclose level areas of ground. It's reminiscent of the Pictish stronghold of *Dunadd (page 96)*, but it hasn't been excavated, so there is nothing to suggest when it might have been built. Worth seeing, though.

Reached by a farm track from the minor road to Neriby, not far from Bridgend.

Kildalton Cross

Historic Scotland • Free • Open access at any reasonable time

This remarkable stone cross dates to the late 700s and is similar in style to the crosses of Iona. It stands in the grounds of a small ruined church of the late 1100s, with quite a few West Highland carved stone slabs scattered around.

In the churchyard at Kildalton. Signposted.

Tiree

Dun Mor broch

On farmland • Free • Open access at any reasonable time

A quite well-preserved broch, its ring of walls still over 2m (7ft) high in places. There is a guard cell on one side of the entrance passage, and a ledge on which a floor may have rested. The gallery in the thickness of the wall was accessed not only by a doorway, which led to a stair, but also by two smaller openings, presumably so that it could be used for storage. These little openings were blocked when a later house was built inside the broch. It has been excavated and is thought to date to about 50 BC.

On a rocky knoll by the shore a short walk from Vaul.

Oronsay

Oronsay Priory

On farmland • Free • Open access at any reasonable time, depending on the tide

The tidal island of Oronsay is just off the southern tip of the island of Colonsay and can be reached on foot when the tide is out. Near the farm are the fairly extensive remains of a priory founded by John, Lord of the Isles in the 1300s. The buildings date mostly to the late 1300s and early 1400s, but were partially restored in 1883.

Another attraction is the superbly carved Oronsay Cross, which is covered with the most astonishingly delicate interlaced foliage and has a relief figure of Christ on the front. There is also a particularly good collection of carved stone grave-slabs.

On the island of Oronsay, off Colonsay.

Lismore

Tirefour broch

On farmland • Free • Open access at any reasonable time

A rather fine broch on the east coast of the island, with excellent views of the sea and mountains. Its walls stand as much as 5m (17ft) high, but the interior has not been excavated. It's reached by a longish walk (about an hour) from the ferry from Port Appin on the mainland, so it would make a good afternoon out.

Also of interest is the parish church, built in 1749 in the ruined choir of a cathedral of the 1300s. Most of the original features were obliterated in the conversion, however.

About 2.5 miles (4km) from the Port Appin ferry landing, along the track to Balnure.

And...

Eileach an Naoimh, *an island west of Luing (owned by Historic Scotland; there are no formal access arrangements)* – The notable thing here is an unusual pair of beehive cells from an early Christian monastery. There's a later chapel, too.

Skye & the Western Isles

including Lewis, Harris, North Uist, South Uist and Barra

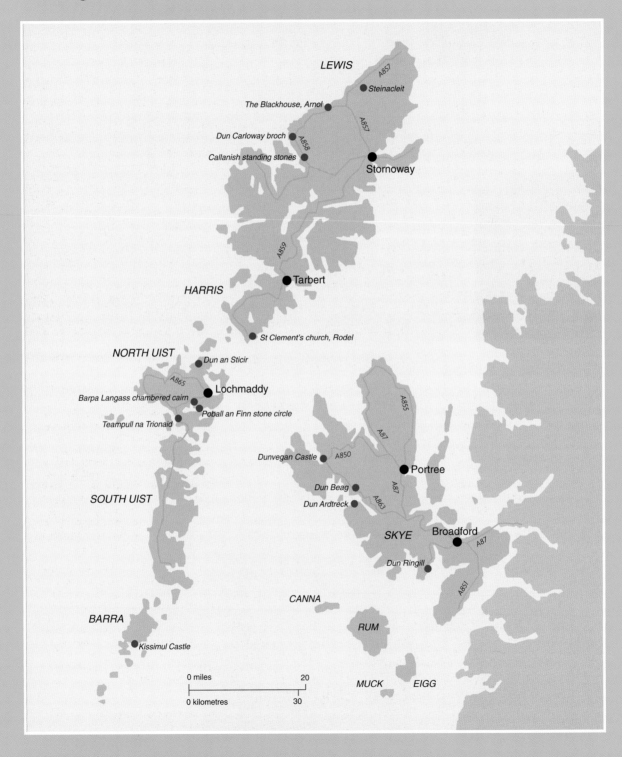

LEWIS

Steinacleit

The Blackhouse, Arnol

A857

A857

Dun Carloway broch

A858

Callanish standing stones

Stornoway

A859

Tarbert

HARRIS

St Clement's church, Rodel

NORTH UIST

Dun an Sticir

A865

Lochmaddy

Barpa Langass chambered cairn

Poball an Finn stone circle

Teampull na Trionaid

Dunvegan Castle

A850

A855

A87

Portree

Dun Beag

A87

Dun Ardtreck

A863

SOUTH UIST

SKYE

Broadford

Dun Ringill

A87

A851

CANNA

BARRA

RUM

Kissimul Castle

0 miles   20

0 kilometres   30

MUCK   EIGG

Using the cliffs as a ready-made defence on the seaward side, Dun Ardtreck is an unusual semi-circular broch.

Skye

There are several minor ruined castles scattered around Skye, and a grand house which used to be a castle; but none of them is especially noteworthy. What the island does have, however – besides the superb scenery for which it is justifiably famous – is a host of the intriguing iron age fortifications known as brochs and duns, many of which are in splendid locations and reached by very pleasant walks.

Dun Ardtreck

On privately owned land • Free • Open access by footpath at reasonable times only

In a superb clifftop setting, with views across the bay of Loch Brachadale and out over the open sea to the Western Isles, this is an extremely interesting ruin in quite a decent state of preservation.

The broch is reached by a path which continues to the end of Ardtreck Point to visit the lighthouse. At the start, the route isn't obvious; but it is an accepted path,

and in fact it seems to be a popular stroll with dog-walking locals.

Built in a naturally strong position on a rocky knoll and semi-circular in plan, the dun is basically a half-broch: excavations have shown that the walls never made a complete circuit, since the natural defences provided by the 20m (70ft) high cliffs on the seaward side were more than adequate.

The dun has typical broch features, including galleries in the thickness of the wall which could be accessed from inside the dun. The entrance passage is equipped with door-checks and a guard cell.

Follow the B8009 through Carbost; turn left for Fioscabhaig (Fiskavaig), then turn first right along the minor road towards Ardtreck Point. Just before the road ends at a gate to a house, park considerately at the roadside.

Walk down the gated farm track to the right. Follow the track as it passes to the right of the house, then cross a stile over a fence to the left. Cross the field and pass through a gate to pick up the footpath to the dun.

Left: the Black Cuillins seen from the coast near Elgol (see Dun Ringill, over the page).

115

Dun Beag

Dun Beag is probably the easiest of Skye's brochs to visit, and it's also reasonably well preserved.

Historic Scotland • Free • Open access at any reasonable time

Of all the brochs on Skye, this is by far the easiest to get at – it's near a main road, with a large car park provided, from where it's just a short walk to the monument – and it's also just about the best preserved. The ruin has been cleared of fallen stone, and the remaining wall is even tidier in its construction than most Skye brochs, with dressed stone laid in neat courses.

It's not quite a typical broch: there isn't a guard cell in the entrance passage, though there is a chamber on either side of the entrance once you get inside the broch, and from one of these chambers, a flight of stairs leads up. On the far side of the broch there's an 'intra-mural' gallery.

The location is also unusual; the broch is in a fairly commanding position, but most are much closer to the sea.

Its name means 'little fort', and there are traces of a hillfort known as Dun Mor ('big fort') nearby.

Signposted by the A863 north of Bracadale. Car park on seaward side of road; cross the road for a short uphill walk to the broch.

Dun Ringill

By a public footpath • Free • Open access at reasonable times only

The road to Elgol, from the largely charmless but useful town of Broadford, passes plenty of spectacular scenery, including the pink granite mountains known as the 'Red Cuillins'; but it's a far from welcoming landscape. How nice, then, to find this pleasant coastal walk with views of the less spectacular, but still beautiful, hills of southern Skye.

The goal of the walk is a small but interesting dun that sits on an irregularly shaped rocky outcrop. It's not easy to make out the shape of the exterior wall, and much of the building is ruined, but the beauty of this dun is that the entrance passage survives pretty much intact.

All is not quite as it seems, however, since the dun was refortified in early medieval times: the entrance passage was lengthened at the inner end, and two stone buildings were put up inside the fort.

Whatever the historical ins and outs, Dun Ringill is an interesting curiosity and provides an excellent excuse for a very enjoyable stroll.

From the B8083 Broadford-to-Elgol road, turn left at Kilmarie down a minor road signposted for the old churchyard.

Left: the notable feature of Dun Ringill is the long entrance passage, still with its roof slabs.

See also…
The castles of Skye

Dun Scaich Castle

On private land; free, open access at reasonable times only. North of Tarskavaig.

Minimal ruin of a castle of the MacDonalds which you can view from outside only. Said to have been the fortress where the Irish epic hero Cuchulainn came to learn the martial arts.

Duntulm Castle

Local council; free, open access at any reasonable time. Overlooking Tulm Bay, next to the A855 at the north end of Trotternish.

This is the most pleasant and most accessible of Skye's three minor castle ruins. Though there's not much of the castle to see, it stands on a north-facing headland from which the views to the Western Isles are very fine on a clear day. As an added incentive, there's a very good pub nearby, too: it goes by the imaginative name of the Duntulm Castle Hotel.

The castle was owned by the MacDonalds, who moved here from Dun Scaich in the early 1600s to consolidate their possession of the much-fought-over Trotternish peninsula. A ditch cuts off the headland: just beyond the ditch is the ruined barrel vault of the basement of a rectangular building which is thought to be the oldest part of the castle. A small tower added in the 1500s stood nearby until as recently as 1990, when it collapsed in a storm.

Dunvegan Castle

Privately owned, ££££, usual hours. Signposted just north of Dunvegan on the A850.

Far less a castle and far more a stately home, this is not a particularly attractive building and it's not very grand inside. What it is, however, is expensive, which is a great shame, because a visit here is one of the few things to do on a rainy day on Skye.

The seat of the MacLeods of Dunvegan and Harris, Dunvegan developed over many years,

Below: Duntulm Castle.

starting as a keep in the 1300s and ending with the addition of a barracks block in the late 1700s before being rebuilt in the mid-1800s in a plain and fairly ugly variation on the Scots Baronial style.

Knock Castle (Caisteal Camus)

On private farmland; access at reasonable times only. By the A851 north of Armadale, on the shore of Knock Bay. Reached by the farm track past the farmhouse and down to the shore.

Standing on a little rocky knoll on the seashore behind a farm is this unimpressive little ruin which is said to be the only example of a hall house in Skye and the Western Isles. The hall house is an early, simple type of castle consisting of a basic keep with a hall on the first floor and cellars below.

There's really not very much to see, and you'll have to brave the farmer's over-enthusiastic mob of sheepdogs to get here. Frankly, it's not worth it.

And…

Rubh' an Dunain chambered cairn

On the headland south of Loch Brittle, reached on foot from the minor road to Glenbrittle.

A superb long walk with fine views of the Cuillins leads to this well-preserved neolithic tomb. It's a round trip of about eight miles and takes five hours: full details are in a reasonably priced booklet called 'Walks from Glen Brittle', one of a series by Charles Rhodes, which is available from the tourist office in Portree.

The cairn is round, with a curved forecourt lined with upright stones, and has a short entrance passage leading to a roughly oval chamber. Several of the roofing slabs of the passage are still in place. Excavations in the 1930s found the bones of five adults in the chamber, as well as neolithic and bronze age pottery, chips of flint and quartz, and pieces of pumice stone.

Another interesting feature nearby is a rock-cut ditch known as 'the Viking canal', which leads from a small loch to the sea. The experts scoff at theories that it was cut for boats, saying that it's too small, and suggesting instead that it had some kind of industrial use. It's thought to be medieval.

See also…
The other islands

Barra

This remote little island at the southern end of the chain of the Western Isles is well known for its peace and quiet, as well as for its wild flowers in spring. It's not the easiest of places to get to: the daily ferry from Oban takes about seven hours and only sails direct to Castlebay on Barra every second day, calling in first at Lochboisdale on South Uist every other day, which adds a couple more hours to the trip. You can fly from Glasgow, if you don't mind that the plane lands on the beach.

Kissimul Castle

Privately owned • £££ • Limited hours (May to September, Weds and Sats)

This is one of the most picturesque castles in Scotland, standing on a little island in the middle of Castle Bay. The three-storey tower and most of the curtain wall date to the early 1400s, with later additions in the courtyard. Other buildings were pulled down to be used as ballast for ships.

The family seat of the MacNeils, it was restored by a descendant of the family in the late 1960s. Visitors are ferried out to the castle two days a week to look over the plain interior.

And…

There's an interesting chambered cairn called **Dun Bharpa** at the north end of the island, and a ruinous dun called **Dun Cuier** not far away at Allasdale. You might also like to visit the medieval **Kilbarr church** on the slopes of Ben Eoligarry, which is not well preserved but has two decent chapels and a number of carved stones.

South Uist

Linked to Benbecula and North Uist by main roads on causeway, this island has lots of scenery, but not much historic stuff. There's a standing stone at Bein a' Charra, near Stoneybridge, but the island's main attraction is the **Kilpheder aisled roundhouse**, which is a ruined iron age wheelhouse.

The remarkable stones of Callanish: four stone rows meet in a circle with a tall 'pillar' in the centre.

Lewis & Harris

Although they are physically joined, these two 'islands' have had separate identities since medieval times, when they were owned by different clans. The 'border' is to the north of the high mountains of Harris, which is mostly wild scenery. Lewis boasts several famous ancient monuments which are popular with coach trips.

Callanish standing stones

Historic Scotland • Free • Open access at reasonable times only

This extraordinary arrangement of tall, thin stones is deservedly famous, but also suffers as a result; this is one of the prime destinations for coach parties on Lewis and, as at Stonehenge in England, access arrangements could do with a rethink.

Dated to about 3000 BC, it's a circle of stones with a single tall stone (4.8m or 15ft high) in the middle and four stone rows leading off (a double row, or avenue, to the north). The rows run roughly north, south, east and west, but this might not be deliberate; it could simply be because the ridge on which the stones are set runs north to south. A chambered tomb, set between the central 'pillar' and the east side of the circle, was added about 100 years after the monument was built.

Remarkable though this arrangement is, the stones themselves are even more striking, composed of a pale grey stone called Lewisian gneiss that weathers with a grain almost like wood. They would probably look very fine by moonlight: ghostly and ethereal. However, even the tallest weighs only 5 tons and could have been hauled up by just 20 people.

There are several smaller stone circles in the area, the two most notable of which are reached by a short walk from the main road (A858) just south of Callanish.

Signposted from the A858 about 15 miles west of Stornoway at Calanais (Callanish). Free car park at the visitor centre; short walk to the stones.

Left: Cnoc Fillibhir is one of several small circles associated with the main monument at Callanish.

Dun Carloway broch

Historic Scotland • Free • Open access at reasonable times only

One of the best ruined brochs in Scotland, not so much for the height of the tallest piece of surviving wall, which juts into the sky like a monstrous fragment of broken eggshell, as for features like the entranceway and the internal staircase.

To enter the broch, you must stoop low under a large lintel stone and shuffle along a short entrance passage with a guard chamber on the right. Inside – where you get a much better impression of the interior space a broch offers than in many similar ruins – there are openings to two other chambers and to the stairs, which you can climb to a height of about 2.5m (8ft) above ground level.

Higher up on the interior wall, you can see a ledge which would presumably have supported an upper floor.

Signposted off the main A858 road just south of the village of Carlabhagh (Carloway). A car park is provided next to the new visitor centre.

Below: Dun Carloway is one of the best-preserved brochs in Scotland, with stairs you can still climb.

See also… Lewis and Harris

The Blackhouse, Arnol

Historic Scotland, ££, usual hours. Signposted from the A858 at Arnol, on the north coast.

It's astonishing to think that this thick-walled, primitive-looking house (*pictured above*), in which the animals lived under the same low roof as the people, was built only in the 1800s and was lived in until 1964. The pre-industrial lifestyle of the islanders had basically changed little since the iron age, and nothing is more evocative of it than the smell of the peat blocks burning on a hearth of stone slabs in the main room of the house. This is a truly remarkable place, and well worth seeing for yourself.

Clach an Trushal

In the village of Ballantrushal, off the A857

A very impressive single standing stone some 6m (20ft) in height.

St Clement's church, Rodel

Historic Scotland, free, open access during usual hours. Clearly signposted at Rodel, South Harris.

This attractive little church of the 1500s (*pictured above*) contains two fine tombs, one of which is covered in outstanding, intricate carvings. This tomb was built in 1528 for Alexander McLeod of Dunvegan, though he didn't die for another twenty years. Besides admiring the splendid carvings, you can also climb up the church tower – a rare treat – though you can't get out on the roof.

Steinacleit

Historic Scotland, free, open access at any reasonable time. Clearly signposted up a track off the A857 near Shader.

The experts aren't at all sure what this severely wrecked assemblage of stones represents, though it may be a barrow and/or a house. Oddly attractive, if not actually interesting.

The chambered cairn of Barpa Langass stands out against the bleak scenery with a primitive grandeur.

North Uist

Dismissed by some guidebooks because its scenery isn't as spectacular as that of Lewis or Harris, North Uist is nevertheless a pretty place in its own way, though its moorland can be a little bleak. The fertile, low-lying land has attracted settlers for thousands of years, leaving a great wealth of archeological sites. The island is also known for birdwatching and otters.

Barpa Langass chambered cairn

On moorland • Free • Open access at any reasonable time

One of the most interesting chambered cairns in Scotland. Where so many cairns have had their stone robbed, Barpa Langass is an impressively big pile of rocks with an excellent roofed passage that you can crawl a short way into (if, that is, you're brave enough to dive into the tumbledown entranceway; peering in with the help of a good, bright torch might be wiser).

The cairn measures about 25m (80ft) across and 4m (13ft) high, with a kerb of small upright stones running all the way round it. There are traces of a facade around the entrance, though the stones have collapsed.

The entrance passage is about 4m (13ft) long and faces east, but is blocked by a couple of fallen roofing stones, so that the oval chamber inside can no longer be reached, though it is still intact.

About 5 miles south-west of Lochmaddy on the A867, just as the road rounds the only hill for miles. A rough car park is provided; the path to the cairn leaves from the roadside, crossing the fence by a stile which is not in good repair.

Poball an Finn stone circle

On moorland • Free • Open access at any reasonable time

A not too long (perhaps half an hour) and very pleasant circular walk, marked by striped posts, leads from the cairn at *Barpa Langass* (*above*) around the side of the hill and turns left past the hotel to this slightly ragged stone circle. It's not all that thrilling in itself, but it has good views across the loch to the hill of Eaval.

By footpath from Barpa Langass (above).

Left: the ragged stone circle of Poball an Finn has excellent views to the south-east.

Dun an Sticir

On farmed moorland • Free • Open access at any reasonable time

This great little site is tremendously good fun to visit, provided you don't mind relying on your own surefootedness to save you from a soaking. Decent waterproof boots are a wise idea.

It's quite a well-preserved broch, built on an island in a lake and reached by a causeway of stones. Actually, you have to cross two causeways; one, composed of large stepping stones, leads from the shore to a small island, and a second, made of lots of little rocks, brings you to the dun. It's on this second stretch that good footwear comes in really handy.

Like many others, the broch was also used in medieval times, when some kind of rectangular house was built inside it. It is said to have been the refuge of a rebel clan leader called Hugh MacDonald.

By the B893, where the road to Newtonferry and the Berneray causeway turns off. Walk to the southern shore of the lake.

Below: to get to the ruined broch of Dun an Sticir, you have to cross two causeways of stones.

☐ *See also...*

**Teampull na Trionaid
(Church of the Trinity)**

Turn off the main road at Carinish by the present church; footpath leads through the gate and garden of the house (not the farm).

A ruined church (*pictured above*) which might date as far back as the 1200s, it's historically important but not really hugely interesting. There used to be an old sheepdog at the house who loved to play fetch: if he's still there, throw something for him!

☐ *And...*

If you're spending some time on North Uist, there are many more ancient monuments to track down, including an interesting neolithic barrow called **Unival chambered cairn** and another island fortification of the iron age, **Dun an t-Siaman**. There's also an unusual chambered cairn at **Clettraval** with an iron age **wheelhouse** nearby.

Highland

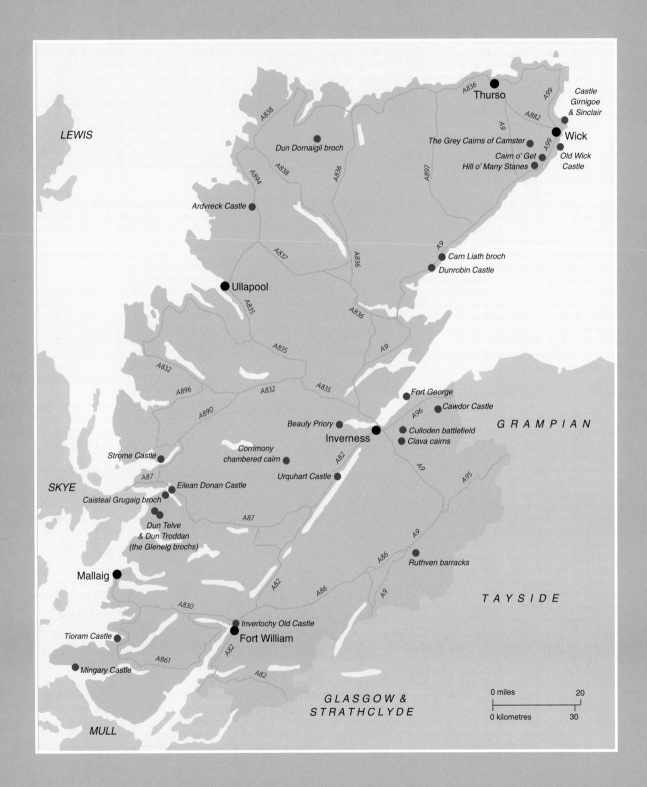

LEWIS

Thurso

Castle
Girnigoe
& Sinclair

Dun Dornaigil broch

The Grey Cairns of Camster

Wick

Cairn o' Get

Old Wick
Castle

Hill o' Many Stanes

Ardvreck Castle

Carn Liath broch

Dunrobin Castle

Ullapool

Fort George

Cawdor Castle

GRAMPIAN

Beauly Priory

Culloden battlefield

Inverness

Clava cairns

Strome Castle

Corrimony
chambered cairn

SKYE

Urquhart Castle

Eilean Donan Castle

Caisteal Grugaig broch

Dun Telve
& Dun Troddan
(the Glenelg brochs)

Ruthven barracks

Mallaig

TAYSIDE

Inverlochy Old Castle

Tioram Castle

Fort William

Mingary Castle

GLASGOW &
STRATHCLYDE

0 miles   20

0 kilometres   30

MULL

122

Caisteal Grugaig broch

Forestry Commission land • Free • Open access at any reasonable time

Not far (by car) from the notable brochs of *Glenelg (page 128)*, this is a smaller ruin with a lot of appeal, reached by a pleasant drive along the south side of Loch Duich. The remains are a bit overgrown, but that's not a bad thing, because they feel like your own private discovery.

A rushing stream at the foot of the broch would have provided fresh water, and the view through a gap in the trees shows that the broch-dwellers could have monitored traffic at the junction of three sea lochs.

Even though it's small, the ruin has all the usual broch features. The entrance has an impressive lintel over the door, and there are door checks and bar-holes in the entrance passage as well as a guard cell.

The rocky surface inside the broch is far from level, so the 'scarcement', or projecting ledge, low on the interior wall would have supported a wooden floor for the usual ground-floor living quarters.

From the A87 at Shiel Bridge, follow the minor road to Letterfearn; park in one of the large laybys near the end of the road. At the end of the road, follow the path through the forestry: it's an easy walk of about 15 minutes.

Carn Liath broch

Historic Scotland • Free • Open access at any reasonable time

A good warm-up for the excellent brochs of Orkney, if you are heading that way, and a pleasant stopping-off point on the main road north whatever your destination,

with fine views to the Grampian hills. Good sea access is usually a factor in the sites chosen for brochs, and was clearly a priority here, but the low coastline on this site offers no natural defence, so the broch's builders surrounded their tower with a substantial outer wall. A passage roofed with stone slabs led from a gate in the wall right up to the door of the broch.

Inside the broch, a doorway opposite the entrance leads to stairs which you can climb to emerge on the wall. A ragged lining of stonework that runs all round the interior is the remnant of a later house built inside the broch after its partial collapse.

Signposted by the A9 north of Golspie. Walk down to the southern end of the layby to cross the main road, then follow the path to the broch.

The overgrown Caisteal Grugaig isn't a big broch, but it has plenty of interesting details to look at.

 **See also… Beauly Priory**

Historic Scotland, ££, usual hours; right in the middle of the attractive little town of Beauly, near Inverness.

Although the church here can never have been an especially splendid building, it is, at least, quite well preserved, whereas the rest of the priory with which it was associated has long since vanished. The ruined church offers keen students of religious architecture an opportunity to study details which must have been seen as really quite sophisticated for this far north; but for the rest of us, it is not a particularly interesting place to visit.

The priory belonged to an obscure French order called the Valliscaulians, who had three establishments in Scotland: the others were at *Ardchattan* (*Argyll & Bute*) and at Pluscarden in Moray. The order was founded in 1205 at Vallis Caulium in Burgundy, which translates as 'Valley of the Cabbages'.

Left: a stair leads out on to the ruined wall of Carn Liath broch, a small but interesting ruin in a pleasant setting beside the sea.

Clava cairns

Historic Scotland • Free • Open access at any reasonable time

Arguably Scotland's prettiest group of ancient monuments, this set of three distinctive neolithic cairns stands in a wooded glade – a setting which enhances the serenity of the monuments. It's not far from the battlefield of Culloden and the town of Inverness, both very much on the Highland tourist trail, so don't be surprised by the number of visitors who turn up: but they don't stay long, so if you would like the place to yourself, just sit tight for a few minutes.

The cairns are outstanding examples of a local variety of burial monument found all over this region, particularly in the more fertile land of the Nairn district, to the east. What distinguishes this 'Clava type' of cairn is a kerb of stones

Above: the north-east cairn is the handsomest of the lot. Look out for a fine cup-and-ring-marked stone on the north side of the kerb that runs right round the cairn.

Left: the central cairn has a larger chamber, but it has no passage. The chamber may have been filled in as soon as it was built.

around the edge of the cairn, and a circle of standing stones surrounding it.

Of the three cairns here, the two at either end are alike in that they both had a passage leading to a chamber which would have been corbelled inward and topped with a capstone. The one in the middle, however, did not have a passage and is consequently known as a ring

cairn. It is thought that the chamber would have been filled in and covered over as soon as it was built. All three cairns would have stood more than 3m (16ft) high before they were ruined.

Another remarkable feature of the central cairn is a unique arrangement of three stone causeways leading from the edge of the cairn to three of the standing stones that surround it.

Look out, too, for a remarkable set of cup-and-ring markings on a stone in the kerb of the north-east cairn (the one nearest the car park); and note the way that the entrances of the passages and the biggest stones of the kerbs all face towards the south-west, the direction of the midwinter sunset.

Signposted off the B9006 east of Inverness, near Culloden battlefield. Note that the site is also known as Balnuaran of Clava.

Left: the south-west cairn also has a passage facing south-west, towards the midwinter sunset.

Castle Girnigoe & Sinclair

*In care of Historic Scotland • Free • Open access
at any reasonable time*

This dramatic ruin in a spectacular coastal
setting is well worth seeing, though its
crumbling condition and the cliffs that
drop sheer from its walls make it a place
to explore only with great care. It owes its
unusual double name to a tradition that a
substantial tower built in 1607 and often
known as Castle Sinclair was in some way
a replacement of the older Castle Girnigoe,
but in reality it was an enhancement of it.

The castle was the seat of the Sinclairs,
who were Earls of Caithness. The most
prominent remnant is a tower built of
near-black local flagstone with vivid red
sandstone trimmings, put up by William,
Earl of Caithness in the late 1400s.
Dangerous to enter, it blocks access to the
older castle ruins on the headland beyond.

*Follow the minor road to the lighthouse at
Noss Head, north of Wick; from the end of the
road, it's a signposted walk of 10 minutes.*

Castle Girnigoe & Sinclair is in a dangerous condition, but it has a splendid setting on a rocky headland.

Cawdor Castle

Privately owned • ££££ • Usual hours

This castle has no connection with the
historical Macbeth, though the Thanes
(and later Earls) of Cawdor have lived
here since the late 1200s. Maybe the
Shakespearean connotations help draw the
crowds, but this would be a popular spot
in any case: it's right on the tourist trail,
and it's one of Scotland's most appealing
examples of a castle that has developed

*Below: Cawdor Castle has developed over the years
into a comfortable and appealing stately home.*

into a grand but comfortable stately home.
Admission is distinctly too expensive, but
there's a lot to see and do in the grounds.

The original thick-walled tower dates
from about 1380, and it's surrounded by
four ranges of accommodation, two of
which were built in the late 1500s and
modified in the 1670s, and two of which
were added in the 1800s.

The castle is still in the family, and two
of the most engaging things about it are
the pleasantly conversational descriptions
of each room written by the present Earl,
and its lived-in feel. Modern art hangs
alongside the family portraits; cosy sofas
mingle with the antiques. Very nice.

Well signposted on the B9090 east of Inverness.

*Corrimony is a 'Clava' type of chambered cairn,
surrounded by a circle of standing stones.*

Corrimony chambered cairn

*Historic Scotland • Free • Open access at any
reasonable time*

This is the only other decent example of
the Clava type of cairn (*see opposite*), and
it's rather good fun. Just as at Clava, a lot
of the stone that once covered the cairn
has been robbed, leaving the chamber
exposed; but here there is still a roof over
the passage, so you can crawl down it to
emerge in the chamber.

The walls of the chamber still stand to
more than shoulder height and are corbelled
so that they curve inward, making it tricky
to climb out. Excavations in 1953 found a
crouched burial under the chamber's
cobbled floor.

Nearby, the RSPB has recently started
to restore the native wildwood in a new
nature reserve, and this is a very pleasant
spot for a walk.

*Signposted on a minor road off the A831 west of
Drumnadrochit, between Braefield and Cannich.*

Eilean Donan Castle

Privately owned • £££ • Usual hours

One of Scotland's most famous castles, thanks mainly to its picturesque setting on a small island by the shore of Loch Duich. It's so photogenic that it appears on nearly as many postcards as the Queen's head.

You may be surprised to learn, however, that this is, strictly speaking, a house built in the early 1900s. The original castle here, based on a tower of the late 1300s, was being held by Spanish troops as part of a minor Jacobite uprising in 1719 when three British frigates sailed up the loch and pounded it to rubble with cannon-fire.

It remained a ruin for 200 years, but in 1912 a descendant of the MacRae family, who had held the castle since the early 1500s, decided to rebuild it. An accurate restoration was impossible, because no plans survived: but within weeks of the castle's completion in 1932, a detailed set of drawings from around 1700 turned up.

The castle has been refurbished again in recent years and is now more or less fully open for visitors to wander where they will (a vast improvement over the guided tours of former years). If you take it for what it is – a country house of the 1930s – it is a very pleasant place to visit, coping pretty well with its large numbers of visitors.

By the A87 on the north shore of Loch Duich.

Below: Eilean Donan, pictured on many a postcard, is in reality a country house of the 1930s.

The stout old castle of Inverlochy stands on the edge of Fort William, with Ben Nevis in the background.

Inverlochy Old Castle

Historic Scotland • Free • Open access at any reasonable time

This is an excellent example of a castle of the 1200s – of which there aren't all that many in Scotland – with thick stone walls and fat round towers. But what makes it particularly pleasing is that it's like a classic toy castle: a square of walls, with a tower at all four corners and gates in two of the walls.

It's a shame that its unappealing setting, on the industrial outskirts of Fort William, and a continuing programme of restoration currently give it a neglected air. With luck, the end of the work and a tidy-up of the surroundings should restore its dignity. The riverside location, with Ben Nevis as a backdrop, could be very pleasant.

Built by the Comyns in about 1280, the castle later passed to the Gordons. It was of great strategic importance, along with *Dunstaffnage* in *Argyll*, in resisting the might of the Lords of the Isles.

Signposted off the A82 just north of Fort William town centre, south of its junction with the A830.

Fort George

Historic Scotland • £££ • Usual hours

This is one of the most remarkable pieces of historic military architecture in Britain, though that doesn't necessarily mean it's as interesting to visit as you might hope: the fort is on such a vast scale that it can all be a little difficult to take in, while the details on a more human scale – such as the interiors of certain buildings – are a bit disappointing.

The trick, then, is to try to appreciate the bigger picture. Fort George was built between 1748 and 1769 following the Jacobite rising of 1745, in which the British army's two most important fortifications, at Inverness and Fort Augustus, were both destroyed by artillery. The new fort incorporated all the latest ideas in European military architecture in an attempt to make it impregnable.

The main defence is a massive circuit of ramparts, fronted by stone walls but made of earth, so as to absorb the impact of artillery projectiles. The exterior walls are all angled so that no corner is safe from the defenders' gunfire. Deep under

Huge earth ramparts surround a village of elegant Georgian buildings at the remarkable Fort George.

the ramparts are a number of 'casemates': bomb-proof, brick-vaulted barracks which could shelter the entire garrison.

The approach to the fort, through an outwork called the Ravelin, is, in itself,

Once the only way into the fort, this long bridge is heavily defended.

quite remarkable. You start by crossing a short bridge over an outer moat, which brings you to a sort of island, like the barbican of a medieval castle. You then cross a longer bridge over a wide expanse of inner moat to reach the main gate.

Incidentally, the fort is still in full use by the army (who use a new gate punched through one of the ramparts). This means that you may get your bag searched and it does restrict access to the buildings, but it also means you may get to see drills taking place in the parade ground.

Buildings that you do get access to include: a barrack block with reconstructions of infantry quarters of several different periods; the magazine, with its immensely thick walls; the Lieutenant-Governor's and Fort Major's house, with its Adam fireplaces, which is used for a regimental museum; and the chapel which stands on its own at the far end of the fort.

The fort stands on a headland that juts out into the Moray Firth, and if you're lucky, you might spot one of the Firth's resident bottlenose dolphins. Gulls nest in the moats in early summer, and protective parent birds sometimes buzz visitors!

Near Ardesier on the B9006. Signposted from the A96 east of Inverness.

The brochs of Glenelg

Mainland Scotland's finest examples of these castles of the iron age

Facing the Isle of Skye across a narrow stretch of water is an odd slice of country: isolated, but also civilised and pastoral. There's even a decent pub. You can get here in two ways: either on the rickety two-car Kylerhea ferry from Skye, or by the hill road from Shiel Bridge, which climbs a spectacular set of hairpin bends to a fine viewpoint before dropping down to the coast. The road was built by the British army in the 1720s to improve access to the fort-like barracks at Bernera (see *Ruthven barracks, opposite*).

South of the village of Glenelg, a minor road heads away from the coast, up a surprisingly sheltered river valley, and in this hidden valley you will find two of the best-preserved brochs in Scotland.

The second tallest broch in Scotland, Dun Telve looks almost complete from some angles.

Dun Telve

Historic Scotland • Free • Open access at any reasonable time

The walls of this fairly spectacular broch still stand up to 10m (35ft) in height, which is higher than any other broch bar the incomparable *Mousa* in *Shetland*. From some angles, the structure looks almost complete, but the parade is rained on a little when you go round the back and discover that more than half of the broch has collapsed. Ah, well.

It's a good place for examining the standard hollow-wall construction methods used in brochs, with gaps left in the interior wall apparently to reduce the weight of stone pressing down on weak spots like the doorway. The inner and outer walls are joined by flat slabs which act as floors in about five galleries inside the wall. It seems that only the lowest of these galleries was used, probably for storage; its walls have been carefully finished, whereas the higher galleries are full of nasty, sharp stones sticking out of the walls.

A unique feature of this broch is the 'scarcement' or ledge right up at the top, which would have supported a top floor or a roof. There is also the more usual scarcement lower down to support a floor at first storey level. Other features include the corbelled cell and stairway which lead off from either side of a doorway inside the broch.

Signposted on a minor road south of Glenelg: park in the large layby just before the broch.

Dun Troddan

Historic Scotland • Free • Open access at any reasonable time

This broch stands on a terrace on the hillside, rather than on the valley floor. Perhaps it's not quite as spectacular as its near neighbour, but Dun Troddan is still well worth seeing. One part of its wall stands as much as 7.6m (25ft) high.

An excavation of 1920 found a few small items such as spindle-whorls and a glass bead, but its most thought-provoking discovery was a set of post-holes around a central hearth on the floor of the broch. The post-holes would presumably have held timbers to support a wooden floor. This is the only case in which actual evidence for an internal wooden structure in a broch has been found.

Just a short walk (5 minutes) further up the road from Dun Telve.

Left: Dun Troddan stands on the hillside a short way away from Dun Telve. Just inside the entrance is a fine corbelled guard-chamber.

Ruthven barracks

Historic Scotland • Free • Open access at any reasonable time

One of four barracks blocks built not long after the 1715 Jacobite rebellion, when the British army was attempting to impose its control on the Highlands. The army's plan was to exert its influence from a heavily defended line of communication running from Fort William to Inverness along the south-eastern side of the Great Glen. Major-General Wade's military roads, with their attractive stone bridges, are relics of the same turbulent period.

The shells of the two main barracks blocks are pretty much intact, though the roofs, floors and windows are all missing. Since these are just domestic buildings, the interiors are not terrifically interesting, but you do get an idea of how spartan the existence of the infantry troops billeted here was: they lived, cooked, ate and slept in one cramped room, often shared with wives or camp followers. A visit to the reconstructed barracks rooms at *Fort George (see page 127)* will help fill in the details if you are interested.

The two blocks are surrounded by a fairly low curtain wall, with a wide walkway all round it supported on open vaults that could be used for storage. Outside the wall is a stable block which dates to 1734, when a force of 30 dragoons was drafted in 'to serve as a convoy for money or provisions… as well as to retain that part of the country in obedience'.

Another similar barracks can be seen from a distance at Bernera, near *Glenelg (see overleaf)*, but there is no public access.

Signposted on the B970 just east of Kingussie.

The infantry barracks at Ruthven were built in 1719 to help suppress support for the Jacobite cause.

Strome Castle

National Trust of Scotland • Free • Open access at any reasonable time

There are traces here of a tower house and a courtyard wall, but so completely ruined are they that it's more of a viewpoint than a historic site. The ragged stonework of a single archway frames a fine view of Skye and the pointy Cuillin hills. The castle, built in the mid-1400s, was destroyed by English soldiers in 1602 after a siege in which it was taken from the MacDonalds.

On the north shore of Loch Carron: signposted from the A896 at Lochcarron village.

■ *See also… Old Wick Castle*

Historic Scotland; free, open access at any reasonable time. On a dead-end minor road along the coast from the southern side of Wick: there is a signpost from the main road, but none after that, so you will have to find your own way. The castle is 10 minutes' walk from the layby at the end of the road.

This early stone tower is remarkable for its primitive simplicity, and for little else. It was probably built in the late 1100s or early 1200s, when Caithness was held by the Norse Earls of Orkney. The clifftop here is a popular spot for local people to walk their dogs, and the trip along to the castle is a fairly pleasant stroll.

Left: there isn't much left of Strome Castle, but it's a grand spot for views of Skye.

The Grey Cairns of Camster

The long cairn is an enormous structure incorporating two earlier cairns, each with its own burial chamber.

Historic Scotland • Free • Open access at any reasonable time

The resonant name sets an appropriately dramatic tone for this remarkable pair of neolithic monuments. The Grey Cairns are two of the best-preserved chambered cairns in Britain, and they stand on a forbidding slice of moorland in country so remote that a single house features on the map as if it were a village. Yet there's an intimate quality to the location, too, and it's not at all an intimidating site to visit.

The enormous Long Cairn, stretched out along the ridge, is 60m (nearly 200ft) long and incorporates two chambered tombs, both very like the nearby Round Cairn. Both the chambers can still be reached by crawling or shuffling down the unusually long passages. You don't need a torch, since the chambers are lit by skylights in their roofs, but you'll find one useful for examining the interior of the passage.

The long cairn was formed by building a drystone retaining wall around a pair of round cairns and then piling stones on top, resulting in a distinctive humped profile. Excavations showed that at each end of the cairn there was originally a horned forecourt, and these have been restored.

Right: the beautifully constructed round cairn, with the long cairn visible on the ridge beyond.

The one at the top end is particularly intriguing, if the restoration is accurate. It has steps up to what looks like a low stage running along the end of the cairn, which surely must have been the venue for some kind of ceremony.

Though less dramatic, the round cairn is just as extraordinary. The entrance passage and the chamber are even more impressive, with some terrific stonework using vast megalithic slabs and pillars. The corbelled roof is practically complete, which is a very rare thing to find. The tomb had been filled in after it was last used, and excavations found human and animal bones, pottery and flint.

Signposted on a minor road which runs north from the A9 west of Lybster; it's about 5 miles to the cairns, which stand near the road.

See also, nearby…

This north-western corner of Scotland is full of interesting prehistoric monuments, at least two of which are close to the Grey Cairns of Camster and well worth seeing while you're here…

Cairn o' Get

Historic Scotland, free, open access at any reasonable time. Signposted a short way along a minor road off the A9 at Whaligoe; park sensibly and follow the striped posts that mark the path to the monument (about 15 minutes, steadily uphill).

This neolithic cairn is basically a ruined version of a chambered tomb like the ones at the Grey Cairns. Most of the stones that covered the cairn have been taken away, so the passage and chamber are exposed. It's a little bit like a cutaway diagram of one of the Grey Cairns: handy for getting a better understanding of the anatomy of those impressive tombs.

The cairns of the region are built to a distinctive pattern, with similarities to other neolithic cairns in Scotland but with quite significant differences, too. The passage leads first to a kind of antechamber formed by a pair of stone slabs (very like the dividing slabs in the 'stalled cairns' of Orkney). Beyond is the chamber, its back wall formed by a large slab laid back at an angle (which again is very reminiscent of Orkney's stalled cairns).

Like the long cairn at Camster, the Cairn o' Get was originally a simple round cairn, but it was later incorporated into a large, rectangular cairn with dramatic horned facades at each end (though in this case the cairn was nothing like as big as the Camster long cairn, and there's not very much of it left).

Given an OS map and a decent pair of boots, you can explore the moorland here in search of a number of other ancient monuments: more chambered cairns, bronze age burial mounds, an iron age fort, even a fan-shaped arrangement of standing stones similar to the Hill o' Many Stanes. The big stone structure behind the Cairn o'Get, however, is a dam built in the 1800s to provide water for a mill.

Below: the Cairn o'Get is a ruined version of a chambered cairn very similar to the Grey Cairns.

Above: rows of tiny standing stones fan out across the slope at the mysterious Hill o' Many Stanes.

The Hill o' Many Stanes

Historic Scotland, free, open access at any reasonable time. Signposted off the A9 just north of Clyth; park in layby opposite the monument.

This is an intriguing monument. Essentially, it's pretty much what the name suggests: a hillside covered with standing stones. The stones are arranged in about 22 rows which fan out as they drop down the slope, so there's a sort of focal point at the top of the hill where the rows converge.

To visit, it's not quite as impressive as it might sound, because the stones are surprisingly titchy – little more than knee-high – and quite a lot of them are missing. But it's certainly a fascinating puzzle. What could it have been? There is a theory that it was a complicated lunar observatory, but this would be hard to prove. Other similar arrangements of stones are known, and some have a burial cairn at the 'focal point', but there isn't one here.

And…

Here are more prehistoric monuments to visit in Caithness, not far from the Grey Cairns…

Achavanich standing stones, *beside the minor road that runs from Lybster to the A895 Thurso road (Local landowner, free, open access at any reasonable time)* – A most unusual and quite well-preserved horseshoe or part-oval of standing stones, thought to be from the bronze age. Note that the flat, slab-like stones are set edge-on to the centre of the monument, whereas in stone circles they are always face-on.

Cnoc Freiceadain long cairns, *signposted footpath leaves the minor road between Achreamie to Shebster, off the A836 west of Thurso (Historic Scotland, free, open access at any reasonable time)* – Somewhat further afield, near the north coast. Two impressive horned neolithic cairns set at right-angles to each other. No chambers are visible; the cairns have not been excavated.

Coille na Borgie chambered cairns, *beside the minor road to Skelpick, off the A836 south of Bettyhill (Local landowner, free, open access at any reasonable time)* – Much further afield, this time. The remains of several cairns, but they are little more than big piles of rocks.

Yarrows archeological trail, *signposted from the A9 at Loch of Yarrows, south of Wick (Local landowners, free, open access at any reasonable time)* – Back in the locality of the Grey Cairns, this is a well thought-out walk guided by a leaflet available from the tourist office in Wick. A round trip of a couple of hours visits a broch, several neolithic cairns, a standing stone, a hilltop enclosure and an iron age settlement. None of the monuments is especially exciting, but it's a pleasant stroll.

Urquhart Castle

Historic Scotland • £££ • Usual hours

It's almost inevitable that this, a ruined castle overlooking the best stretch of Loch Ness for monster-spotting, should be one of the Highlands' busiest coach-trip destinations, and in the peak summer season it gets unbearably busy. The rest of the time, though, it handles large numbers of visitors with relative ease. You might have to queue for the narrow spiral stair in the tower-house, but you should be able to get a quiet corner by the water all to yourself.

In truth, it's not the most entertaining castle to visit. It's a little too ruinous, with too few interior spaces to explore. But it is, nevertheless, a rare example of a large medieval castle in Scotland, and it's a pleasant spot besides.

Obvious highlights are the gatehouse, one side of which has a dungeon cut deep into the rock, and the tower house of the early 1500s (its turrets probably added in the 1620s) which is now the outstanding feature of the castle.

One side of the tower has collapsed, so there are no floors; but you can climb a stair that takes you up to parapet height for excellent views out over the loch. And since the entrance to the tower is on the first floor, you can also go down the stair to the vaulted cellars on the ground floor, where an unusual postern gate leads out into the main castle ditch.

There are many other buildings inside the castle walls, but most of them are so ruined that it's hard to tell what they were. What's more interesting is the overall plan of the castle. A massive ditch protects it from attack on the landward side, but by the shore of the loch, a water gate allows access to a small beach. Protected by wings of the castle on either side, this beach could be used to land fresh troops and supplies even when the castle was under siege, as actually happened in 1689, when a garrison holding the castle for the king found the landing to be 'very safe'.

The castle was abandoned not long after this siege, and it is thought that at least parts of it – such as the gatehouse – were blown up to prevent it from being of use to Jacobite rebels.

By the A82 just south-east of Drumnadrochit; car park on site, but during peak periods an overflow car park in the village operates – it's 15 minutes' walk away.

Urquhart Castle, on the banks of Loch Ness, is one of the most romantic castles of Scotland.

See also…

These two castles are a fair way off the beaten track and you can't gain access to the interior of either, but both are well worth seeing.

Mingary Castle, Ardnamurchan

On private land, free, open access to view exterior only at any reasonable time. Down a minor road to the Mingary estate, off the B8007 east of Kilchoan; a car park is provided.

A formidable ruin standing on an outcrop of solid rock on the shore of Kilchoan Bay. Its high walls of rough stone, with the round corners typical of castles on the west coast, give it a darkly purposeful air. It consists of a tower and a roughly triangular enclosure of walls parts of which date to the 1200s.

Although the castle is on private land, the estate provides a car park and a footpath down to the shore. It's well worth the 10-minute walk.

A good way to get to Kilchoan is by ferry from Tobermory on Mull, which takes about an hour.

Tioram Castle, Moidart

On private land, free, open access to view exterior only at any reasonable time. Reached by a minor road to Cul Doirlinn, off the A861 near Acharacle; the turning is north of the turn to Shielfoot, over a river bridge and past the turn to Moss. Again, the estate generously provides a car park.

This is a magical location for a castle. A narrow, twisty minor road brings you to a peaceful, beautiful, hidden-away spot on the shores of Loch Moidart. The castle is on an island, reached on foot via a sandy causeway which can only be crossed when the tide in the sea loch is low.

It's an interesting ruin, too, but recently access to the interior was suspended after a safety inspection found it to be dangerous. Since repairs would be expensive, it's not likely that they will be carried out with any great urgency.

The castle itself is very similar to Mingary, consisting of a five-sided enclosure of high walls with rounded-off corners, built in the early 1200s. A tower-house and other buildings were added in the interior at later dates.

And…

Above: Mingary Castle.

Ardclach bell tower, *on a minor road off the A939 near Redburn* (*Historic Scotland, free, ask for key at Fort George*) – This tiny building on a hill seems to have been a watchtower-cum-prison. Dates to 1655. Cute and in attractive countryside, but getting hold of the key is extremely bothersome.

Ardvreck Castle, *on the shores of Loch Assynt, off the A837 north of Ullapool* (*on private land, free, open access at any reasonable time*) – The ruinous but romantic remains, in a splendid wild setting, of a tower house probably built in the early 1500s.

Ballone Castle, *near Rockfield, south-east of Portmahomack, overlooking the Moray Firth* (*private land, view from shore footpath only*) – A pretty substantial ruin of a Z-plan tower-house with one round tower and one square. It is under restoration, and can only be viewed from the shore.

Castle Stuart, *on the B9039 west of Inverness* (*privately owned, open occasionally*) – A posh tower of the early 1620s, rebuilt in 1869, which is now a hotel. It's sometimes open to the public.

Culloden battlefield, *signposted on the B9006 west of Inverness* (*National Trust of Scotland, free access to battlefield but fee for visitor centre, usual hours*) – The moor where the Jacobite cause was wiped out in 1645. There's not much to see, but the memorials to the Highland clans are quite touching.

Dun Dornaigil broch, *on a minor road south of Hope on the north coast* (*Historic Scotland, free, open access at any time*) – Quite a big ruined broch: the walls stand 7m (22ft) high over the door, but the interior is filled with rubble. Worth seeing.

Dunrobin Castle, *beside the A9 north of Golspie* (*privately owned, £££, usual hours in summer only*) – This extraordinary chateau-like confection owes more to rebuilds in the mid-1800s and early 1900s than it does to the original tower of the 1300s that's buried underneath. Open as a stately home (part of the Great Houses of Scotland scheme). Fine gardens.

Fortrose Cathedral, *signposted in the middle of Fortrose* (*Historic Scotland, free, open access during usual hours only*) – Fragmentary and disappointing ruin consisting of part of an aisle of the cathedral church, and an undercroft from one of the buildings of the cloister. Of no real interest.

Keiss Castle, *on footpath from Keiss harbour, north of Wick* (*on private land, no access to the interior*) – Dramatic ruined tower of the late 1500s on a clifftop.

Kilravock Castle, *near Inverness* (*privately owned, £££, open occasionally*) – Old-fashioned hotel in a tower of 1460; tours are offered, but the lovely wooded grounds may be visited free of charge.

Left: Tioram Castle.

Grampian

Aberdeen and the north-east

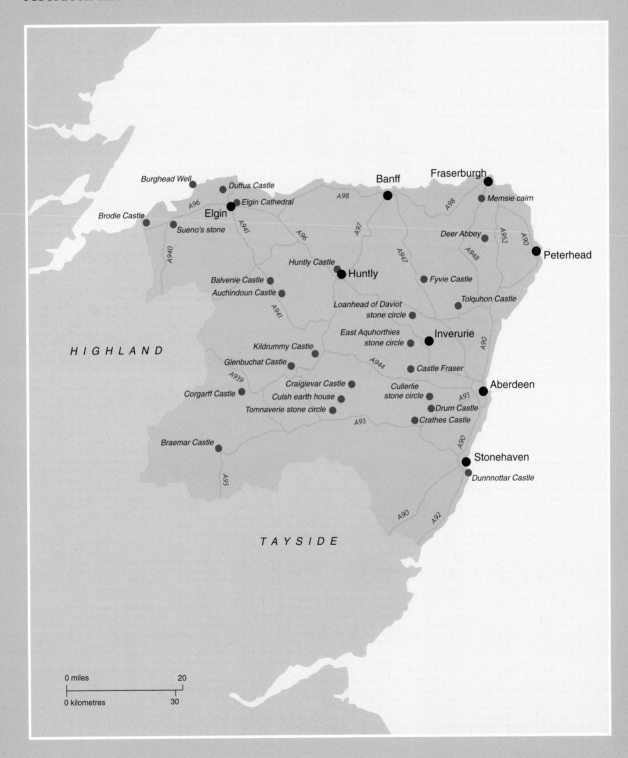

Burghead Well

Duffus Castle

Banff

Fraserburgh

A98

A96

Elgin Cathedral

Memsie cairn

A98

A952

A90

Brodie Castle

Elgin

Sueno's stone

A941

A96

A97

Deer Abbey

A948

Peterhead

A940

A947

Huntly Castle

Balvenie Castle

Huntly

Fyvie Castle

Tolquhon Castle

Auchindoun Castle

A941

Loanhead of Daviot
stone circle

HIGHLAND

East Aquhorthies
stone circle

Inverurie

A90

Kildrummy Castle

Glenbuchat Castle

A944

Castle Fraser

A939

Craigievar Castle

Cullerlie
stone circle

Aberdeen

A93

Corgarff Castle

Culsh earth house

Drum Castle

Tomnaverie stone circle

A93

Crathes Castle

A90

Braemar Castle

Stonehaven

A93

Dunnnottar Castle

A90

A92

TAYSIDE

0 miles   20

0 kilometres   30

Auchindoun Castle

Historic Scotland • Free • Open access to view exterior only at any reasonable time

A big, dangerous, crumbling pile of rock with its gates bricked up, Auchindoun is currently awaiting restoration (and looks as if it could be in for a long wait). Still, it looks extremely dramatic against its backdrop of bleak moorland.

The castle, which stands within the earthen ramparts of an iron age hillfort, is basically an L-plan tower house with a curtain wall. It was built in the late 1400s by Robert Cochrane, who was court mason of James III and designed the Great Hall at *Stirling Castle* (*see page 90*).

By the A941 south of Dufftown; park by the road and it's a walk of 15 mins, starting quite steeply, up the signposted track.

Balvenie Castle

Historic Scotland • £ • Usual hours, Summer only (beginning of April to end of September)

Balvenie is a fine-looking castle at the heart of whisky country, its oldest walls dating to the 1200s.

Frequently enveloped in the sour smell of mashing whisky coming from the famous Speyside distillery next door, this is a handsome castle tucked away amidst the trees of its own grounds. It isn't quite as interesting on the inside as it looks from the outside, but it's still good value.

The oldest part is the impressively massive circuit of curtain walls, dating from some time in the 1200s. In the mid-1500s most of the east side (the front) was demolished and a grand accommodation range known as the Atholl Lodging was built, incorporating a large round tower at the north-east corner.

The southern end of this range offers the most memorable feature of the interior: a big, dark space under a large vault,

where there was a two-storey kitchen. Also worth noting is the unusual double-door 'yett' (iron gate) in the entranceway.

The prominent feature of the castle's history (apart, naturally, from the fact that Mary Queen of Scots visited) is that it was always owned by unsuccessful upstarts who eventually received a good kicking from the king. It was originally the seat of the 'Black Comyns', Earls of Buchan, who were defeated by Robert the Bruce in May 1308; and later in its career it was the home of the 'Black Douglases', whom James II destroyed in 1455.

Clearly signposted on the north side of Dufftown, just off the A941 (the Elgin road). Free car park (private cars only) is straight up the castle drive.

See also... **Ballindalloch Castle**

Privately owned, £££, usual hours (Easter to end of September). Signposted on the A95 near Bridge of Avon.

Generations of alterations have pretty much swamped the original tower house of 1546, eventually producing a pleasant family home with bright, airy rooms and soft, pastel-hued, feminine interiors reminiscent of a very fine country house hotel. Rewarding if you enjoy stately homes with a lived-in feel.

Left: Auchindoun Castle is bricked up and awaits restoration, but it's worth seeing.

See also… **Burghead well-chapel**

Historic Scotland; free; key from a nearby house at reasonable times only. Signposted on the main road in the town of Burghead.

The wee town of Burghead stands on a headland that was once occupied by the largest known Pictish fort, built some time after 300 AD and destroyed by fire in the 800s. Its ramparts were decorated with stone carvings of bulls, dug up in the 1800s when the ramparts were quarried for stone to make repairs to the harbour.

Another surprise discovery was an old rock-cut well, found by engineers looking for a source of drinking water. Investigating tales that there was a spring here, they found a pool cut in the rock with a flagstone walkway round its edge and steps down to it.

Initially thought to be Roman, the well – or shrine – is now believed to be an early Christian monument of the Pictish era, possibly used for baptisms. It's an interesting monument: a little dark, dank and eerie, but well worth experiencing for yourself.

Brodie Castle

National Trust for Scotland • £££ • Usual hours

The speciality of this region is this type of grand, comfortable, beautifully furnished castle-cum-stately-home, and most are in the care of the National Trust for Scotland. Each one has a slightly different character – *Fyvie (page 145)* is ornate and baronial in a very Victorian way, whereas *Crathes (page 139)* has an austere 1600s style – and Brodie's distinctive quality is that it is the friendliest and most pleasant of the lot.

Brodie also has a special claim to fame in its superb collection of pictures, which practically makes it an art gallery disguised as a castle. Specialising in late Victorian and twentieth century art, but also featuring some older English paintings, the collection was put together by the parents of the 25th Brodie of Brodie, who gave the castle to the Trust in 1980. Quite recently, the laird was still doing occasional stints as a volunteer guide, which must really have brought the place to life for visitors.

The Trust has renovated the house, but has mostly kept it as it was after the Second World War, in the most recent phase of its long career. The result is that it still feels like a welcoming family home as well as being a collection of historic objects and interiors that has gradually accumulated over 400 years. From the

It's really a grand stately home rather than a castle, but Brodie is a friendly and charming place to visit.

moment you step through the front door and wander into the library – where french windows open onto the lawn and a croquet set is at hand, ready to be used – you can imagine living here.

The formal rooms on the first floor are very grand indeed. The dining room is very dark, but rich, with a plaster ceiling painted to look like wood. Next door is a small sitting room with astonishing blue wall coverings, bright as a jewel, and its own very old plaster ceiling. From here on, the paintings are the most eyecatching thing in most of the rooms, though the nurseries on the top floor are good fun.

As with many of the Trust's castles in the region, the grounds are open when the castle isn't and are a great attraction in themselves. There's a tearoom, and an excellent wooden fort for kids to play on. Also worth looking in on is the dairy, in an outbuilding at the back of the house, which has a surprisingly interesting little display on Victorian cheese-making.

Historically there is little to say about the castle, which started life as a Z-plan tower in the 1560s, was enlarged in the 1820s and was remodelled a while later.

Beside the A96 west of Forres, east of Nairn.

Castle Fraser

*National Trust for Scotland • £££ • Slightly
limited hours (daily in July & August)*

This particularly large and grand-looking
tower house is, like *Craigievar* (*overleaf*),
from the very last days of castles. It gives
the impression of having been modernised
in the Victorian era, but in fact it looks
much as it did in the early 1600s.

Somewhere underneath is an old tower,
thought to date to before 1454, when the
king set aside land here to form a barony
and gave it to Thomas Fraser. Work began
on a new residence in the 1570s, but the
plan changed several times before finally,
in 1618, work finished on the Z-plan tower
with two low wings. Its dominant feature
is the seven-storey round tower, which
you can climb to the top of (via the small
stair-tower which you can see in the photo)
to emerge on the flat roof.

The interiors are furnished with a
predominantly Victorian feel, but the
original layout of the building is never far
from the surface. Probably the most
memorable room is the library, converted
from two rooms in 1839, which occupies
the whole top floor of the main block.

*Signposted on a minor road south of the B993
at Craigearn (or from the A944 at Dunecht).*

**Below: the star-shaped fortification that surrounds
the tower at Corgarff gives it a unique appearance.**

*The exterior of the grand-looking Castle Fraser
has some particularly pleasing decorative details.*

Corgarff Castle

Historic Scotland • ££ • Usual hours

The unusual appearance of this tower is a
result of its conversion in 1748 into a
military barracks-cum-fort protected by a
star-shaped fortification. Its clean lines are
very appealing, standing out sharply
against the bleak landscape of this high
moorland region.

The tower was rebuilt from a total ruin
in the 1960s. Inside, it's smaller than
you'd think. It has three storeys above a
basement: the first floor houses the ticket
office (where the friendly custodian keeps
a small peat fire burning, creating that
evocative smell), while the second has a
reconstruction of a barracks room (very
basic, with beds and little else) and the
third features an exhibition on General
Wade and the army in the 1700s.

Signposted on the A939 west of Corgarff village.

Craigievar Castle

Craigievar Castle, one of the last tower houses to be built, is in remarkably original condition.

National Trust for Scotland • ££££ •
Usual hours

This extraordinary tower house was built in the 1620s and has altered very little in the years since. It is remarkable not just as a fine example of a castle from the very last days of castle-building, but also because so many of its original fixtures and fittings are so well preserved.

Craigievar was built by William Forbes, who, as a merchant trading with the Baltic, had earned himself a fortune and the nickname 'Danzig Willie'. Much of the wood for the panelled interiors was brought from eastern Europe in his own ships.

His home was really far more a house than a castle, but it was defended by a wall around a courtyard (more commonly known as a 'barmkin'). Just one of the small corner towers of this wall survives.

The castle has attracted tourists since the middle of the 1800s – Queen Victoria and the American writer Henry James are amongst those whose signatures appear in the visitors' book – but after it was opened to the public by the National Trust for Scotland in the 1970s, the trickle of visitors turned into such a flood that the delicate materials of the interior were threatened. The castle was closed for a major programme of restoration in the mid-1990s, and is now open again only under strict limits.

Visits are by guided tour only, and in very small groups (so if you go at a busy time of year you may have to wait your turn or be disappointed altogether) and the Trust doesn't publicise the castle at all. The guides are excellent, friendly and knowledgeable, and they point out lots of details that you simply wouldn't have picked up for yourself.

Craigievar has many original features, from the iron 'yett' (gate) at the front door to the 'screens passage' on the approach to the hall – the only one to survive in any Scottish castle. Particularly notable are the plaster ceilings, dated 1625 and 1626, which use some of the same mouldings as the ceilings at *Kellie* and *Glamis* castles.

But it would be a mistake to think that the place has not changed since the day it was built. Part of its appeal is the way little changes have been made over the years, from the Victorian plumbing (with a bath squeezed into an old box bed) to the excellent 20th century studio pottery scattered around the place.

Signposted on the A980 south of Alford.

Crathes Castle

National Trust for Scotland • £££ • Usual hours

Crathes boasts two outstanding features, either of which would be enough on its own to ensure the castle's lasting fame: it has superb painted ceilings, which are almost as old as the building itself, and it has very beautiful walled gardens.

These attractions have made it one of the Trust's busiest properties, but it copes well with its large numbers of visitors. Admission to the castle itself is controlled by the issue of timed tickets, but there is plenty to keep you occupied while you wait: you can visit the gardens, pop in to the restaurant or the gift shop, or stroll in the extensive grounds, where there are nature trails varying in length from just a quarter of a mile to four miles. Actually, you could easily spend a whole day here.

Construction of the tower house started in the 1550s and was completed in 1596. Later additions include a Queen Anne wing of the early 1700s and a Victorian one, but both burned down in a fire in 1966 and only the earlier one was rebuilt.

The interiors are furnished sparingly, with an emphasis on early objects. There's even a pair of armchairs dated 1597 which were part of the castle's original furniture. One room worth noting is the long gallery on the top floor, where the lords and ladies walked when bad weather kept them in. Look out, too, for the jewelled ivory horn hanging in the hall, said to have been a gift from Robert the Bruce in the 1300s.

Ultimately, though, the painted ceilings – at their finest when depicting legendary knights in the Room of the Nine Nobles – and the equally colourful and imaginative gardens are both so marvellous that the rest rather pales into insignificance.

Signposted on the A93 east of Banchory.

Crathes Castle, built in the late 1500s, has glorious medieval painted ceilings which are almost as old.

Cullerlie stone circle

Historic Scotland • Free • Open access at any reasonable time

This smallish monument lacks the drama of its larger cousins, but it does have a pleasing symmetry to it, and its fat little boulders are curiously appealing.

It was built in the late bronze age on a thin finger of solid ground surrounded by boggy marshland. The monument consists of a small circle of eight standing stones, in the middle of which were placed eight little cairns: seven around the outside, and one slightly larger one in the middle.

The cairns started off as rings of stones, looking rather like campfires. In each one, branches of willow were burned, then a handful of cremated bone was placed in the middle before smaller stones were piled up to form the cairn.

Signposted on a minor road off the B9125 south of Garlogie, not far from Drum Castle (overleaf).

See also… Delgatie Castle

Privately owned, ££, usual hours (summer only). Signposted off the A947 north of Fyvie.

Rather an eccentric little spot. As a Victorian conversion of a tower house of the 1570s, it has none of the style, luxury and comfort of nearby *Fyvie Castle* (*page 145*), but view it as a folly of indeterminate age and it has a definite faded charm. Looked at in this way, some of the peculiar features of the place – like the way the wall has subsided where large windows were fitted in an attempt to turn the hall into an elegant drawing room – begin to seem colourful rather than merely shabby.

The castle does, however, boast one truly outstanding feature – a painted ceiling in one of the upstairs rooms which is thought to date to the 1590s and is one of the finest you'll see, in no way inferior to the splendid ceilings at *Crathes Castle* (*this page*).

Left: the bronze age stone circle at Cullerlie is one of the region's most appealing ancient monuments.

Culsh earth house

Historic Scotland • Free • Open access at any reasonable time

It's really just a hole in the ground, but it's an interesting one. This is a well-preserved souterrain – an underground passage built in the iron age and used for storing grain or some other kind of agricultural produce.

There are quite a few souterrains around, but what makes this one particularly worth seeing is that it's still roofed with big slabs of stone and covered over with earth. And it's a large one, too – high enough to stand up in. You'll need to bring a good torch, because the passage curves and daylight doesn't reach the end.

Signposted beside the B9119 east of Tarland.

The earth house at Culsh is an underground passage some 14m (18ft) long, and is well worth exploring.

Drum Castle

National Trust of Scotland • £££ • Limited hours (summer months and afternoons only)

Like many other castles, Drum developed from a grim tower into an elegant house – but it did so in a most unusual way. In the early 1600s the Irvine family, who had lived at Drum since the early 1300s, simply built a new mansion alongside the old tower, which they left standing there, intact but empty. In a final twist to the tale, a further remodelling in the Victorian era

Below: the original tower at Drum Castle is one of the oldest in Scotland and is very well preserved.

saw a hole knocked through the massive wall of the old tower so that its first floor hall could be turned into a library.

The result of all this activity is a pleasing little group of buildings with lots of interesting features. The Jacobean house has a number of Victorian alterations, such as enlarged windows and a door in the south front leading out on to the lawn, and the interior has a late Georgian or early Victorian feel to it (as compared with, say, the early 1600s air of *Crathes*, or the baronial late Victorian swagger of *Fyvie*). The usual furniture and portraits are the main attraction, but look out for the

watercolour sketches by Anna Forbes Irvine in a room off the drawing room.

The tower, dating to before 1290, is one of the oldest in Scotland. It's reached from outside in the garden, by a stair up to the first floor: inside, it has a wonderfully rough and archaic feel, which makes it great fun to explore. A narrow spiral stair leads down to the basement and up to an upper hall, with wooden steps to the roof; but you can't get to the library on the first floor, which can only be reached from inside the house.

Signposted off the A93 south-west of Aberdeen.

Duffus Castle

The ruined tower of Duffus Castle still looks pretty good from this side, but the far wall has fallen away.

Historic Scotland • Free • Open access at any reasonable time

There's something extremely satisfying about the sweeping earthworks of this long-abandoned ruin, with the gentle slopes of the castle mound standing out from the unusually flat farmland that surrounds it.

The landscape makes a lot more sense when you discover that at the the time the castle was built, this was not fields, but water and marshy ground. The castle stood beside a tidal estuary called Loch Spynie, which dried up many years later after its mouth silted up. The boggy ground all around has been drained and reclaimed as farmland, creating the flat landscape that you see today.

Incidentally, the bishop's palace known as *Spynie Castle* (*see page 148*) also stood near the shore of Loch Spynie, and at the ticket office there you can see a map that shows the extent of the loch at the time.

Both the motte (the higher mound on which the keep stands) and the raised bailey of the castle are largely artificial, built up mostly from gravel. When the first castle was built here in the mid-1100s, the only structures were of timber; but in about 1300 a curtain wall was built around the bailey and the motte was topped by a thick-walled stone tower. The mound was just not solid enough to hold up the tower, and one whole wall has collapsed. It's not known how soon the problem occurred, but there are signs that smaller fractures were repaired before the whole thing fell apart, and the fact that there were no later improvements to the accommodation in the tower suggest that it might have been abandoned quite early on.

Near the tower are the foundations of a range built in the 1500s which included a hall and the usual reception rooms as well as a kitchen and cellars. More interesting to look at, though, are the cobbled road that leads up from the castle gate and the well-preserved brick-lined oven on the far side of the bailey.

The reason Duffus is here at all is that in 1130, King David I suppressed the fiercely independent Pictish province of Moray and redistributed the lands owned by its earl to his supporters, giving the land at Duffus to a Flemish knight called Freskin, whose descendants took the title 'de Moravia' (of Moray) and became one of the region's most powerful families.

Signposted from the B9012 north-west of Elgin.

See also… St Peter's church, Duffus

Historic Scotland; free, open access to the exterior at any reasonable time and to the interior during usual hours only (key available from a nearby house). Signposted in the village of Duffus, on the B9012 north-west of Elgin.

This substantially intact but roofless ruin is in an attractive sheltered setting in Duffus village, about half a mile from the castle. Although there was a church on this site before 1226, the oldest parts of the present building are a porch, built in 1524, and the barrel-vaulted basement of a rectangular tower, which is slightly earlier.

The body of the church follows the long, narrow plan of the earlier structure, but dates mostly from the 1700s. The interior was arranged in the usual Presbyterian style, with a pulpit in the middle of the south wall and galleries round the other three sides. A feature typical of that period is the 'laird's loft', which has the added luxury of a fireplace.

Dunnottar Castle

Privately owned • £££ • Usual hours

The extraordinary location of this castle, on a promontory so precipitous that it's like an island of rock rising sheer out of the sea, is immensely striking – far more so than the ruin itself, really.

It's a place that will appeal as much to anyone with an interest in geology or in birdwatching (there are puffins on the cliffs in spring and early summer) as to historians. You don't have to pay for

The superb setting of Dunnottar meant that even in later days, it was safe from all but the heaviest cannon.

admission to the castle to enjoy the spot, either. If you are happy to look at the castle from afar, you can wander down the path from the car park to the clifftop, and stroll along a path that leads along the cliff, from where you get fine views both of the castle and of the dramatic coastline.

Hardy souls who wish to visit the castle will plunge down the steps (very steep, and very hard work on the way back up) almost to sea level before climbing through

a narrow defile where the gatehouse is set. Beyond this, the headland opens out into a broad and fairly flat area, around the edges of which is a scatter of diverse ruins from all sorts of different periods.

The tower house on the landward side of the headland, built in the late 1300s, is an early L-plan design with cellars on the ground floor (later converted to a kitchen) and a hall on the first floor. The side-tower of the 'L' originally contained a cellar downstairs with a kitchen next to the hall on the first floor. The building is fairly well preserved and has some interesting details, but it's rather dank and unpleasant inside because it's a lair of seabirds.

Elsewhere are various ruined ranges of assorted later dates. Amidst the ruins, it's a surprise to find the restored drawing room in the North Range with a panelled ceiling. None of it is especially interesting.

The castle was the property of the hereditary Earls Marischal of Scotland until Cromwell destroyed the place in May 1652 following a lengthy siege.

Signposted from the A92 south of Stonehaven, on a minor road that leads into the town.

Left: the tower house is a fairly early one, dating from the late 1300s, and is in decent condition.

Pictish carved stones in Grampian

The extraordinary monuments of one of Scotland's native peoples

This region, to the north and east of the Grampian range, is just as much a part of the Pictish heartland as the area south and east of the mountains (*see 'Pictish symbol stones in Tayside', page 161*) and is similarly scattered with the remarkable carved stones created by the Picts in the early Christian era.

You come across these stones in all sorts of places. There's a good one in the grounds of *Brodie Castle (page 136)*, well preserved by having been buried in the ground for many years; and there's a weathered but interesting example, with what looks like a hunting scene on it, inside *Elgin Cathedral (overleaf)*.

Several outstanding stones in the area are in the care of Historic Scotland and are described on this page.

The Maiden Stone

Historic Scotland • Free • Open access at any reasonable time

A tall, graceful cross carved in the late 700s or early 800s AD, this is one of the most pleasing of all the stones. Next to the ring-headed cross is a human figure flanked by two monstrous fish, thought to represent Jonah and the whale. The rest of it is very ornate, but the back of the slab has simple panels with typical Pictish symbols: notched rectangle and Z-rod, 'swimming beast' (or dolphin), the mirror, and the comb.

Stands beside the minor road that leads from Chapel of Garioch to the A96 at Whiteford.

Picardy symbol stone

Historic Scotland • Free • Open access at any reasonable time

Standing incongruously in a field, this is thought to be one of the oldest stones because the symbols on it are simple shapes, simply carved. It has a distinct crude charm. Another good reason to come here is to see the impressive rows of trees that line the roads, which were presumably planted to give shade.

Indicated by a sign at the side of the minor road that runs north-west from Insch towards Largie.

Left: the superb Sueno's Stone is of unrivalled size and splendour. Its intricate carving tells the story of a battle, probably between Scots and Picts.

Sueno's Stone

Historic Scotland • Free • Open access at any reasonable time

This stone is on a truly monumental scale, standing more than 6.5m (20ft) high, but even more impressive than its sheer size are the extraordinary scenes it depicts.

On the front is a cross (though there is also a scene thought to be the inauguration of a king). On the back is a narrative made up of a series of battle scenes, thought to be the story of a battle in the 800s AD at which the Scots defeated the Picts.

On the eastern outskirts of Forres, signposted from the A96 at its junction with the B9011.

See also...

Brandsbutt symbol stone

Historic Scotland; free, open access at any time. In the middle of a housing estate on the north side of Inverurie, signposted from the A96.

Sadly, this early carved stone was broken up and used in a field wall, and has had to be stuck back together, so it's hardly glamorous; but it has one unique feature, which is an inscription in the Celtic runes known as ogham.

Dyce symbol stones

Historic Scotland; free, open access at any reasonable time. Of the B977 north of Dyce.

In the ruined parish church there are two stones: one of the older style, with simple symbol carvings, the other newer and featuring a Celtic cross.

Elgin Cathedral

Historic Scotland • ££ • Usual hours

Not so much an attractive ruin as a loose collection of attractive *pieces* of ruin. There are lots of interesting things to see, but they don't quite add up to an outstanding building.

Some features of the architecture are pretty extraordinary, though, starting at the beginning with the amazing doorway

The elegant east end of Elgin Cathedral – it's very similar in style to Whitby Abbey in Yorkshire.

at the west end of the church, decorated with seven layers (or 'orders', to use the jargon) of arches. It's very striking.

Also at this end of the church is a pair of intact towers which, in characteristic Scottish style, you are encouraged to climb up. Stairs lead to the top floor of both towers, but you can't get out on the roofs and the views are obscured by

wooden grilles in the windows. The two towers are linked at first-floor height by a gallery, which you can walk across, overlooking the interior of the church.

Other notable pieces include the east end of the church (at its best when seen from outside), the stunningly pretty vaulted ceiling in the south choir aisle, and the intact chapter house; it has some ugly windows, but the shafted central pillar and vaulted roof are gorgeous, like a stylised tree sculpted in stone.

The cathedral was founded as late as 1224, when the bishop moved operations to Elgin from smaller churches around Loch Spynie, but the bishops continued to live at *Spynie Palace* (*see page 148*).

Following a fire in 1270 that destroyed most of the original church, the cathedral was redesigned in a splendid new style. In 1390, however, it was burned down by Alexander Stewart, Earl of Buchan, known as the Wolf of Badenoch. It was never quite the same again, and after the reformation in 1560 was left to decay.

Signposted on the east side of Elgin city centre.

Left: the interior of the church, seen from the gallery that crosses between the two towers.

Fyvie Castle

*National Trust of Scotland • £££ • Usual hours
(grounds open all day every day)*

This glorious stately home is the ultimate
in Victorian baronial excess, done with
such panache that you have to laugh out
loud at some of the final flourishes.

The architectural history of the place is
long and complicated (and in any case is
of little relevance, since it's now really a
Victorian house); but it's basically a long
row of towers, the earliest and solidest of
which dates to before 1400, with various
wings added. The last major addition was
the Leith Tower in 1890.

Whereas many of the region's castles
have been in the same family for centuries,
Fyvie has changed hands lots of times,
usually for money rather than as a result
of political upheaval. The second most
recent purchase, in 1889, had a very
romantic twist. In 1433, the castle's owner,
Sir Henry Preston, died and Fyvie was
inherited by his youngest daughter; when
she married, the castle passed to the
Meldrum family. In 1596, it was sold to
Alexander Seton. Sir Henry's second
daughter, meanwhile, had married into the
Forbes family of Tolquhon; and in 1889,
14 generations later, a descendant of hers
named Alexander Leith, who had made his

fortune in the steel industry in the United
States, finally bought Fyvie back.

Inside the castle, a series of grand rooms
boasting paintings by artists such as
Gainsborough, Romney, Reynolds and
Raeburn culminates in the ostentatious
Drawing Room and neighbouring Gallery,
the latter dominated by a vast self-playing
organ installed here in 1900.

There's a delightful dramatic touch at
the end of your visit, when you emerge on
the lawn at the front of the house: having
entered round the back, you have no idea
how big and grand the place looks from
out here, and the effect is very pleasing.

Off the A947 at Fyvie, north of Oldmeldrum.

Glenbuchat Castle

*Historic Scotland • Free • Open access at any
reasonable time*

This modestly sized but attractive Z-plan
tower house built in 1590 is a pleasant one
to visit. It has a typical layout, with the
kitchen on the ground floor and hall above;
the first floor was later divided, probably
in the early 1700s, to create a separate
drawing room and dining room.

Off the A97 south-west of Kildrummy.

*The pleasing little tower house at Glenbuchat is an
excellent example of a later Z-plan tower.*

*Below: the exuberant grandeur of Fyvie Castle is
very appealing. Inside, it's really a Victorian house.*

Huntly Castle

Historic Scotland • ££ • Usual hours

One of the grandest ruins in the country and a thoroughly enjoyable one to explore. The outstanding structure is the vast range known as the palace, which was built in the 1550s and enhanced around 1600 by the addition of a series of splendid oriel windows on the top floor and lots of ornate flourishes inside and out.

There has been a castle here since the early 1100s, when the king gave land to Duncan, Earl of Fife, as part of a plan to secure the road north through Strathbogie to Elgin and Inverness. The 'motte' (mound) of this early castle still stands, and the later buildings were put up in its raised bailey.

The grand palace at Huntly: the lettering on the frieze, dated 1602, is the name of the marquis and his wife.

The Gordons of Huntly were installed here in the early 1300s by King Robert I (Robert the Bruce) after the previous owner backed the wrong side at the battle of Bannockburn. They built a thick-walled L-plan tower house here in the early 1400s, but only its foundations remain; it was blown up by King James VI in 1594 after the sixth Earl of Huntly joined an ill-advised revolt against the king.

Other buildings in the courtyard have gone the same way as the tower house, though destroyed by the ravages of time rather than by gunpowder, leaving only a bakehouse and brewhouse in decent nick. But this lack of other structures hardly

matters when the grand, highly decorated palace range awaits your attention.

The basement level, built in the 1460s, has three cavernous vaulted cellars and a dark prison reached by a narrow corridor. The upper levels date from the 1550s: kitchen and stores on the ground floor, hall and lord's private chambers above, and a grand suite of rooms on the top floor.

The icing on the cake is the decorative stone-carving throughout, not least the splendid armorial panel over the front door; but also worth noting is the painting on the wall of the first-floor Great Chamber.

Signposted in Huntly, off the A96.

Kildrummy Castle

Historic Scotland • ££ • Usual hours

Arguably the classic era of castle-building in Britain was in the late 1200s and the early 1300s, when thick-walled round towers and wide moats were in vogue. Scotland doesn't have so many castles of this kind: *Bothwell Castle* near Glasgow, *Inverlochy Old Castle* in the Highlands and *Caerlaverock* in Dumfriesshire are all of roughly the same era and in roughly the same style, but Kildrummy was much more the archetypal castle of the period.

It's a shame, then, that this castle isn't better preserved: most of the fat, round towers have been reduced to little more than the level of their foundations and there are no upstairs floors to be explored. It's unquestionably still worth seeing – apart from anything else, the remains are very picturesque and in a lovely, peaceful country setting – but it's not as thrilling as you might hope (particularly if you've visited similar castles in Wales).

The best way to get a clearer idea of how the castle might have looked in its heyday is by strolling round outside the walls to the back, where the highest stretch of wall runs up to the most intact of the towers, the Warden's Tower.

The great builder of castles of this kind, especially in Wales, was the English king Edward I, and there is an intriguing theory that he might have been involved here too. Edward twice visited the castle: in 1296, when it was still under construction, and again in 1303. Shortly after the second visit, the king made a big payment to his mason, Master James of St George, possibly for work carried out here. The argument is given weight by similarities between Kildrummy and Edward's castle at Harlech which Master James also designed.

If so, then Edward must at the time have been on friendly terms with the castle's owner, the Earl of Mar; but by 1305 the earl had died and was succeeded by his infant nephew, putting the castle in the hands of the boy's guardian, Robert the Bruce.

During the wars of 1306, Bruce sent his wife and children to Kildrummy for safety; but they were forced to flee when an army under Edward, Prince of Wales, marched here and successfully besieged the castle.

Surprisingly, the castle was occupied into the early 1700s. The last Earl of Mar, John Erskine, supported a Jacobite rising and in 1716 was forced to flee to France.

Signposted off the A97 at Kildrummy, west of Alford and some distance south of Huntly.

■ *See also…* **Memsie cairn**

Historic Scotland; free, open access at any reasonable time. Just off the B9032 in Memsie, south of Fraserburgh.

This extraordinary cairn is an impressively large pile of stones with a very satisfying shape to it, almost like a modern work of environmental art rather than an ancient monument. It's a good reminder of how dramatic such cairns would have looked at the time they were built, standing out from the flat country all around.

The only slight fly in the ointment is that the basis of the cairn is probably from the bronze age, but it has almost certainly been added to by farmers clearing rocks from their fields in the last couple of centuries, so it isn't quite all it seems. Cute, though.

Below: the shattered walls and towers of Kildrummy. The three tall lancet windows were in the chapel.

Spynie Palace

Historic Scotland • £ • Usual hours

This interesting ruin is good value anyway, but especially so if you buy a combined admission ticket with Elgin Cathedral. The site is dominated by the substantial remains of David's Tower, a particularly large and grand example of the plainest sort of rectangular tower house. Around it is an almost complete circuit of walls with a couple of towers and a good gateway, and against one of the walls is the site of a pretty sizeable great hall.

The palace was the official residence of the bishops of Moray. In the 1100s, when records of the bishopric were first made, the bishops seem to have carried out their religious duties at several small churches in the area, but in 1208 a church here at Spynie was established as the cathedral. Even after it was replaced in 1224 by the new cathedral at Elgin (*see page 144*), the bishops continued to live at Spynie.

The palace stood right on the shore of Loch Spynie, which in those days was a sea-loch deep enough for fishing boats and merchant ships (it is now mostly drained). The original timber buildings which made up the bishop's palace were replaced some time in the 1300s by stone walls with round towers, but most of this work has been buried by later structures.

The big tower was started in about 1470 by Bishop David Stewart, after whom it is named, and was finished by his successor in about 1480. It was built right on top of one of the old round towers, which makes the basement rather interesting: a tunnel-like corridor leads to a cellar beneath the new tower, but you can also still get into the basement of the old tower, which,

An immense tower house of the late 1400s, known as David's Tower, dominates the ruin of Spynie Palace.

naturally enough, is a circular space. It's really quite odd.

On the ground floor, the space inside the tower is really rather impressive, partly because none of the floors is in place and a lot of original whitewashed plaster has survived, giving the place a light and airy feel. A spiral stair in one corner leads all the way to the top of the building for a vertiginous view of the courtyard.

Elsewhere in the palace, the most striking feature is the great hall, which occupies most of the north wall of the courtyard. This was clearly a very splendid building: the sheer size of it is impressive, and a single surviving corbel carved to look like a man with a beard is an extremely fine piece of work.

Signposted on the A941 north of Elgin.

Tolquhon Castle

Historic Scotland • ££ • usual hours

Just as the guidebook suggests, this is a very charming and picturesque little ruin; but it's pushing its luck a bit in claiming for itself the title of 'castle', because it's mostly a mansion of the 1500s.

The oldest element is a heavy, plain rectangular tower house of the early 1400s known as the Preston Tower, which is thought to be named after Marjorie Preston (second daughter of Sir Henry, the owner of nearby *Fyvie Castle*) who in 1420 married Sir John Forbes, heir of Tolquhon. This older tower was completely upstaged by the later rebuilding, which is dated very accurately in an inscription: 'All this warke excep the auld tour was begun be William Forbes 15 Aprile 1584 and endit be him 20 October 1589'.

The 'warke' of William Forbes was a residence that abandoned the traditional tower house layout in favour of a mansion made up of four ranges around a courtyard. At the back was the house (kitchen and cellar on the ground floor, hall and private reception room above); down either side ran long wings, which on the ground floor consisted mostly of practical rooms such as stores and brewhouses, but on the first floor allowed room for a luxurious gallery that ran the whole length of the building; and on the end was an ornate gatehouse.

After a couple of centuries of neglect, the result is an attractive and interesting little ruin which is well worth visiting.

Signposted down a minor road off the B999 north-west of Pitmedden.

Left: Tolquhon Castle is an attractive, elaborately ornamented house; the original tower is on the left.

See also...

Braemar Castle

Privately owned, £££, usual hours (summer only). By the A93 just north of Braemar.

This squat L-plan tower house, built as late as 1628, owes its unusual appearance to a revamp as an army barracks in 1748 (the same time that *Corgarff Castle* was given similar treatment). The turrets were given flat tops with battlements, and a star-style outwork was constructed. The garrison was withdrawn in 1797 and the castle was reoccupied ten years later. What's on show now is a shabby Victorian residence with a few interesting early details but not much in the way of elegance or splendour. Pretty dull.

Deer Abbey

Historic Scotland; free; open access during usual hours only. By the A950 west of Mintlaw.

There's not much left of this Cistercian monastery beyond the outline of the church and the lower parts of a few domestic buildings. The ruins seem more like follies in the context of the pleasant grounds; it's a lovely spot for a stroll on a sunny afternoon.

Dunideer hillfort and castle remains

On a hill west of Insch, visible from miles around; approached by a path up the north side of the hill.

The hillfort here had a roughly rectangular rampart of stone which was burned at some time and was partly vitrified (the stone has melted and fused so that it's like glass). A simple rectangular tower

Above: Deer Abbey.

thought to be part of one of the oldest stone castles in Scotland was built inside the fort in the early 1200s, using some stone from the ancient rampart. One wall of it survives sufficiently well to retain a first-floor window. It's a good place for a walk.

Peel Ring of Lumphanan

Historic Scotland; free, open access at any reasonable time

Impressive earthwork castle of the 1200s consisting of a large 'motte' (mound) with traces of a building on top, surrounded by an outer ditch and rampart, the whole now ringed by trees. It's an extremely pleasant and atmospheric spot. Macbeth was killed nearby in 1057.

Braemar Castle.

And...

Auchindoir St Mary's Church (*Historic Scotland; free, open access at any reasonable time*), *by the B9002 just off the A97 south of Rhynie* – One of the best medieval church ruins in the country, roofless but complete, with a smashing early Gothic arched doorway and a richly ornamented sacrament house (a cupboard-like feature near the altar).

Deskford church (*Historic Scotland; free, open access at any reasonable time*), *off the B9018 in Deskford, north-east of Huntly* – A small, roofless church ruin notable solely for its richly carved sacrament house (see previous entry).

Doune of Invernochty motte, *off the A944 near Strathdon* – The predecessor to *Kildrummy Castle* is this vast oval motte surrounded by a ditch and bank. The mound is topped by a thick stone wall, and the remains of a large rectangular building are thought to represent a medieval church.

Kinkell Church (*Historic Scotland; free, open access at any reasonable time*), *on a minor road off the B993 south of Inverurie* – A ruined church of the 1500s with an ornate sacrament house dated 1524 and the splendid tomb of a knight killed in 1411.

St Machar's Cathedral transepts, Aberdeen (*Historic Scotland and church authorities; free, open access to the exterior of the building at any reasonable time*), *in Old Aberdeen* – The ruined transepts of the cathedral are in the care of the state, but the nave and towers are still in use as a church.

Loanhead of Daviot, with the big recumbent stone and its taller flankers towards the back of the circle.

Recumbent stone circles

An attractive variety of monument, unique to this region.

The 'recumbent stone' circle (that is, a circle of stones which features a single recumbent stone) is a speciality of this part of north-eastern Scotland, though certain of its distinctive features are occasionally found elsewhere (see, for example, *Auchagallon stone circle* on the Isle of Arran).

The principal features of this fascinating type of monument are that the standing stones are graded in height, getting taller towards the southern side of the circle, where a single large, slab-like stone is set on its side rather than upright. This is the recumbent stone, and it is flanked by two taller uprights which are invariably just a little higher than the recumbent.

These circles are one of the few unchallenged examples of astronomic alignments in prehistory, showing a consistent interest in the rising or setting of the moon in the southern sky . The circles are aligned towards the south and always

have an uninterrupted view of the horizon in this direction; the recumbent stone, with its two flankers, is always positioned so that it frames the moon when viewed from inside the circle.

Particular importance seems to have been accorded to the recumbent stones, which are often of enormous size and composed of a type of stone that isn't easy to get hold of. The largest known, in a circle at *Old Keig* (*see opposite*), is thought to weigh 61 tonnes and must have been brought more than six miles (10km) from the nearest source of this type of rock.

The interest in the position of the moon is widely accepted to be a feature of the late neolithic era or the early bronze age, contrasting with the alignment of earlier monuments (such as the incomparable chambered tomb of *Maes Howe, Orkney*) on the midwinter sunset. Very broadly, recumbent stone circles are thought to date to the centuries around 2000 BC.

Loanhead of Daviot stone circle

Historic Scotland • Free • Open access at any reasonable time

This is the classic recumbent stone circle. It's one of the largest, it's the most famous, it's a thoroughly pleasant place to visit, and it has been fully excavated so that a fair bit is known about its history.

The setting is on an open hillside with extensive views to the north, but the trees that shelter the monument obscure the views to the south that the people who built the monument were interested in. This seems something of a shame, particularly since the hills over that way have a very dramatic appearance.

The recumbent stone is a particularly grand one, split dramatically in two by frost. As usual, it is positioned at the southern side of the circle, just to the west of south: if you imagine the compass as a clock with north at 12 o'clock and south at six, the recumbent is between six and seven.

It's worth taking a closer look at the stone to the east of the east flanker, which has cup marks carved on it.

Dating evidence suggests that the circle was built around 3000 BC. Roughly a thousand years later, a ring cairn with a tidy kerb all round it was built inside the stone circle: the excavations found pottery and deposits of cremated human bone. Additionally, small stone cairns were placed at the bottom of six of the stones.

In later years, a cremation cemetery was placed next to the circle, consisting of a low wall with two opposing entrances: inside, twenty deposits of cremated bone, some of it buried in pits and some in urns, represented the remains of more than thirty people, including children.

Signposted on a minor road off the B9001 north of the village of Daviot.

Easter Aquhorthies stone circle

Historic Scotland • Free • Open access at any reasonable time

The location here is superbly dramatic, with the hillside setting offering the usual open views to the south, but also with a powerful sense of being placed in relation to the tall, spiky hills behind. The circle shows the usual alignment, slightly to the west of south.

Of particular interest here are the different types of stone used in this circle, which seem to have been carefully chosen for their colour and texture. Of nine stones in the circle, eight are of pink porphyry and one is of red jasper; the two tall flanking stones, meanwhile, are of grey granite, and the recumbent stone is composed of red granite.

Signposted along a minor road from the A96 on the western side of Inverurie. It's a gentle uphill walk of no more than five minutes from the car park to the monument.

At Easter Aquhorthies, the grey stone of the flankers contrasts with the pink stones in the rest of the circle.

Tomnaverie stone circle

Historic Scotland • Free • Open access at any reasonable time

This circle is not quite as well preserved as the others, but in 1999 it was excavated prior to a restoration the following year, with the intention of replacing some of the fallen stones in their original positions.

Again, the choice of location is superb: the circle stands on a small ridge with views in all directions, as if you're right in the middle of a massive bowl of hills.

To the south of the B9094 near its junction with the B9119 south of Tarland. Walk up the track and veer left where it levels out.

☐ *See also…* **more recumbent stone circles**

Garrol Wood stone circle

In Forestry Commission woods south-east of Banchory, signposted on a minor road between the B974 at Bridge of Feugh and the A957.

A circle that consisted originally of ten (now nine) red stones and a grey recumbent, with a later ring cairn in the middle. There are lots of circles all along the River Dee, and just 500m (550 yds) to the north-west of this one is another good example, Eslie the Greater.

Old Keig stone circle

Reached on foot near the quarry at Old Keig, off the B992 east of Alford.

The massive recumbent stone made of gneiss (*see the introduction opposite*), along with two of its flankers and one other stone, is all that remains of a circle which originally measured about 20m (22 yds) across.

Sunhoney stone circle

Reached on foot up the track to Sunhoney Farm, off the B9119 west of Echt.

This is the best of the rest, with a circle of eleven stones more than 25m (almost 30 yds) in diameter and a fallen recumbent, the surface of which is covered in cup marks. Again, a ring cairn was later added inside the circle.

Left: the beautifully positioned circle at Tomnaverie during excavations in 1999.

Tayside

Including Perthshire, Kinross & Angus

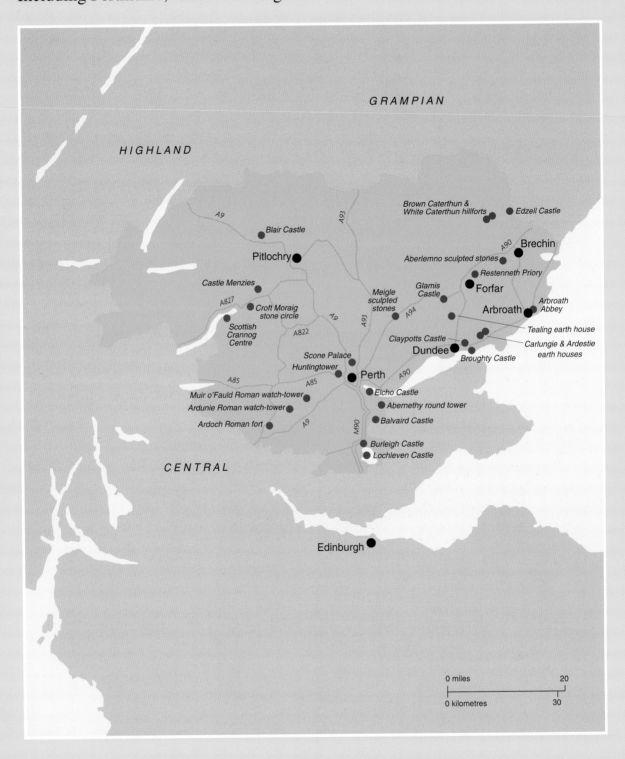

GRAMPIAN

HIGHLAND

A9

Blair Castle

A93

Brown Caterthun &
White Caterthun hillforts

Edzell Castle

Pitlochry

A90

Brechin

Aberlemno sculpted stones

Restenneth Priory

Castle Menzies

A827

Croft Moraig
stone circle

Meigle
sculpted
stones

Glamis
Castle

A94

Forfar

Arbroath
Abbey

Scottish
Crannog
Centre

A9

A822

A93

Arbroath

Tealing earth house

Claypotts Castle

Carlungie & Ardestie
earth houses

Scone Palace

Dundee

Huntingtower

Broughty Castle

A85

A85

Perth

A90

Muir o'Fauld Roman watch-tower

Elcho Castle

Ardunie Roman watch-tower

Abernethy round tower

Ardoch Roman fort

A9

M90

Balvaird Castle

Burleigh Castle

Lochleven Castle

CENTRAL

Edinburgh

| 0 miles | | 20 |
| 0 kilometres | | 30 |

Arbroath Abbey

Historic Scotland • ££ • Usual hours

This is a massive place, not just in the vast scale of the ruined church, but also in the resonance of the historical events that took place here. In 1320, Scottish nobles gathered at the abbey to sign the Declaration of Arbroath, a resounding statement of their intention never to submit to English rule (*see below*).

As you approach it from the street, the ruined abbey looks extremely substantial: the west end of the church, with the main door in it, soars solidly upwards, and the gatehouse range on the right looks completely intact. Once you're through the door and inside the church, however, you find that there's actually not that much of it left. It's slightly disappointing, but not severely so: the size of the church is still impressive, and there are enough interesting bits still standing to keep you here for a wee while.

One of the great things about Scottish abbey ruins – and this compares very favourably with English ones – is that the authorities seem perfectly happy to let you climb up anything that's there to be climbed. The obvious attraction in this respect at Arbroath is the surviving end wall of the south transept, which is the only part of the church to survive to something like its full height and stands alone in precariously monolithic style.

The immense abbey church at Arbroath still has a great deal of grandeur despite its ruinous condition.

A stair leads to a gallery halfway up the wall, looking down over the interior of the church: it's slightly precarious and very good fun.

Beyond the transept, the buildings of the cloister have more or less disappeared, with the exception of the substantially intact abbot's house, which has a nice vaulted undercroft filled with bits of carved stonework from around the site.

The south transept of the church stands alone: it's impressive, if a little precarious-looking.

A couple of other intact buildings in the gatehouse range are used to house an introductory exhibition and video.

The abbey was founded in 1178 by King William the Lion, who was buried there in 1214, though the church was only finally completed and consecrated almost 20 years later, in 1233.

Easily found in the town of Arbroath.

The Declaration of Arbroath

Long after the victories of Robert the Bruce had secured Scotland's independence as a nation, the English king, Edward II, continued to claim that Scotland owed him homage. The bad news for the Scots, though, was that Edward had the support of the Pope who, as head of the church, was the leading authority in such matters. Bruce, however, refused to take delivery of letters summoning him to appear before the Pope at Avignon, because they were addressed to 'Our beloved son Robert who says he is king of Scotland'.

On April 6th, 1320, Bruce's nobles gathered at Arbroath Abbey to sign a letter to the Pope which expressed their support for their king.

Historically the Declaration of Arbroath was of little importance, but its words resound through the centuries: "So long as one hundred of us remain alive, we will never in any degree be subject to the dominion of the English. Since not for glory, riches or honours do we fight, but for freedom alone, which no man loses but with his life."

The 'earth houses' of Angus

Not houses at all, but underground grain stores…

It's never seriously been suggested that these intriguing subterranean passages, more properly known as souterrains, were *really* houses under the earth: it is widely accepted that they were used by iron age farmers to store food.

The souterrains of Tayside are larger than the ones found in the Northern Isles (such as *Grain earth house, Orkney*) and seem to date from around 100-200 AD (rather than 400 BC). Since these dates coincide with the Roman occupation of the area, it is thought that these Tayside earth houses were used to store vast amounts of grain for the Roman army.

Three fine examples, set close together in the country near Dundee, will give you a clear picture of Tayside souterrains.

The souterrain at Carlungie is the largest of the three, and its tunnel has several branches.

Ardestie earth house

Historic Scotland • Free • Open access at any reasonable time

The remains of houses stand inside the curve of this souterrain, and you can see a tunnel of some kind – a 'back door' when the main entrance was sealed? – leading down from one of the houses into the passage. There's what must be a drain in the well-paved floor.

By the A92 north of Monifieth, in a field north of the road and west of the B962 to Newbigging. Park by the verge of the 'B' road; walk along the main road to the path to the monument.

Left: next to the entrance of the souterrain at Tealing is this stone with a cup-and-ring carving on it.

Below: at Ardestie, a 'tunnel' leads up to one of the houses that sit in the curve of the souterrain.

Carlungie earth house

Historic Scotland • Free • Open access at any reasonable time

This is a large souterrain, and has a fairly elaborate shape: a long curve with two branches off to the side. There's what appears to be a vent at one point, and there is a very obvious 'secret passage' leading up from the middle of the tunnel to the interior of one of a group of huts inside the curve.

From the A92, go north on the B962; turn first right on to a minor road, then first right again, and park by the verge: a signposted footpath leads across a field to the monument.

Tealing earth house

Historic Scotland • Free • Open access at any reasonable time

The simplest shape of the three, making a single, oval loop around a house. It is of particularly solid construction with stout door jambs which are still intact. Look out for a stone by the entrance with bronze age cup-and-ring markings.

At Tealing village, off the A90, 3 miles north of Dundee. Signposted to Tealing dovecot; for the earth house, continue down the farm track past the dovecot for about 40m (50 yds) and you'll soon see a signposted gate on the right.

Balvaird Castle

Historic Scotland • Exterior: free, open access at any reasonable time • Interior: ££, limited opening (weekends in July and August)

Perched stylishly on the top of a hill, this is a handsome L-plan tower house of 1500 with a gatehouse added in 1581. It's such a pleasant little building that it's well worth seeing, even when the interior isn't open (though access outside the proper opening times is on a somewhat unofficial basis).

The castle was the home of the Murray family, Earls of Mansfield, before they moved to *Scone Palace (see page 167).*

By the A912 north of Gateside; there's a small car park by the road below the castle (use the entrance when the car park is shut).

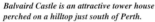

Balvaird Castle is an attractive tower house perched on a hilltop just south of Perth.

Blair Castle

Privately owned • £££ • Usual hours in summer (April to October)

The original castle was demolished in the 1700s and rebuilt as a Georgian mansion, then in the 1860s the whole lot was rebuilt again in the Scots baronial style, resulting in a big, bold Victorian house with lots of rooms stuffed with nicknacks. Nicest are the bathrooms, from the earliest days of hot running water, and the small top-floor bedroom used by Queen Victoria herself.

For all its grandeur, Blair has been too indelicately developed as a tourist attraction to be very appealing. And it has the pushiest peacocks you'll ever meet...

Off the A9 and B8097 near Blair Atholl.

Below: one of Scotland's more heavily developed tourist attractions, Blair Castle is a vast mansion.

See also... Abernethy round tower

Historic Scotland, free entry, key from nearby shop during usual hours; signposted off the A913 in Abernethy town centre.

An extraordinary building, this is one of only two Irish-style monastic towers surviving in Scotland; both of them are in this region.

The tower was built in about 1000 AD as a place of refuge in times of crisis for the Celtic Christian community which it served. It would originally have had a series of wooden floors which were reached by ladders, but it can now be climbed all the way to the top by a solidly built metal spiral stair case.

Set in a quiet little town, preserved in fairly original condition and with an interesting Pictish carved stone at its foot, the Abernethy round tower is very pleasant to visit.

The region's other surviving round tower is attached to the cathedral at Brechin: it's not in quite such good, original condition as this one, and it isn't open on such a regular basis.

Broughty Castle

Historic Scotland and local council • Free •
Usual hours

Built on what was originally an island
– it's now more of a peninsula – and
gaining a faint touch of glamour from its
seaside setting, this tall, thin tower is not
so much a castle as a Victorian fort.

The original tower here was built some
time before 1500 and was captured by the
English in 1547. It was retaken by the
Scots only three years later but, probably
because it had been damaged in the process,

Its seaside setting, and the interesting local museum in the tower, make Broughty Castle well worth a visit.

it was allowed to decay. It was rebuilt in
about 1600, but damaged again in 1650
and again it was just left to rot. Finally,
in 1855 the ruin was bought by the British
government at a time when the nation
lived in perpetual fear of French invasion,
and it was used as the base for a new fort.
This remained in use right up to the
Second World War, so the defences were
altered several times; probably the best
original Victorian feature is the
drawbridge balanced by huge weights.

The interior of the tower is not terribly
castle-like. It houses a local museum with
modest but interesting exhibits on themes
such as whale-hunting and local wildlife.
Particularly interesting is a model of the
amazing roll-on, roll-off railway ferry that
gave the town of Broughty Ferry its name.

All in all, the castle is pretty good value.
(Well, it's free…)

On the seafront in the centre of Broughty Ferry,
just west of Dundee on the A930.

Burleigh Castle

Historic Scotland • Free • Key from nearby
house at reasonable times only

Use the big iron key to unlock the big iron
gate and you can examine the vaulted cellar
on the ground floor before climbing the
steps to the paved first floor of this small,
roofless three-storey tower house. Sadly,
there's not a lot to see up there except
pigeon droppings. The tower dates to about
1500 and is connected by a stretch of wall
to a later round tower, to which access is
not permitted. Details of where to get the
key are displayed at the site.

Right next to the A911 immediately to the west
of Milnathort; signposted from the town.

Left: there's not a lot to see at Burleigh Castle,
though you are allowed inside the square tower.

Brown Caterthun & White Caterthun hillforts

Historic Scotland • Free • Open access at any reasonable time

Scotland has plenty of hillforts, some of them in spectacular settings, but it doesn't have any with the kind of vast, sweeping earthen ramparts that you find on hillforts in the south-west of England. This is one of the few Scottish hillfort sites to offer a similar sense of scale and drama, and these qualities make it a very rewarding place to visit.

There are two forts here, sitting on neighbouring hilltops, and they get their names from the colour of their ramparts. The Brown Caterthun's gentle contours are covered in brown heather, while the White Caterthun has ramparts built of stone which have collapsed into heaps of pale rubble on the summit.

Some hillforts are hard work to get to, but these two are pretty easy. The road runs right between the two: park the car in the large layby, and it's a gentle uphill walk of about 10 minutes to either summit. The more interesting of the two forts, by

quite a long way, is the White Caterthun. Its stone ramparts are not especially high, but it's easy to trace the whole circuit of them around the oval hilltop, and you can see that this must have been a pretty formidable fort. Traces of other earthen ramparts further down the slope are thought to be the remains of an earlier phase of construction.

The Brown Caterthun is not nearly as easy to make sense of (and the views aren't as good, either). It has widely spaced ramparts with an unusually large number of entrances, and it might not have been a defensive enclosure at all.

The White Caterthun has stone-built ramparts which have collapsed into piles of rubble.

North-west of Brechin, south-west of Edzell: signposted on minor roads near Little Brechin and Tigerton from the A90.

Right: the ramparts of the Brown Caterthun are widely spaced and much less distinct.

Castle Menzies

*Privately owned by a charitable trust • ££ •
Usual hours (summer only)*

The traditional seat of the Menzies clan
was abandoned and rotting in the 1950s
when descendants of the clan established a
charitable trust to buy and restore the ruin.
Just as well they did, too, because it's an
enjoyable place to visit.

The interior of the castle is still in the
process of being restored (and looks as if
it will be for some time yet) with work
going ahead on details such as wood
panels and ornate plaster ceilings in the
grander rooms. Although this means that,
in places, the castle is a bit of a building
site, the overall effect is a rather pleasing
combination of tidied-up ruin (like the sort
of castle that Historic Scotland cares for)
and a kind of 'behind the scenes' version
of a furnished castle. It is to be hoped that
the restoration will not be taken too far.

The original tower, completed in 1577,
was later expanded with the building of
two additional ranges: an accommodation
block was added at the back in the early
1700s, and a west wing was built at the
side of the castle in the 1840s. The earlier
of these two was considered unsafe and
was demolished when the restoration of
the castle started, but the Victorian wing
has been kept, and houses a teashop.

Before you go in, it's worth lingering
and taking a good look at the attractively
detailed stonework of the exterior, with its
rich carvings over the dormer windows.
The door in the angle of the towers still
has its iron 'yett' (exterior gate), but it was

*Below: Castle Menzies is a classic Z-plan design,
with projecting towers at back left and front right.*

Small, pretty, and tricky to understand, Croft Moraig stone circle is an intriguing jumble of boulders.

replaced by a new front door as part of the
early 1700s rebuilding. Many of the grander
details of the interior decor – particularly
the ornate plaster ceilings and the wood
panelling mentioned above – date from
the same phase of rebuilding, and the
restoration has focused on these.

Historically, the castle's main claim to
fame is an association with Bonnie Prince
Charlie, who stayed here in January 1746
and is said to have slept in a small room
just off the main spiral stair on the second
floor of the south tower. At the head of
half his rebel army, the Young Pretender
was heading for Inverness, where he
would be defeated at Culloden in April.
On display in Castle Menzies is a bronze
copy of the prince's death mask.

Signposted off the A827 at Weem, near Aberfeldy.

Croft Moraig stone circle

*On private land • Free • Access permitted at
reasonable times only*

This small, pretty stone circle is a jumble
of stones which piled up during several
different phases of construction. It's a
pleasant thing to look at, but it's tricky to
make sense of. It has, however, been
excavated, which means that at least some
of its history is known.

The site was in use from about 3000 BC,
for roughly a couple of thousand years.
The original monument was a rough circle
(or possibly a horseshoe-shaped setting)
of timber uprights about 9m (30ft) across.
This was replaced by a small oval of eight
boulders, which still stands as the inner
ring of the monument.

Also thought to be a part of the second
phase of construction is a low rubble bank
that runs round the outside of the monument,
turning it into a little henge. There are
more standing stones associated with this
bank, and one large boulder on the south-
eastern side of the monument is
particularly worth paying attention to,
because it's covered with primitive
carvings: 23 of the simple scoops known
as cup marks, and a couple of rings.

The last phase of construction was
another circle of stones surrounding the
inner oval. At the same time, two outlying
stones were placed just outside the
monument on the east side, forming a kind
of gateway. Two grave pits were found
just beyond these stones.

*On the southern side of the A827 a couple of
miles east of Kenmore (at the end of Loch Tay)
and west of Aberfeldy. The monument is in a
field next to the entrance to Croftmoraig Farm;
parking is difficult, so please be considerate.*

Edzell Castle

Historic Scotland • ££ • Usual hours

The castle is nice: it's a pleasing complex in red sandstone, consisting of a tower house and the ruins of its attendant ranges. But the thing that really steals the show here is the garden.

'It really is the most extraordinary thing of its kind,' says the guidebook gleefully, referring not to the clipped hedges and formal planting of the garden itself (it was restored in the 1930s) but to the walls that enclose and shelter it, which are decorated with a remarkable series of carved panels.

The tower house was built in the early 1500s to replace an earlier timber castle, the mound or motte of which can be seen a few hundred metres away. In 1558 it was inherited by David Lindsay, who at the time was just eight years old. In 1562, aged twelve, the young laird received as his guest Mary Queen of Scots, who stayed here for two nights and called a meeting of her Privy Council (probably it gathered in the hall on the first floor of the tower house). In 1580, another royal guest at the castle was James VI of Scotland, who knighted its lord the following year.

Sir David Lindsay was something of a Renaissance man, organising large-scale industrial projects (such as planting

The formal garden at Edzell is remarkable not so much for its modern planting as for its original stonework.

forests and starting up mines) as well as redeveloping the house and laying out the walled garden, which he started in 1604, just six years before his death.

Built into the walls of the garden is a simple heraldic design, with planting-boxes cunningly arranged so that the flowers would fill in the colour. The design also incorporates nesting-boxes for songbirds.

The carved panels cover three educational or improving themes: the liberal arts (from grammar to astronomy), the planetary deities (Mars, Venus and so on) and the cardinal virtues. Most have titles to help you identify them; some are direct copies of engravings, so you can compare the charmingly wobbly and naive versions in the garden with the sophisticated printed originals reproduced on notices. It's all very good fun.

The tower house itself is entertaining, too, though it's not especially big or grand. From the cellars in the basement, a stair leads to the hall on the first floor. You can also climb a small spiral stair that would have led to the private rooms above, but there are now no upstairs floors. Next to the tower are two ruined ranges.

Signposted from the B966 at Edzell village.

☐ *See also…* **Claypotts Castle**

Historic Scotland, ££, limited opening times (weekends in July and August only). On the western side of Dundee, near Broughty Ferry, signposted from the A92 to Arbroath.

Almost twee enough to be an ornament in the garden of one of the suburban bungalows that surround it, this pretty tower house of about 1570–80 is a most unusual variation on the Z-plan design. Its main tower is flanked by two round towers with rectangular rooms corbelled out at the tops. Shame it's not open more often.

Elcho Castle

Historic Scotland • ££ • Usual hours

Elcho Castle is a beautifully preserved example of a later tower house, and is immense fun to explore.

This place is great. It's one of Scotland's most enjoyable castles to explore, with a particularly intriguing line in staircases (most of which bring you out on the roof), and it has an interesting history. Yet it gets hardly any visitors, which is inexplicable.

It's basically an L-plan tower house, consisting of a main block and an offset tower, though a second subsidiary tower makes it more like a 'T'. There's no record of when it was built, but a good clue is provided by a bill for ironwork dated 1570. (Incidentally, the survival of the original iron grilles over the windows is one of the castle's more remarkable features.)

The layout is absolutely typical of a modern castle. On the ground floor are the kitchen and cellars, which are dark and gloomy because the windows were kept small for security reasons. Most of the castle's residents and guests would have passed from the front door straight up the wide, graceful main spiral stair to the hall on the first floor. The lord's private reception room was through a door at the far end. From the hall floor, three small spiral staircases led to private rooms on the second floor and in the towers.

Each of the three staircases emerges on the roof, which is one of the main things that make the castle such fun to explore. One comes out on a walkway that loops round the front tower to a point right over the door. Another – the one that starts from the laird's chambers at the back of the castle – gives access to a short walkway between two little turret-top rooms known as 'cap houses', which are equipped with fireplaces to keep the guards warm. There's even a latrine up here.

One reason the castle is in such good condition is that it was the home of the earls of Wemyss (pronounced 'Weems') up until the 1780s, and was maintained even after that: it had a new roof in 1830.

The best way to find out more about the castle's history is to chat to the custodian, who will tell you about William Wallace hiding in the nearby marshes, and the little girl whose ghost haunts the castle.

Signposted down the minor road to Rhynd and Fingask off the A912 just south of Perth.

Pictish symbol stones in Tayside

The intriguing legacy of the people who once ruled Scotland…

This area of Scotland was at the heart of Pictland (Pictish kings were crowned on the Mote Hill at Scone, near Perth) so it's no surprise to find that the region is rich in the remarkable carved stones that are the Picts' main legacy.

The stones are often found in groups which presumably mark communities. The later stones are often crosses and were probably associated with Christian settlements, but the art of stone-carving would have flourished under the patronage of wealthy nobles, so where there's a set of stones, there may also have been the residence of a Pictish king or earl.

Once you've seen a few of the earlier stones, you'll start to recognise the strange and intriguing symbols that appear on them. It has been suggested that the most likely purpose for the stones is as grave-markers, and that the symbols may represent words, possibly important individuals' names – but it's a hard one to prove unless some surprising new evidence comes to light.

Aberlemno sculpted stones

Historic Scotland • Free • Any time

One of the best places to see Pictish stones still standing in the open air, with three stones of different ages right by the road and another one in the churchyard. One of the stones is a good example of a simpler early stone, bearing symbols such as the serpent, the Z-rod and double-disc, the mirror and the comb. Another is a superb carved cross with a battle scene on the reverse which shows the battle of Dunnichen in 685 AD, where the Picts defeated the Angles.

Beside the B9134 Forfar to Brechin road.

Meigle sculpted stones

Historic Scotland • ££ • Usual hours

A collection of 27 stones, all found in the village, is housed in an old school. These are all later, Celtic Christian carvings from the late 700s onwards. Some of them are really beautiful, but it's not quite the same seeing them in this museum-like environment.

On the A94 between Coupar Angus and Glamis.

St Vigeans sculpted stones

Historic Scotland • Free • Key from nearby house during usual hours only

A collection of 32 stones thought to have been created for a monastery. Again, they date from the 700s onwards and include some fantastically good carving.

Signposted from the A933 north of Arbroath.

This tall, finely carved cross-slab at Aberlemno features a battle scene on its reverse.

See also…

The Dunfallandy Stone

Historic Scotland; free, open access at any time; signposted just to the south of Pitlochry.

Rather a fine carved stone with human figures as well as symbols, now protected by a glass shelter.

Eassie sculpted stone

Historic Scotland; free, open access at any time; inside the ruined church at Eassie, near Glamis.

A cross-slab in Celtic style on one side, Pictish on the other, showing animals, humans and angels.

Fowlis Wester sculpted stones

Historic Scotland; free access in usual hours only; in the village church, off the A85 east of Crieff.

Two large stones: one is worn but interesting, the other is particularly well preserved.

St Orland's Stone

Historic Scotland; free, open access at any time; signposted off the A928 north of Glamis.

An early Christian cross with Pictish symbols on the other side, standing in a field.

Left: this older stone from Aberlemno features a number of classic Pictish symbols: the serpent, the Z-rod with double-disc, and the mirror.

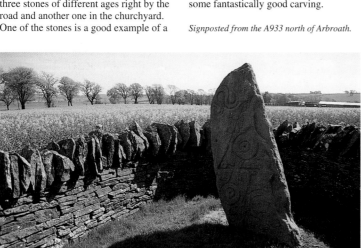

One of the most attractive castles in Scotland, Huntingtower was originally two separate towers.

The 'Raid of Ruthven' and other tales

The most notorious episode in the castle's history was the 'Raid of Ruthven', which took place in August 1582 (at the time, the castle was still known as the House of Ruthven).

A group of rebel noblemen, including the Earl of Gowrie, who at the time was the laird of the castle, kidnapped the young king, James VI, while he was staying overnight in Perth. They brought him back to the castle and held him here for ten months.

Their intention, it seems, was to free him from the influence of the Duke of Lennox and the Earl of Arran, until now his chief advisers, who were both Catholic sympathisers. As long as they had the king in their power, the group of conspirators effectively ruled the nation.

After the king eventually escaped, in June of the following year, he seemed to make light of the incident; but that was not enough to save Gowrie's bacon. In April 1584, a group of rebel nobles seized Stirling Castle and held it for a short while before fleeing to England. Gowrie had not been involved, but he received word that he was being accused of taking part; he got as far as Dundee, on his way out of the country, when he was arrested. He was beheaded at Stirling on May 2nd.

In 1600, the king completed his revenge by obliterating the Gowrie title and renaming the castle 'Huntingtour'.

Huntingtower

Historic Scotland •££ • Usual hours

Perth is a lucky place where castles are concerned, with two superb tower houses just a few miles from the town centre. *Elcho Castle* (*previous page*) is possibly a bit more enjoyable to visit, but this one runs it a close second.

Known as the House of Ruthven until 1600, when the king changed its name as part of a bid to wipe out all trace of its former owners, the castle played its part in several of the more unsavoury episodes of Scottish history in the late 1500s.

One very unusual aspect of the place is that it's actually two separate towers. The two were only joined in the 1700s, when a little linking range was built between them and large windows were fitted, in a bid to make the whole thing look like a single grand house.

There's a theory that the odd two-tower arrangement dates from 1480, when the estate was split between two sons of the then laird, who both wanted to set up their own, separate household; but that's really little more than guesswork.

The older of the two is the Eastern Tower (on the right in the picture above), which was built as a gatehouse and was converted into a residential tower house around 1500. The Western Tower is an L-plan design and was constructed not long afterwards.

One of the nice things about a visit here is that the two towers still have quite distinct identities, so it's a bit like having two castles to explore. In both cases, you can climb a stair all the way to the roof and emerge on a paved roof-walk that leads right round the tower. Smashing!

The interiors are not especially grand, but there are a few treats in store. The hall on the first floor of the Eastern Tower has several interesting features, including a fine wooden ceiling painted with tempera in about 1540, and flowing wall-paintings which are thought to be older still.

Outside the towers, there's not much left of the other buildings known to have stood in the yard, which included a fairly grand one-storey banqueting hall with big windows and a huge fireplace. These other buildings were already crumbling by the 1760s, but the main block must have remained in pretty good condition, since in 1805 it was sold to a local man who used it as accommodation for workers at his cloth-printing factory.

On the western outskirts of Perth, off the A85 Perth-Crieff road, just west of the A9.

Lochleven Castle

Historic Scotland • ££ • Usual hours

One of the most thoroughly enjoyable castle-visiting experiences in Scotland is the boat trip to this small tower house on an island in a loch. The tower itself is possibly not the most interesting building you'll ever come across, but it does have a pretty remarkable history.

The ferry leaves from a jetty in a pleasant park that runs down to the shore of the loch near the little town of Kinross. The ferry fare is included in the entrance fee to the castle, but it's not an expensive place to visit. The ferryman recommends that you come earlier in the year so as to avoid the worst ravages of midges.

The first castle on the island was built at the time of the English invasion under Edward I in the 1290s, and may actually have been established by the English. The circuit of curtain walls is thought to date to this time. William Wallace is said to have captured the castle, slaughtering the 30 Englishmen and five women he found here, and in 1313 Robert the Bruce stayed on the island.

The basic, primitive tower was put up in the early 1300s and is unusual in that its only entrance was by a wooden stair to the hall on the second floor. The kitchen was below this on the first floor, with a cellar in the basement reached only by a trapdoor.

Below: the tower house on an island in Loch Leven where Mary Queen of Scots was imprisoned.

The first glimpse of baronial Glamis Castle at the end of its long, tree-lined drive is a memorable sight.

On the third floor was a private apartment, and a fourth floor was added later.

The room on the third floor was where Mary Queen of Scots stayed when she was imprisoned here in 1567 following her defeat by rebel Scottish lords. In May 1568, she escaped; the story goes that a young lad called Willie Douglas, who looked after the boats, locked the garrison in the tower and threw the keys in the loch while Mary got away. In the 1800s, a large bunch of keys which could only have come from the castle was found in the water near the island.

Signposted from Kinross town centre.

See also… **Glamis Castle**

Privately owned, £££, usual hours (Apr to Oct). Signposted on the A928 and A94 near Dundee.

The childhood home of Elizabeth Bowes-Lyons – now better known as Queen Elizabeth, the Queen Mother – is one of Scotland's most magnificent mansions, but its origins as a squat, powerful tower of the 1300s are not far below the surface – particularly in the thick walls and barrel-vaulted ceiling of the original great hall, now the Drawing Room.

Visits are by guided tour only, and the wealth and splendour on display will not be to everyone's taste; but if you fancy a touch of classic over-the-top Scots baronial living, then this is the place to find it.

Restenneth Priory

Historic Scotland • Free • Open access at any reasonable time

This is a pleasant if undistinguished ruin, consisting of the chancel and tower of the church of an Augustinian priory, plus a couple of big, plain walls from the priory's domestic buildings. It's a peaceful spot, and you won't regret going to take a look; but equally, it won't detain you for long.

Signposted on the B9113 east of Forfar.

Scottish Crannog Centre

Charitable trust • ££ • Usual hours (summer only, May to October)

Scattered across Britain are quite a few reconstructions of ancient houses, from Celtic round houses to Saxon halls. At their best, they're like living museums; and this is certainly one of the best.

It's a reconstruction of a bronze age crannog, a house built on an artificial island so that it could easily be defended. Inevitably a lot of guesswork went into the design, but the nearby site on which it

Below: the reconstructed crannog on Loch Tay, looking particularly beautiful on a May morning.

Restenneth Priory is a quietly attractive ruin in a peaceful slice of countryside not far from Forfar.

was based was investigated in immense detail by diving archeologists, and the posts that hold up the house were placed exactly in the pattern of the originals, so the start point, at least, was correct.

It's a fascinating site, made even more interesting by the enthusiasm of the young archeologists who run the place. All kinds of remarkable things were found by the excavators, including, would you believe, traces of bronze age butter in a wooden butter dish.

A memorable and thought-provoking insight into bronze age living.

At Kenmore, at the eastern end of Loch Tay.

See also...

Brechin Cathedral round tower

Historic Scotland and church authorities; free; limited hours. In Brechin town centre.

The other of the region's ancient monastic round towers (*see Abernethy Round Tower, page 155*), this one is less readily accessible (it's often closed) and is not in quite such original condition (it has a large cathedral attached to it). The interior of the church is pretty interesting, though.

Dunkeld Cathedral

Historic Scotland and church authorities; free; usual hours. In Dunkeld, off the A9 north of Perth.

Dunkeld is a beautifully preserved historic town, with a small visitor centre run by the National Trust of Scotland to introduce you to the story of the town's restored buildings.

The choir of the old cathedral is still in use as the parish church, but the nave and tall bell-tower are attractively semi-ruinous. There are interesting traces of medieval paintwork in the ground-floor room of the tower. The best thing about the place, though, is the setting, with a smooth lawn running down to the wide, fast-flowing River Tay.

St Serf's church, Dunning

Historic Scotland and church authorities; free; limited hours (weekends only). In the village of Dunning, south of Perth.

The simple Romanesque architecture of this ancient parish church is very pleasing, and the tall, thin, square church tower is unusual. Worth seeing.

Scone Palace

Privately owned, £££, usual hours (April to October); signposted off the A93 just north of Perth.

This grand house of the early 1600s, the family seat of the Earls of Mansfield, was given a major facelift in the 1800s to make it look a little more castle-like. The interiors are extremely rich, dripping with fine furniture and ornaments, but are a little too carefully arranged, as if they are the work of a crack team of professional interior decorators, making the place feel more like a splendid hotel than a home.

The grounds are pleasant, with a good maze and a Douglas fir grown from a seed sent from America in 1826 by the man who discovered the tree.

Perhaps the main historic attraction, however, is the famous Moot Hill, where kings were crowned from Pictish times onward, Scottish parliaments met, and the Stone of Destiny stood. It's a low, flat-topped mound with a small, fairly modern chapel in the middle, and frankly it's not very exciting.

Perth

This pleasant city has always been very much at the heart of historic Scotland, and played an important part in several major episodes. The park known as **North Inch** is where the Jacobite forces gathered in preparation for the armed uprisings of 1715 and 1745. On the steps of **St John's Kirk** in the town centre, John Knox roused the Protestants in 1559. **Balhousie Castle** on Hay Street, to the north of the North Inch park, is a grand castle-like house of 1862 which is now home to the regimental museum of the Black Watch (*free, usual hours*).

Dunkeld Cathedral.

Below: Scone Palace.

And...

Alyth Arches, *Alyth, near Blairgowrie* – Monument marking the site of St Molag's church, said to date to before 600 AD.

Drummond Castle Gardens, *off the A822 north of Muthill (privately owned, £££, afternoons only May to October)* – Parts of a tower house of the 1400s were incorporated into the gatehouse of a later mansion and can be seen from the extensive and elaborate formal gardens laid out in the early 1600s.

Dunsinane Hill, *south-east of Collace off the A94* – A steep footpath up the north side of the hill leads to this iron age fort with fine views. It has a huge inner rampart with traces of vitrification (suggesting that the rampart was laced with timber and at some stage was set on fire) and three small outer ramparts.

Innerpeffray Chapel, *signposted off the B8062 south-east of Crieff (Historic Scotland, free, open access during usual hours only)* – Collegiate church of 1508 in pretty good condition.

Muthill Old Church, *Muthill, south of Crieff (Historic Scotland, free, open access at any reasonable time)* – Large ruined church mostly of the 1400s, with a tall Romanesque tower.

Pass of Killiecrankie, *Killiecrankie (National Trust of Scotland visitor centre, £, open usual hours, May to October)* – Site of a Jacobite battle, but also a famous beauty spot.

St Mary's church, *Grandtully, near Aberfeldy (Historic Scotland, free, open access at any reasonable time)* – Church of 1500s with excellent painted ceiling from the 1630s.

Tullibardine Chapel, *signposted off the A823 north of Gleneagles (Historic Scotland, free, open access at any reasonable time)* – One of the least-altered small medieval churches in Scotland, dating from 1446 and said to be very pleasing.

Wade's bridge, *Aberfeldy* – One of the most attractive stone-built bridges on General Wade's military road, designed in 1733 by Robert Adam.

A series of ditches defends the eastern side of Ardoch Roman fort, with a causeway crossing to the gate.

The Romans in Tayside

At the northern limits of the Roman Empire

In 83 AD, not much more than 30 years after their invasion forces first landed on the south coast of England, the Romans won a huge battle in northern Scotland at a place they called *Mons Graupius*.

The site of this battle has long been thought, purely on the similarity of the names, to have been somewhere in the Grampian mountains. In recent years, by identifying the scant traces of marching camps, archeologists have managed to track the progress of a Roman army up the east coast through Aberdeenshire, and it is now thought that the battle took place somewhere near the Moray Firth.

The architect of the victory was the then Governor of Britain, Julius Agricola, who had been campaigning in Scotland since 79 AD. He had already built two major supply routes up the east and west sides of southern Scotland to reach the estuaries of the Clyde and Forth rivers:

later, the narrow stretch of land between these two firths would be crossed by the Antonine Wall and held as the northern frontier of the Roman empire.

The territory further north which Agricola had conquered was held by the Romans for a while after 83 AD, but the withdrawal of troops to deal with problems on the Danube frontier stopped any chance of further advances and soon led to a withdrawal to the Forth-Clyde line. In 98 AD, following some kind of military disaster in Britain, the troops were pulled back even further, to the frontier which by 128 AD was firmly defined by the construction of Hadrian's Wall.

After Hadrian's death, his successor, Antoninus Pius, decided to push the frontier back up to the Forth-Clyde line, and his new wall was finished by 143 AD. Forts to the north of this wall played an important role in keeping the natives quiet.

Ardoch Roman fort

On private farmland • Free • Open access at any reasonable time

Even though only the earthen ramparts remain, this is one of the most impressive Roman forts you are likely to see. The area enclosed by the ramparts is the classic 'playing card' layout, and there is a raised area of ground right in the middle that presumably indicates the usual buildings (the headquarters building, commander's house and so on) which would have been built from timber on stone foundations.

The southern and eastern sides have the natural defence of the slope to protect them and are guarded only by the outer rampart, but the western and northern sides are strengthened by an impressive series of ditches with causeways crossing to the gates of the camp.

The fort is believed to date to roughly 150 AD and to be a northerly outpost of the Antonine Wall.

Off the A9 north of Dunblane, beside the A822 just north of the village of Braco. Either park in the village and walk up to the fort, or park in the large layby on the opposite side of the road beyond the fort, and walk down to it.

Gask Ridge watch-towers

From the camp at Ardoch, an important military road led north and west, across the River Earn and along this ridge to a point on the River Tay just north of Perth. It was probably a vital route for bringing in supplies from the sea, and it was guarded by a series of watch-towers.

Traces survive of many of these watch-towers, and three of them are in the care of Historic Scotland (though only the two detailed below can easily be visited: access to the third, which lies in between, is only possible with permission from the manager of the estate on which it stands).

Confusingly, the towers are sometimes referred to as 'signal stations', which they were not: if this were their function, they wouldn't need to be so close together. Essentially, they were just small, timber-framed towers with projecting balconies from which sentries could get a view over the surrounding country. Each one was surrounded by a wall of turf and a ditch.

A slight hump in the ground is the only visible trace of the Ardunie watch-tower. It's not a thrilling sight.

Ardunie Roman watch-tower

Historic Scotland • Free • Open access at any reasonable time

Unfortunately, there's practically nothing to see. The only visible remains are traces of a roughly circular ditch, with a raised area of ground inside where the tower would have stood, and a faint raised area around where spoil from the ditch would have been thrown up into a bank. The site has not even been excavated.

Take the minor road from the A9 west of Perth towards Kinkell Bridge; turn right (to the north)
through Trinity Gask; where the road bends 90 degrees to the right to follow the Roman road, look for the signposted track on the left. Ardunie watch-tower is about 20 minutes' walk straight along the track. Park carefully on the roadside.

Muir o'Fauld Roman watch-tower

Historic Scotland • Free • Open access at any reasonable time

As far as visible remains are concerned, there is no great difference between this and the Ardunie site, but there are certain differences in the setting: it stands in a clearing in the forest, reached by a well-surfaced forest track, so it's a bit easier to reach, though once you're here the site is rather boggy. Again, there is nothing to see but a shallow ditch around a raised area of hummocky, tummocky ground.

Ease of access suggests that this might be the better one to visit, but the longer walk to the Ardunie site makes it seem more rewarding and the views across open country on the way are more interesting than anything you'll see in the woods here.

From Trinity Gask, take the Perth-to-Kinkell Bridge road towards Perth; after about a mile, the road bends sharp left and then sharp right, at which point the track to the watch-tower leaves to the left. Park carefully on the roadside.

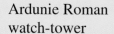 *See also…*

Blackhall camps

Near Braco, just to the north of the Roman fort at Ardoch (opposite).

In the fields to the north and north-east of the fort there are traces of six temporary marching camps, the outlines of which overlap each other and the fort. Some of them may be earlier than the fort and date to the period after Agricola's campaign and before the withdrawals of 98 AD.

Left: the Muir o'Fauld tower, standing in a boggy clearing in the forest, is no more exciting.

Orkney

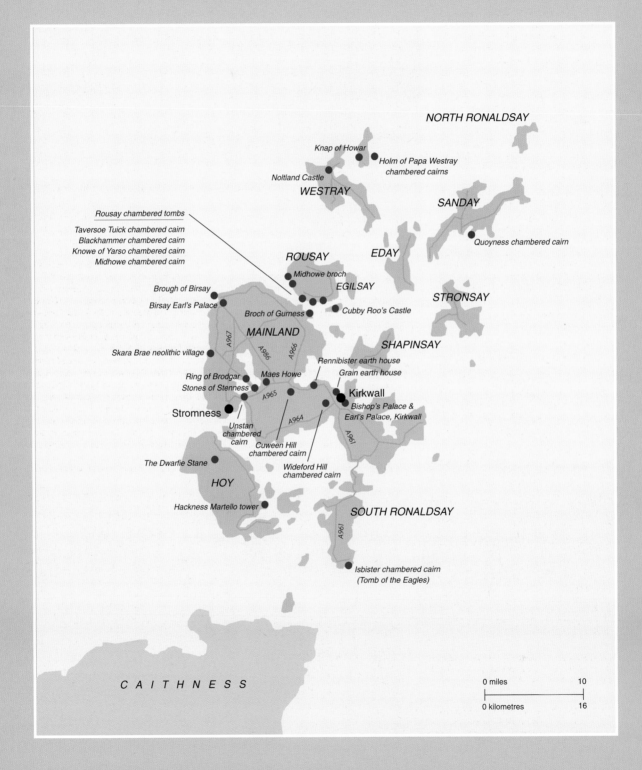

NORTH RONALDSAY

Knap of Howar

Holm of Papa Westray
chambered cairns

Noltland Castle

WESTRAY

SANDAY

Quoyness chambered cairn

Rousay chambered tombs

Taversoe Tuick chambered cairn
Blackhammer chambered cairn
Knowe of Yarso chambered cairn
Midhowe chambered cairn

ROUSAY

EDAY

Midhowe broch

EGILSAY

STRONSAY

Brough of Birsay

Birsay Earl's Palace

Broch of Gurness

Cubby Roo's Castle

A967

MAINLAND

SHAPINSAY

A986

A966

Skara Brae neolithic village

Rennibister earth house

Grain earth house

Ring of Brodgar

Maes Howe

Stones of Stenness

A965

Kirkwall

Stromness

Bishop's Palace &
Earl's Palace, Kirkwall

Unstan
chambered
cairn

A964

A961

Cuween Hill
chambered cairn

The Dwarfie Stane

Wideford Hill
chambered cairn

HOY

Hackness Martello tower

SOUTH RONALDSAY

A961

Isbister chambered cairn
(Tomb of the Eagles)

CAITHNESS

0 miles   10

0 kilometres   16

Birsay Earl's Palace

Historic Scotland • Free • Open access at any reasonable time

This castle-like ruin was actually a grand and sumptuously decorated house built in 1574 by Robert Stewart, Earl of Orkney, to a fashionable design of four ranges around a courtyard. Each range had two storeys: the working rooms on the ground floor had tiny windows, but the important rooms on the first floor – the hall, the lord's chamber and a trendy long gallery in the west range – were lit by big gable windows projecting from a steeply pitched roof.

From outside the walls, you can get a fair idea of how the house looked; but in truth the ruin is fragmentary and there's not all that much to see.

Birsay was home to the rulers of Orkney from Pictish times right into the Norse era. The *Orkneyinga Saga* says that a certain Earl Thorfinn had his main residence here, and in about 1050 he 'built and dedicated to Christ a fine minster, the seat of the first bishop of Orkney'; but Kirkwall's rise to prominence was inevitable once work began on the new cathedral in 1137.

Signposted on the A966 at Birsay village, at the north-western tip of Mainland.

The Earl's Palace at Birsay, described in 1633 as 'sumptuous and stately', fell out of use in the late 1600s.

Bishop's Palace & Earl's Palace, Kirkwall

Historic Scotland • ££ • usual hours

The Orkney capital is a friendly, attractive little town with a healthy quantity of historic buildings, and just next door to the superb Norse cathedral of St Magnus you'll find these two ruinous residences (both covered by one admission ticket).

The larger and more splendid of the two is the Earl's Palace, built in about 1600 by the tyrannical Earl Patrick Stewart and said to be the finest example in Scotland of a Renaissance building. Indeed its vast windows suggest airy, elegant rooms and extravagant decoration. It's rather an enjoyable building to explore: interesting details include those fine oriel windows lighting the Earl's private apartments, and a particularly appealing well by the door.

The palace seems fairly complete as an L-plan building, if a little small, but it is thought that it might have incorporated the buildings of the Bishop's Palace into a courtyard design not unlike *Birsay* (above).

The Bishop's Palace, over the road, is less exciting to look at, being little more than a shell. It's worth noting the different construction methods in the lower courses: these foundations are thought to be from the original bishop's hall, built when the cathedral was started in the mid-1100s and so the oldest secular building in Kirkwall.

That original palace was in disrepair by the 1300s but was rebuilt by Bishop Reid in about 1550, when the superb Round Tower was added. It's round on the outside, but the rooms are square. A spiral stair takes you to the top, from where there are great views of Kirkwall and the cathedral.

In the centre of Kirkwall, next to the cathedral.

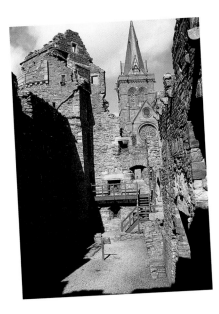

Above: the interior of the Bishop's Palace in Kirkwall isn't much to look at, but there are superb views of the cathedral from the top of the Round Tower.

Right: the neighbouring Earl's Palace, built by the tyrannical Earl Patrick Stewart, is said to be the most graceful Renaissance building in Scotland.

169

Broch of Gurness

Historic Scotland • ££ • Usual hours

In a fantastic coastal setting, with fine views over to Rousay and a sandy bay a short walk away, this is a very classy broch indeed. What makes it special is not so much the broch tower itself, but rather the defended village of six houses that clings to it for protection, the whole thing encircled by a triple rampart. It's a bit of a jumble, but you can make out six houses, each consisting of one main room and one

Above: at the Broch of Gurness, the buildings that surround it are as interesting as the tower itself.

store or shed, with an open yard outside. The approach to the broch up a walled 'street' is impressive: inside the tower, the scattered remnants of stone fixtures hint at a sophisticated interior design.

A later Pictish 'clover leaf' house was removed during excavations and has been reconstructed near the ticket office.

Signposted from the A966 by the school at Evie.

Brough of Birsay

Historic Scotland • ££ • Open all year round: hours vary with tide

This tidal island can only be reached on foot in the two hours each side of low tide. Times when it's safe to cross are broadcast every morning on Orkney Radio or can be obtained from the tourist offices in Kirkwall or Stromness, or by phoning a number shown on a sign by the car park at the Point of Buckquoy (which, by the way, is a great place for rock pools).

On the sheltered landward side of the island are the remains of a Norse village built on the ruins of earlier Pictish houses. Apart from the ruined church, which dates from the early 1100s, there is not much more to see than the outlines of buildings, but Norse settlements are rare in Britain, so it's certainly worth a look. In particular, the remains of the earlier Norse houses higher up the slope give a good idea of what these long, hall-like houses were like. Items of Norse date to look out for include the paved entranceway, the smithy, and a possible sauna; and don't overlook the small Pictish well covered by a stone slab.

Signposted a short way north of Birsay village.

Left: The Brough of Birsay is a tidal island with excellent rock pools and traces of a Norse village.

Cuween Hill chambered cairn

Historic Scotland • Free • Open access at any reasonable time

It's places like this, as much as grand sites like *Maes Howe* and *Skara Brae (overleaf)*, that make Orkney special. What appears to be just a hole in the ground is actually the entrance passage (a longish crawl or shuffle, but well worth it) to a *Maes Howe* type of tomb: not especially large, but easily high enough to stand up in, and very finely built from flat stone slabs.

Four cells open off the main chamber, one of them with a second compartment. Excavations in the 1800s found bones of eight people, along with 24 dog skulls, which suggests that the dog might have been a totem for the people who built and used the tomb, just as the sea eagle probably was at *Isbister (this page)*.

Incidentally, with typical Orkney generosity, a torch is provided at the site, so you shouldn't need to bring one.

Signposted off the A965 just west of Finstown: follow the farm track up to the car park.

Cuween Hill: looks like just a hole in the ground, but it's actually one of Orkney's finest chambered tombs.

It's not much to look at from the surface, but when you go underground, Grain earth house is excellent.

Grain earth house

Historic Scotland • Free • Key and torch from nearby shop during usual hours only

This is a particularly fine example of the smaller, northern variety of 'souterrain', an underground passageway and chamber which would have been hidden under an iron age farmstead and would almost certainly have been used for storing food (*see also 'The earth houses of Angus' on page 154*). It's rather good fun to crawl down the long tunnel, and the chamber supported by stone pillars is a particularly handsome design. Again, a torch is provided for your use. There is a similar souterrain at *Rennibister (page 175)* but it's not quite as entertaining as this one.

Signposted off the A965, in the industrial estate east of Kirkwall: a 15-minute walk from town.

Isbister chambered cairn (Tomb of the Eagles)

On private land • ££, including entrance to 'museum' and a short talk • Usual hours

This clifftop tomb was excavated by the farmer who owns the land, and is now operated as a mildly eccentric tourist attraction by the family. A brief talk in the small site museum offers visitors a chance to handle a neolithic skull. Near the path to the tomb is the only excavated example of a 'burnt mound', where fire-blackened stones covered a bronze age cooking place. The tomb itself, in a spectacular setting with its entrance facing out to sea, is similar to *Unstan (page 175)*. As well as the remains of over 300 people, it also contained the bones of sea eagles.

Signposted on the B9041 in South Ronaldsay.

Above : just off the path up to the tomb at Isbister is Liddle Burnt Mound, where a pile of shattered, fire-blackened stones were used in the bronze age to boil a tank of water for cooking. The building is either a dwelling or a communal cook-house and was excavated in the 1980s.

Below: the entrance to Isbister chambered cairn is on the far side of this low mound, facing the sea.

Maes Howe

Historic Scotland • ££ • Usual hours

If you had to pick out the finest ancient monument in Britain, this would probably be the one. A large mound in a field – which in fact is what 'Maes Howe' means – covers a beautifully built chambered tomb of the neolithic era.

The stonework inside the tomb is just astonishing, not only because some of the stone slabs used are vast, but also because the structure is so carefully designed and tidily constructed.

Visits are by guided tour only, because this is too important a monument to be left to fend for itself, but that's no bad thing. The guide gives a brief talk, filling in the background detail nicely, and she or he will point out lots of details that you might not notice for yourself. Arrangements are pretty informal: after checking in at the ticket office, which is housed in a interesting old mill, you wander across the field to the tomb and if the door isn't open, you wait a few minutes until the previous party emerges.

The guide will explain several very impressive design features, such as the way the entrance passage slopes gently towards the door to provide drainage, or

A bank and ditch encircle the mound of Maes Howe, the finest neolithic chambered tomb in Britain.

the enormously long stone that makes up most of one wall of this passage. You will also be encouraged to have a go at pushing the enormous blocking stone which acts as a door: vast though it is, the stone swivels easily on a protrusion that acts as a pivot. This 'door' would have been pulled shut from outside using ropes.

The most resonant design feature, though, is the way the entrance passage points towards the midwinter sunset, the direction of which is marked by a standing stone called the Barnhouse Stone. For about 40 days in midwinter, the low evening sun shines right down the passage and strikes the back wall of the chamber. In a bizarre blend of old and new, Historic Scotland now places a 'webcam' video camera so that internet users can watch this happen every day. (Get the web site address by phoning their office in Glasgow.)

This alignment with the midwinter sunset is not especially hard to achieve – all you need to do is be there at the right time and mark it with pegs – but it does show how important midwinter was to neolithic people, just as Christmas is now.

Besides the beautiful stonework of the chamber – with four tall pillars at the

corners and three neatly built cells reached by apertures in the sidewalls – the other extraordinary feature of the interior is a collection of runes scrawled on the stones by Norse visitors in the 1100s. The scratchy inscriptions are mostly just boastful or lewd graffiti, but there are also references to a treasure. These were once thought to be entirely fanciful, since stone age tombs don't contain any treasure beyond pottery and flint; but there is a possibility that the tomb might have been spruced up and used for a Norse burial at some stage in the 800s, and that grave goods from this burial were later robbed.

The tomb must have been empty when the Norsemen carved their runes, but it was filled with earth when archeologists got to it in the 1860s. There was very little left of its contents: a few animal bones and a small piece of human skull were all that was found.

Circumstantial evidence, some of it from an excavation of the ditch and bank encircling the tomb, suggests it was built about 3000 BC and is contemporary with the *Stones of Stenness (opposite)*.

Signposted beside the A965 near Stenness.

Ring of Brodgar & Stones of Stenness

Historic Scotland • Free • Open access at any reasonable time

Both these stone circles are remarkable in different ways, but more remarkable still is their setting. They stand on thin strips of land between two lochs: the freshwater Loch of Harray to the north-east, and the Loch of Stenness, which meets the sea at a narrow gap near *Unstan* (*overleaf*), to the south-west. With flat farmland all around, and the hills of Hoy a misty blue in the distance, it makes for an extraordinary landscape of water and sky.

It is suggested that ideas of duality – sky/earth, fresh water/salt water – might have been particularly important to the people who built the circles.

The Ring of Brodgar is the largest stone circle in Scotland, more than 100m (110 yds) across and originally composed of about 60 tall, thin stones set in a perfect circle. Less than half the stones are still in place, and quite a few are broken: just a few years ago a stone was struck by lightning and smashed to pieces.

It's a friendly monument in spite of its scale, and you'll find it difficult to resist walking all the way round. Along the way, don't forget to look at the impressive rock-cut ditch, 9m (30ft) wide and as

Below: even though many of its stones are missing, the Ring of Brodgar is impressively big and bold.

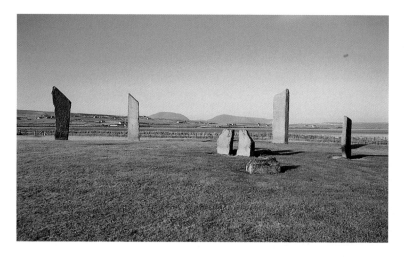

Unusual shapes make the Stones of Stenness very pleasing, but it's the setting that lingers in the memory.

much as 3m (10ft) deep. Look out, too, for a broken stone carved with Norse 'tree runes', which translate as the name Bjorn.

An outlying stone – the Comet Stone – points towards the Stones of Stenness, and there are two other standing stones further on with a fourth – the Watch Stone – nearer to the Stenness circle. It's thought that when the circles were built, you would not have had to cross a stretch of water, as you do now, to go from one to the other.

The Stones of Stenness are charming in their simplicity and always look splendid in a low evening light. Three very tall, thin and interestingly shaped stones still stand from an original circle of twelve, with a henge bank and ditch around. Excavations uncovered a square setting of four stones in the middle of the circle, with traces of stone and timber structures between it and the henge entrance.

A footpath beside the Stenness circle leads to the excavated Barnhouse village, which, like the stones, is thought to date to not long after 3000 BC.

Clearly signposted beside the B9055 off the A965 east of Stromness.

Skara Brae
neolithic village

Inside a 4,500-year-old house at Skara Brae, with beds either side of the hearth and a dresser by the far wall.

Historic Scotland • £££ • Usual hours

Nowhere else can you see neolithic houses some 4,500 years old which still have their furniture in place, and this makes Skara Brae a completely extraordinary site. Just to put it in context (and excuse us for a moment if you're up on your archeology), the neolithic, or new stone age, was the time when people first started settling down and farming the land; so basically this is a village from the first period of history in which people lived in villages.

The reason so much of the furniture inside the houses survives is that it was built of stone. It looks a little crude and Fred Flintstone-ish, but in the absence of any decent source of wood (Orkney's only natural woodland is a scrubby affair of stunted little trees tucked away behind Ward Hill on Hoy) and with so many thin, flat stone slabs lying around, making the furniture from stone would have been the only sensible option.

There was originally an expanse of grassland between the houses and the bay, but the erosion of the coast brought the beach ever closer until eventually sand dunes buried and preserved the houses.

In 1850, the sea finally cut away the dunes and exposed the village again.

The sand preserved not only the houses and furniture, but also a vast range of artefacts including pottery, flint tools, bone tools, beads and pins. Radiocarbon dating showed that the village flourished from about 3100 BC for about 600 years. It was rebuilt several times, and houses from several older phases are still visible: you can tell them apart, though, because they are lower down and cruder.

The final phase was a village of eight houses with dry-stone walls supported by 'midden' – material from the rubbish-piles of the earlier villages, consisting largely of sea-shells – heaped up all round the walls. These are the houses with well-preserved fixtures and fittings: box beds, 'dressers' and cupboards, hearths, and clay-lined tanks which could have been for bait, for fresh seafood or for drinking water.

A covered passage, dug down into the midden, runs between the closely packed houses and gives access to all of them except House 8, which is detached from the rest of the village. House 8 also has a different plan (it's oval in shape) and was found to contain lots of pieces of stone,

many of which had been heated, so it is thought to have been a workshop in which stone tools were made.

The other house that seems different is House 7, which was reached by a long spur off the main passage and apparently had a door that could only be barred from the outside. The doors of the other houses could all be barred from the inside.

Give yourself time to puzzle out some of these details, perhaps with the help of the guidebook, and you should find a visit to the village is a rewarding experience.

Rather less rewarding is the new visitor centre with its café, gift shop and flashy audio-visual exhibition which does very little to help the visitor appreciate the site. A rather better idea is the reconstructed house which now stands just outside the visitor centre. It's surprisingly dark inside, and more spacious than you might expect, but it's also very bare. A more enthusiastic attempt to recreate the sights and smells of the time, perhaps with a fire smouldering in the hearth and fish drying in the eaves, would have added a lot of colour.

Signposted off the B9056 at Skaill, off the A967 north of Stromness.

The souterrain at Rennibister was discovered in the 1920s when a piece of farm machinery fell into it.

Rennibister earth house

Historic Scotland • Free • Open access during usual hours only

This iron age 'souterrain' is very similar to *Grain earth house (page 171)* on the outskirts of Kirkwall, but the passage is smaller and access is by a modern hatch through the roof of the chamber. As at Grain, the storage chamber is tidily built and its roof is held up by stone pillars. There are niches or shelves in the walls.

The souterrain would have been used for food storage by a farmstead above it, and in fact there is still a farm on the site: the chamber was discovered in the 1920s when a heavy threshing machine broke through its roof. The bones of six adults and twelve children were found inside, with no obvious reason for their presence.

Signposted off the A965 roughly halfway between Finstown and Kirkwall.

Unstan chambered cairn

Historic Scotland • Free • Open access during usual hours only

This is an interesting tomb, and it has the advantage that access is relatively easy: it's a short, level walk from the parking place to the tomb, and you don't have to crawl to get in. It stands on a promontory at the mouth of the Loch of Stenness, where fresh water and sea water mix, and it was probably part of the same ceremonial complex as the *Stones of Stenness*.

It's what's known as a 'stalled cairn' (like *Isbister, page171*, and three of the tombs on *Rousay, overleaf*), with pairs of upright slabs dividing the long chamber into five compartments: the end ones originally featured a shelf-like stone slab supported on projecting stones.

Excavations in 1884 found lots of bones and more than 30 pieces of a type of pottery now known as 'Unstan Ware'.

Signposted off the A965 east of Stromness, not far from the Stones of Stenness.

Besides boasting excellent views, Wideford Hill is a good place to see how internal walls held up the cairn.

Wideford Hill chambered cairn

Historic Scotland • Free • Open access at any reasonable time

Great fun to visit, partly because it's on the side of one of Mainland's biggest hills, with fantastic views, and partly because you drop into the main chamber through a modern hatch. Off the sides of the chamber are three cells and a long entrance passage.

An excavation in 1935 investigated the way the cairn was built, and afterwards its internal structure was left exposed, showing the 'revetment' walls that held the cairn up.

Signposted off the A965 just west of Kirkwall. Follow the track up the hill, then park and take the footpath: it's only 10 minutes' walk, but it's a rough path, and steep on the return journey.

See also... Mainland

Click Mill, Dounby

Historic Scotland, ££, usual hours (summer only); signposted beside the B9057 between Dounby and Evie.

A simple type of water mill, with a horizontal paddle-wheel driving the millstones directly, was introduced to Orkney by Norse settlers, and the same basic design remained in use right into the 1900s. This one, built in 1823, is the last surviving example. It has been restored and is working, but the stream that powered it was diverted some time ago, so it has to rely on a small electric motor instead.

Orphir: round church and 'Earl's bu'

Historic Scotland; free, open access at any reasonable time; signposted on a minor road through Gyre, off the A964 east of Houton.

In the early 1100s, Orphir was the home of Earl Haakon Paulsson, who made a pilgrimage to Jerusalem and brought back the idea of building a round church. Remarkably, his church survived intact until 1757 when it was ripped down so that its stone could be used to build a new church. All that now remains is the little half-round apse and a circle of foundations, standing in a tidily kept burial ground.

Nearby are the excavated foundations of a building which is thought to be the Earl's hall or 'bu'. The satisfying thing about this is that it's a link with the recorded past, because the buildings are described in *Orkneyinga Saga*: 'There was a great drinking-hall at Orphir, with a door in the south wall near the eastern gable, and in front of the hall, just a few paces down from it, stood a fine church'.

Left: inside the long chamber at Unstan, you can see how pairs of tall stones divided it into 'stalls'.

Knowe of Yarso tomb stands on a hillside terrace, with views over the Rousay coast and Eynhallow.

Rousay

This is one of the easiest of Orkney's outer islands to get to: the ferries run throughout the day from Tingwall on Mainland, and the trip takes less than half an hour. Rousay is a pleasant and scenic little island, just seven miles long, with heather-covered hills ringed by a fertile coastal strip which has been farmed since neolithic times.

Slightly more to the point, though, the island boasts four rather good chambered cairns and a particularly impressive broch, all strung out along a five-mile stretch of coast.

With a hired bicycle (from the craft shop at the port) you could complete the circuit of the island's main road in a day. There's a café near the port and an inn a couple of miles down the road toward Midhowe (but if you hope to get lunch here it would be wise to phone and check that they are serving).

The Rousay ferry also serves the tiny islands of **Wyre**, where there are the foundations of a strong tower of Norse date (*see Cubby Roo's Castle, overleaf*), and **Egilsay**, which boasts the impressively intact ruin of the round-towered church of St Magnus.

Rousay's chambered tombs

All Historic Scotland • Free • Open access at any reasonable time

Awaiting you on Rousay are four splendid neolithic tombs. One is an unusual variation on the 'Maes Howe' type, while the other three are 'stalled cairns'; the last of these, at Midhowe, is the finest of its kind.

The first three are spaced out along a two-mile stretch starting just five minutes' walk from the ferry landing, so it's not too much trouble to visit these three on foot (and the last of them is right by the pub). You can make a good day of it by walking all the way to Midhowe and back, but the bit in the middle is a rather dull slog along the road. The last leg is much more fun,

hugging the shoreline on a footpath called the Westness Walk, with a detailed leaflet (available free of charge all over the place, including on the ferry) explaining a variety of barely discernible ruined buildings.

Finally, one intriguing aspect of the neolithic tombs on Rousay is that they have inspired a remarkable theory about what the tombs meant to the communities that built them. An eminent archeologist realised that each tomb was in a prominent position overlooking a particular slice of good farmland, and that in each instance, these possible farming territories of the neolithic era were almost identical to an actual farm or croft of the 1800s.

The suggestion, then, is that each tomb would have belonged to a small farming community, possibly an extended family. It is probable that neighbouring groups came together to cooperate on the construction of new tombs.

Please note that the monuments on this page are described in the order in which you come across them as you proceed from the ferry to Midhowe, rather than in the usual alphabetical order.

Left: this trapdoor leads from the upper chamber of Taversoe Tuick to the lower one.

Taversoe Tuick chambered cairn

Set on a small knoll uphill from the road, this is an interesting double-decker tomb in which the roof of a lower chamber has been used as the floor for an upper one.

The modern entrance follows the original passage to the upper tomb. The lower tomb has its own passage, which comes in from the opposite side of the mound, but it's too low and narrow to be used; instead, there's a hole in the floor of the top tomb with a ladder to the lower one. Originally, there was no direct access from one tomb to the other.

Don't miss the unique 'miniature tomb' under a hatch on the seaward side of the mound below the lower entrance passage.

Blackhammer chambered cairn

The first of two quite similar stalled cairns, this was originally entered by a passage from the side, but you now come in through a hatch in a modern concrete roof. Inside, it's similar to *Unstan* and *Isbister* tombs on Mainland, but not in as good condition. It's quite attractive, though. The exterior wall has very neat decorative stonework.

Knowe of Yarso chambered cairn

Very like Blackhammer, except that the entrance is at one end, and it was much better preserved when the archeologists got to it. Lots of human bones were found, and all the skulls were arranged round the

walls of the inner chamber, facing in. There was also an unusually large quantity of red deer bones.

Midhowe chambered cairn

It's the sheer size of this impressive tomb – the monumental scale – that makes it memorable, though the fact that it is indoors also lends it a museum-like gravity.

The chamber is 23m (75ft) long, divided by pairs of slabs into eleven compartments. The walls stand as much as 2.5m (8ft) high, with decorative herringbone stonework on the outside. Excavations uncovered heaps of bone and also complete skeletons: all of the burials were on the eastern side and none were in the first four compartments, which may have had a different ritual function.

Top: the biggest, finest stalled cairn of all, Midhowe was covered by a shed after excavation in the 1930s.

Above: inside Blackhammer chambered cairn, large slabs separating the stall compartments.

Left: the entrance passage to the lower chamber of the double-decker tomb of Taversoe Tuick.

Below: the long mound of Blackhammer cairn stands in a similar setting to Knowe of Yarso.

Midhowe broch

Historic Scotland • Free • Open access at any reasonable time

What's particularly good about this fine broch ruin is the quantity of fixtures and fittings that have survived in the interior. Vast and surprisingly thin slabs of stone have been used, like iron age fibreboard, to partition the ground floor of the broch into two rooms, each with its own hearth, and to create built-in cupboards and cells.

There's no guarantee that all this is the original interior layout of the broch – it might be second-rate revamping by people who occupied the broch after it had started falling apart – but it's certainly interesting. And while you're exploring, note the ledge that supported a wooden upper floor.

Even discounting the interior, the broch is an impressive one. The unusually tall doorway has a particularly fine lintel, and there's a very good guard chamber. It is also surrounded by several interesting buildings, including a small workshop with a hearth used for iron-smelting.

The broch's setting on the rocky shore, just a few metres away from *Midhowe cairn* (*previous page*), is well protected by two deep inlets – known locally as geos – which cut into the rock on either side.

At Midhowe, Rousay; about 5 miles (8km) north of the ferry port.

Right: the foundations of a square tower are pretty much all that's left of Cubby Roo's Castle on Wyre.

Cubby Roo's Castle, Wyre

Historic Scotland • Free • Open access at any reasonable time (depending on ferries)

The tiny island of Wyre, just big enough for three farms, is only a five-minute ferry ride from Rousay. Get the timing right and you can spend about 50 minutes here while the ferry trundles off to Egilsay, which is just enough time to trot up to the castle and have a quick look round.

It's not the most spectacular of ruins, but it is one of the oldest stone-built castles in Scotland, and it's a rare example of a Norse castle. Set on the highest point of the island with clear views in all directions, it was built in the early 1100s by a man named Kolbein Hruga, and is described in

The fabulous broch of Midhowe is remarkable for its interior fixtures as well as its coastal setting.

the *Orkneyinga Saga* as 'a fine stone fort… a really solid stronghold'.

The original castle was a small, square stone tower of which only the basement level survives, with what looks like a water-tank in the floor. Around the tower are the foundations of a jumble of later buildings, and an enclosing wall and ditch are visible where the later buildings haven't covered them over.

Nearby is the ruin, restored but roofless, of a simple chapel of the 1100s which belonged to the owners of the castle.

On the island of Wyre.

Hoy

The Dwarfie Stane

Historic Scotland • Free • Open access at any reasonable time

A big rock with a chambered tomb cut into it, this is a pretty extraordinary one-off. It's also surprisingly pleasing and rather beautifully made. On each side of the chamber is a cell with a carefully carved lip or sill along the bottom of the opening. You can see the grooves made by the pick.

Tombs cut in solid rock are common in southern Europe, but it is unlikely that the inspiration for this one came from so far afield. It might be the work of a single neolithic eccentric.

It's bleak country here at the high end of Hoy; but for a good day's walking, go via Rackwick Bay to the Old Man of Hoy, returning to the Stromness ferry by the path on the other side of Ward Hill.

Signposted beside the minor road to Rackwick, at the northern end of Hoy.

Above: the unique Dwarfie Stane stands in the bleak mountain landscape of northern Hoy.

Westray

Noltland Castle

Historic Scotland • Free • Key from house opposite during usual hours only

It's always fun to take a large iron key and let yourself in through the heavy oak door of a castle like this one. The ground floor is dark and gloomy, with particularly cavern-like kitchens, but when you go up the grand spiral staircase to the great hall on the first floor, the total lack of a roof makes it a lot more airy. Beyond the hall are the laird's private apartments, with more rooms in the adjoining tower.

Dating from the 1560s, the castle has a formidable aspect to it, in keeping with the man who built it – a schemer named Gilbert Balfour who had a hand in all the major plots of the time, including the murder of Lord Darnley. Strangely, work on the castle was never actually finished, even though it was lived in for about 200 years.

A short walk along the road to Noup Head from the Pierowall, in the north of Westray.

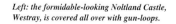 *See also… Hoy*

Hackness Martello tower

Historic Scotland; free, open access at any reasonable time; at Longhope Head, south of the ferry port at Lyness.

The Martello tower, mainstay of Britain's coastal defences in the period just after the Napoleonic wars, was simply a small, thick-walled artillery tower with a big gun on top. The inspiration for it came after a British fleet invading Corsica was stopped in its tracks by a single old, but solid, stone tower armed with a couple of small cannons.

A pair of Martellos was built at the south-eastern end of Hoy between 1813 and 1815 to help defend the harbours against US ships. One has been restored and can be visited, with access to the living quarters on the first floor and to the gun platform on the roof.

See also…Westray

Pierowall church

Historic Scotland; free, open access at any reasonable time; at the north end of Pierowall.

This roofless, ruined church dates mostly from the late 1600s. The main point of interest is not the fabric of the building itself but two tombs, covered with intricate carving, which are set on the wall inside.

Crosskirk church, Westside

Historic Scotland; free, open access at any reasonable time; Westside, near Tuquoy.

A simple chapel of the 1100s in Romanesque style, roofless but otherwise complete.

Left: the formidable-looking Noltland Castle, Westray, is covered all over with gun-loops.

See also…
The other islands

Papa Westray

Also known simply as Papay, Papa Westray is a small island to the east of Westray which can be reached by ferry from the port of Pierowall at the northern end of Westray, or by air from Kirkwall.

Knap of Howar

Historic Scotland • Free • Open access at any reasonable time

These two neolithic houses from around 3500 BC are the oldest known dwellings in north-west Europe. They now stand right on the coast, their doors facing out to sea, but when they were built there was a stretch of grassland between them and the shore. As the coastline was eroded, the houses were buried by sand, which preserved the walls to roof level.

The larger house is divided by a row of stone slabs, separating off a back room which contains a simple hearth and a quernstone for grinding grain. Traces of a wooden bench were found here, too.

A passage leads directly from the larger house to the smaller one, which was split into three rooms: the middle room had a proper stone-built hearth, while the inner room was furnished with stone-built cupboards and shelves.

Below: neolithic houses at Knap of Howar.

Holm of Papa Westray chambered cairns

Historic Scotland • Free • Open access whenever you get the chance

This tiny little island off the east coast of Papa Westray was once a peninsula, but can now only be reached with the help of a boat hired from Papa Westray's community cooperative. At the north end of the island is a ruined stalled cairn, its passage and chamber open to the sky, while to the south there's a massive and extremely interesting tomb of Maes Howe type which consists of a very long passage (20m, or 24 yds, in length) with no less than twelve cells opening off it.

Sanday

Quoyness chambered cairn

Historic Scotland • Free • Open access at any reasonable time

Like the last mentioned, this is another large and extraordinary chambered tomb of Maes Howe type, but this time the headland on which it stands can still be reached on foot. Particularly splendid is the restored entrance, but only the inner 3.5m (11ft) of the especially low entrance passage (it's only about 60cm, or 2ft, high) is still roofed over. Inside, the chamber still stands to its full height of 4m (13ft); only the roof is modern rebuilding.

On the Els Ness peninsula, Sanday; rather too far for a comfortable walk from the ferry port.

And…

North Ronaldsay

Burrian broch, *at the southern end of the island, near the pier* – A decent broch which has been partly incorporated into the stone wall known as the sheep dyke, which runs all round the island. Also of interest on the island are the two large earthworks that divide it into three parts, which are pretty much undateable.

Shapinsay

Burroughston broch, *at the north-eastern tip of the island* – A rather good broch, surviving up to first-floor level and partially restored. Its features include a guard cell at the entrance and a well 3m (10ft) deep. Worthwhile.

Eday

Vinquoy chambered barrow, *on Vinquoy Hill at the north of the island* – Another major chambered tomb of Maes Howe type, with a main chamber and four side-cells. It has been restored, so it's a good one to visit, and there are excellent views from the site.

Calf of Eday chambered barrow, *Calf of Eday (boat trips available from Calfsound)* – Not as much fun to visit because it's ruinous, with its chambers exposed, this long cairn incorporates two stalled tombs of different date: the earlier one is smaller, with just two compartments, while the later one has four.

Eynhallow, off Rousay

Eynhallow church, *on the island of Eynhallow, off the coast of Rousay (Historic Scotland; there are no formal visiting arrangements)* – In the 1800s, only the island's name (it derives from the Norse meaning 'Holy Isle') suggested that there had ever been an early Christian community here: all the buildings had been used as houses since the 1500s, and their true identity was only uncovered in 1851 when a fever epidemic led to the evacuation of the people who lived in them. The remains are in a patchy state as a result, but they include the church and domestic buildings of a monastery and they date to the 1100s.

Egilsay

St Magnus' Church, *(Historic Scotland; free, open access at any reasonable time)* – One of Orkney's most impressive medieval monuments, this is a very large church of the 1100s, roofless but otherwise complete, built in the Romanesque style with a most unusual round tower. It commemorates Earl Magnus, who was killed on the island.

Opposite page: the Stones of Stenness in the early light of a summer's morning.

Shetland

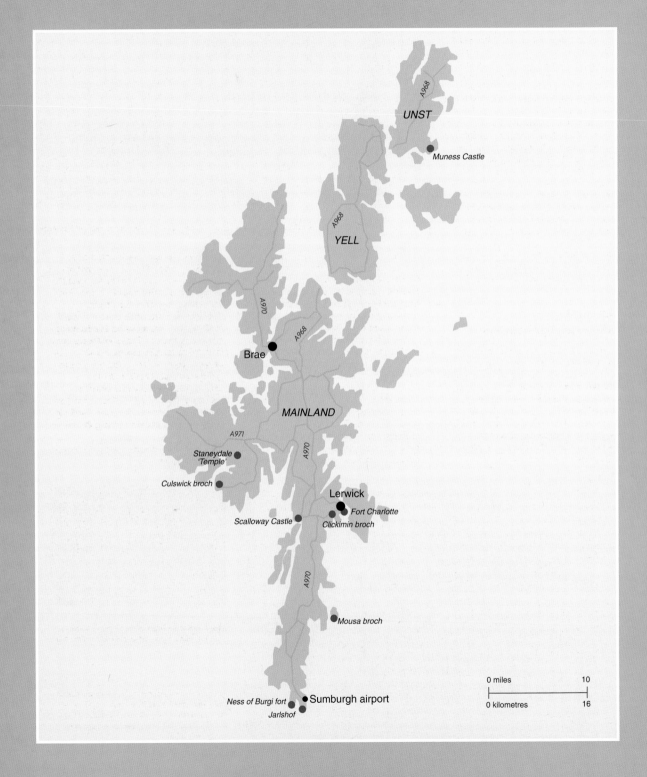

Clickimin broch

Historic Scotland • Free • Open access at any reasonable time

This is a massive and primitive-looking ruin in a slightly peculiar setting on the suburban fringe of Lerwick, Shetland's only town of any size. It stands on what is now a promontory, but was originally an island in a loch reached by a causeway.

The outer wall is actually the rampart of an iron age fort that pre-dates the broch, and what looks like a kind of gatehouse was, in fact, a blockhouse like the one at *Ness of Burgi (overleaf)*. Also visible are the remains of a bronze age farmhouse which was the first building on the site.

The formidable stonework of the broch suggests it was as much a statement of prestige as a defensive structure, and this idea is given weight by an unusual and really quite impractical second entrance high on the lochward wall.

By the A970 Sumburgh road on the southern outskirts of Lerwick; on bus routes, and only 15 minutes' walk from the town centre.

The broch at Clickimin is an unusual mixture of remains, incorporating an earlier iron age fort wall and blockhouse.

Jarlshof

Historic Scotland • ££ • Usual hours

Heaped up on top of each other on this complicated site are remains from lots of different periods, starting with a smithy of the bronze age and ending with a farm of the 1700s. The name, meaning 'the Earl's house' and pronounced as if the initial 'J' were an 'i', was coined by Sir Walter Scott to refer to a ruined mansion of the 1600s which was the only building visible on the site when Scott visited in 1815.

The most unusual structures on the site are the wheelhouses. These strange little round houses date from late in the iron age and were often built inside ruined brochs. They get the name from the series of pillars, like the spokes of a wheel, which held up the roof and partitioned the interior.

Wheelhouses aren't unique to Shetland, but here at Jarlshof is the best place to see them, with two good examples standing among a litter of other structures in the courtyard of an earlier broch. The larger house seems to have been divided in two, but the smaller one beyond is in very good condition, its walls and roof-pillars still standing well over head height. On the inside, it seems as if it would have been rather cramped and gloomy.

Earlier iron age remains on the site include a group of houses with not one but two small souterrains (underground storage tunnels) that you can crawl into: ask at the ticket office for a torch.

The other outstanding feature of the Jarlshof site, from an archeological point of view, is an extensive set of foundations from Norse farm buildings. Norse sites in Britain aren't common – the only one that springs to mind is at *Brough of Birsay, Orkney* – so this is not to be sniffed at, but on the other hand, it's little more than a series of outlines on the ground and not really the most interesting thing to look at.

Signposted off the main road just to the north of Sumburgh airport.

Above: inside the larger of the two wheelhouses at Jarlshof, with a big hearth in the middle of the floor.

Left: towards the front of the picture is the curved outer wall, and beyond it the round roof-hole, of the best-preserved wheelhouse in Britain. It's the most unusual of the many ancient structures on the site at Jarlshof.

Mousa broch

In a fantastic setting on an island teeming with wildlife, the Mousa broch is a unique monument.

*Historic Scotland • Free access to the monument,
£££ for boat trip • Limited hours, summer only*

This unique and extraordinary monument is Scotland's (and therefore the world's) only near-complete example of a broch – a primitive castle of the iron age, dating to around the time of the Roman occupation of Britain. If you do nothing else while in Shetland than make the trip here, you will probably still feel it was worth the trek to this far-flung corner of Britain.

Because the broch stands on the island of Mousa, a visit to the monument is just part of a rewarding half-day out. Boat trips to the island are run from more or less the beginning of May to the end of September; there is only one trip a day, but times vary (morning or afternoon) to fit in with the skipper's hours of work in his proper job. The tourist office in Lerwick can supply a full schedule. There are also evening trips in the summer to see storm petrels: tiny, bat-like seabirds that nest in the broch.

One slight difficulty is that the boat cannot run if the weather is unfavourable; particularly if it's windy. For this reason, it's wise to make the trip as soon as you get a decent opportunity: if you're staying in Shetland for a limited time, there's a danger that the weather may turn bad and you may not get another chance to go.

The locals say that the best time to come to Shetland is in the summer months of June and July. August is prone to fog, while the weather in May and September is rather unpredictable.

Weather allowing, then, the boat takes a party of visitors out to the island, where the captain drops off the passengers and leaves them for a couple of hours. It's an easy walk of not much more than 10 minutes to the broch, and after exploring it you will have ample time to complete a circuit of the island, visiting two sandy bays where seals haul themselves out of the water, and probably getting buzzed by 'bonxies' (great skuas) along the way.

As for the broch... well, it really is pretty special. Inside the high, thick walls, it's surprisingly dark. The most exciting feature of the building, of course, is the stair that runs in the gap between the interior and exterior walls, curving steadily upwards as it travels roughly half way round the broch to emerge on a kind of wall-walk at the top. The stone treads

of the stairs are very narrow and uneven but, taken steadily, it's not a tricky ascent. The idea that the broch still stands to its full height is pretty much confirmed by the fact that the highest part is a kind of covered walkway. This is about 13m (more than 40ft) above the ground.

Back on the ground floor, the most interesting features are three cells with corbelled roofs, each high enough to stand up in, which are reached from the central space by low doors. The original interior features of the broch have been obliterated by the walls, hearth and furniture of a later wheelhouse built inside it.

This broch is mentioned several times in early writings. A story records that an eloping couple sheltered at 'Moseyarborg' ('Bird Island Fort') in 900 AD when their ship was wrecked on the way from Norway to Iceland, and in 1153 a brigand called Erland took refuge here from the pursuing forces of Earl Harald Maddadson, whose mother he had kidnapped.

By ferry from Sand Lodge pier, near Sandwick; most ferry sailings are at times which make it possible to get here by bus from Lerwick.

Muness Castle, Unst

Historic Scotland • Free • Key from nearby house during usual hours only

You might expect Britain's most northerly castle to be a gaunt tower on a clifftop, lashed by sea-spray; but it's actually a domestic little building in a sheltered farmland setting. It's modest in scale, more like a house than a castle; but perhaps it was more impressive when it still stood its original three storeys high. Essentially it's a Z-plan building, with two round towers at diagonally opposite corners of a long central range.

On the ground floor are the usual kitchens and cellars. Tiny windows mean it's dark down here, but with the help of a torch provided by the friendly lady who keeps the key, you should be able to pick out a few interesting details. Upstairs is the main hall, with two private chambers at each end. On the second floor, when it existed, were guest rooms and the lord's bedchamber, the latter reached only by a private stair from the room below.

The comfortable accommodation and some handsome details in the masonry (compare the attractive corbelling under the turrets with that at *Scalloway Castle, overleaf*) suggest that this was quite a classy residence. It was built in about 1598 by Laurence Bruce, a half-brother of Robert, Earl of Orkney and an equally unsavoury character.

Incidentally, the island of Unst is said to be as far north as southern Greenland. To get here from Mainland involves a short ferry crossing to Yell and another to Unst, but ferries are cheap and run regularly.

Clearly signposted on the island of Unst.

Muness, on the island of Unst, is Britain's most northerly castle. Not a lot to come all this way for.

Ness of Burgi fort

Historic Scotland • Free • Open access at any reasonable time

One of Shetland's most unusual ancient monuments, this is a very simple variety of stone-built fortification which is thought to date to the iron age and to be, basically, a kind of poor man's broch, cutting off a rocky promontory to form a crude but effective defended site.

Usually referred to as a 'blockhouse', it's a long, rectangular structure with a doorway in the middle. This doorway leads to an entrance passage that runs right through the building and out the other side. A short way along the entrance passage, you can see door-checks against which the door would have rested, and there's a hole for a drawbar with which the door could have been secured.

Two low doorways, one on each side of the entrance passage, lead to long, narrow chambers, and there's a third chamber at one end of the structure which could only be reached from the outside of the building. But the building was presumably never intended to offer very much in the way of accommodation: it seems likely that its most important role was defensive, as a kind of gatehouse, and some kind of fighting platform on an upper floor would have helped it perform this role.

In front of the blockhouse, you'll notice a rampart, which was originally faced with stone, and a rock-cut ditch. A large, rectangular pile of stones nearby is a stack of rubble cleared from the blockhouse when it was excavated and tidied up.

Even if you are not especially interested in peculiar iron age fortifications, this is an excellent spot for a stroll, with good sea views and plenty of wildlife. You might spot seals on the rocks below. The walk along the headland takes 15 minutes or so and is pretty much level: there is a tricky stretch near the end where the route crosses a rocky ridge, but this has been provided with a kind of chain hand-rail for you to hang on to. It's safe enough.

From the main road near Sumburgh airport, follow the minor road through Scatness to the turning place at the end. Park sensibly, then walk down the farm track along the headland.

Left: the long, low 'blockhouse' at Ness of Burgi is an unusual iron age fort in a dramatic setting.

Scalloway Castle is a fairly modern tower house, with sophisticated details like a 'proper' staircase.

Scalloway Castle

Historic Scotland • Free • Key from nearby shop during usual hours only

This is a very smart, modern castle; one of the last built in Scotland. The Shetland base of Patrick Stewart, the infamous Earl of Orkney and Shetland, it was completed in about 1600, a little before the even more elaborate and sophisticated *Earl's Palace* at Kirkwall in *Orkney*.

Presumably, the villainous earl squeezed a lot of the money out of local landowners to spend on the castle, because it's a handsome building with some rich details in the masonry. On the exterior of the building, for example, look at the neat corbelling under the turrets. Very classy.

Also very grand is the main staircase, which is of the 'scale and platt' variety, composed of straight flights of stairs joined by landings. Far more impressive than an old-fashioned spiral stair.

The ground floor houses the usual ill-lit kitchen (with a very impressive chimney flue) and cellars, and on the first floor is the hall. The end nearest the stair would have been screened off to make a serving area for food brought up from the kitchens.

This is as far as the modern-day visitor can go: from here, spiral stairs would have led to chambers on two more floors. As at *Muness Castle* (previous page), the far end was separated by partition walls so that the chambers there could only be reached by the laird's private staircase.

Thanks largely to trade with Dutch and German fleets, Lerwick quickly grew into Shetland's *de facto* capital, and Scalloway's castle fell out of use by the mid-1700s.

Impossible to miss in the town of Scalloway.

Staneydale 'Temple'

Historic Scotland • Free • Open access at any reasonable time

This unique neolithic building is often still referred to by the speculative title of 'temple' conferred on it by Victorian antiquarians, but in fact nobody has any idea what it was. In serious archeological circles, the description 'neolithic hall' seems to be more in favour these days, and it might have been a meeting-place for the scattered farming communities.

It's certainly quite a large building, which suggests that it may have had some public function. And it had a roof: in the

This neolithic house at Staneydale was oval in shape with a porch protecting the entrance.

middle of the floor are two sockets for big wooden roof-posts, and in one of them fragments of spruce were found, which means the builders must have used a tree-trunk that had drifted all the way across the Atlantic from North America.

The inside of the building is similar to a typical neolithic house, with scooped-out alcoves in the wall. Some of these alcoves had hearths in them. The horseshoe-shaped exterior wall, on the other hand, is very reminiscent of the unique heel-shaped chambered tombs of Shetland. This blend of styles suggests a ritual or ceremonial function for the building. There's also a set of standing stones not far from the entrance to the 'temple', which adds some colour to the theory.

There are quite a few neolithic buildings in the area, and the most interesting one is an oval house which you pass on the way (it's right next to one of the black-and-white-striped waymarking posts). You can see the porch sheltering the entrance and a small 'cell' right at the back of the house. Excavations discovered a hearth in the middle of the room, with alcoves down one side wall and a bench along the other.

Signposted on the minor road to Gruting, off the A971 between Tresta and Walls. Park in the layby and it's a 15-minute walk to the monuments.

Below: the neolithic hall, if that's what it was, at Staneydale was roofed using timbers that had drifted from the other side of the Atlantic.

■ See also…

Culswick broch, with Gruting Voe beyond.

Culswick broch

On farmland, free, open access at any time; as you approach Culswick, take the road on the right that loops around the side of a small valley. A phone box marks the start of a track which sets off past the church and leads eventually to the broch; it's a walk of about half an hour.

The walk to get here isn't actually all that appealing – it's a bit of a trudge along a farm track – but the views along the coast once you arrive are spectacular. The broch is very ruinous but has some fine features, including a door with an impressive lintel.

Fort Charlotte

Historic Scotland, free, open access during usual hours only; signposted by the harbour in Lerwick.

You may wander at will around the large ramparts of this five-sided artillery fort built in 1665 to defend the harbour, but there is no access to any of the buildings. It's interesting, but not vastly so.

St Ninian's Isle

Farmland, free, open access at any reasonable time; signposted from the B9122 at the village of Bigton.

This island, connected to the mainland by a stretch of sand called a tombolo, is one of the most beautiful spots in Shetland. A small chapel of the 1100s is the visible remnant of an important early Christian site, and a major Pictish treasure trove was found here.

The ramparts of Fort Charlotte, Lerwick.

■ And…

Burra Ness broch, *on farmland, reached by a path south from North Sandwick, near Gutcher, on the island of Yell* – Quite a good broch ruin, with walls 4.5m (17ft) thick and a 'scarcement' (ledge to support a floor) visible some 4m (15ft) above the ground.

Gruting school neolithic house, *visible from the road next to the school* – Just over the ridge from *Staneydale (opposite page)*, this is another decent example of an oval neolithic house, with a stone bench along one wall and a small cell at the end opposite the door.

Loch of Houlland broch, *a short walk from the viewpoint by Eshaness lighthouse* – A broch on an island, reached by a causeway. Excellent fun.

Punds Water chambered cairn, *near the farm of Mangaster, off the A970 north-west of Brae* – Mainland's best example of the heel-shaped variety of neolithic cairn which is unique to Shetland, with its roofless passage and chamber clearly visible and with some of its facing walls intact. It's not in the most appealing location, though.

Vementry chambered cairn, *on a small island off Muckle Roe, reached by boat from Vementry farm (boat trips must be arranged in advance)* – This is said to be the finest of Shetland's heel-shaped tombs, with a well-preserved passage and chamber set in a round cairn which, in turn, is surrounded by a heel-shaped platform. The remote location that has kept it safe also makes it a little tricky to visit.

Index of places

Aberdour Castle, Central region 81

Aberlemno sculpted stones, Tayside.....................................161

Abernethy round tower, Tayside...155

Achavanich standing stones, Highland 131

Achnabreck rock carvings, Argyll & Bute 95

Aikwood Tower, Lothian & Borders 46

Alloa Tower, Central region 81

Antonine Wall, Glasgow region 76

Arbroath Abbey, Tayside..153

Ardchattan Priory, Argyll & Bute..112

Ardclach bell tower, Highland 133

Ardestie earth house, Tayside 154

Ardifuir dun, Argyll & Bute 113

Ardoch Roman fort, Tayside...166

Ardunie Roman watch-tower, Tayside 167

Ardvreck Castle, Highland..133

Arran (island of)...104

Auchagallon stone circle, Isle of Arran 105

Auchindoun Castle, Grampian..135

Balgonie Castle, Central region 81

Ballindalloch Castle, Grampian..135

Ballygowan rock carvings, Argyll & Bute 95

Ballymeanoch standing stones, Kilmartin, Argyll & Bute 103

Balmerino Abbey, Central region 83

Baluachraig cup and ring marks, Kilmartin, Argyll & Bute ..103

Balvaird Castle, Tayside 155

Balvenie Castle, Grampian 135

Bannockburn monument, Central region 91

Barcaldine Castle, Argyll & Bute 93

Barpa Langass chambered cairn, North Uist 120

Barra, island of...117

Barsalloch fort, Dumfries & Galloway 69

Bearsden bath-house, Antonine Wall, Glasgow region 77

Beauly Priory, Highland 123

Birsay Earl's Palace, Orkney 169

Bishop's Palace, Kirkwall, Orkney 169

Blackhammer chambered cairn, Rousay, Orkney..................179

Blackhouse (the), Arnol, Lewis 119

Blackness Castle, Central region 82

Blair Castle, Tayside...155

Bonawe ironworks, Argyll & Bute 112

Bothwell Castle, Glasgow region 71

Braemar Castle, Grampian..149

Brandsbutt symbol stone, Grampian.....................................143

Brechin Cathedral round tower, Tayside 165

Broch of Gurness, Orkney 170

Brodick Castle, Isle of Arran 104

Brodie Castle, Grampian...136

Brough of Birsay, Orkney 170

Bibliography

Here are some of the books I have found most useful while visiting Scotland and preparing this book.

• The *Oxford Archaeological Guide to Scotland* by Anna and Graham Ritchie (Oxford University Press, ISBN 0-19-288002-0) is a superb all-round introduction to the ancient monuments of the country, written by two leading experts in a friendly, accessible style, and full of useful information.

• Scotland is fortunate in being covered by a series of regional guides to its historic monuments (covering not just archeology and medieval monuments such as castles and abbeys, but also moving right into the industrial age) published by The Stationery Office (formerly HMSO). Titles in the *Exploring Scotland's Heritage* series that I have found particularly enjoyable are *Orkney* by Anna Ritchie (ISBN 0-11-495288-4), *The Highlands* by Joanna Close-Brooks (ISBN 0-11-495293-0) and *Argyll and the Western Islands* by Graham Ritchie and Mary Harman (ISBN 0-11-495287-6).

• A well-written introduction to castles which is not only entertaining but also very good value is *Castles of England, Scotland and Wales* by Paul Johnson (published by Weidenfeld and Nicholson, ISBN 0-297-83162-3). It has an excellent chapter on Scotland.

• Two good histories of Scotland are the colourful, poetic *The Lion in the North* by John Prebble (ISBN 0-14-003652-0) and the more staid but admirably clear *A History of Scotland* by JD Mackie (ISBN 0-14-013649-5), both of which are published by Penguin.

• Good books from which to start learning about archeology are *Prehistoric Britain* by Timothy Darvill (ISBN 0-7134-5180-7) and *Archaeology of the British Isles* by Andrew Hayes (ISBN 0-7134-7305-3), both published by Batsford. The former is a beginners's introduction; the latter is slightly more intense and is perhaps better suited to students. A very good read is *Before Civilization* by Colin Renfrew (also in Penguin) which explains modern dating methods.

Broughty Castle, Tayside....................................156

Brown Caterthun hillfort, Tayside 157

Burghead well-chapel, Grampian 136

Burleigh Castle, Tayside....................................156

Burrian broch, North Ronaldsay, Orkney 182

Burroughston broch, Shapinsay, Orkney 182

Bute, isle of 111

Caerlaverock Castle, Dumfries & Galloway 61

Cairnbaan rock carvings, Argyll & Bute 95

Cairn Holy chambered cairns, Dumfries & Galloway............62

Cairn o' Get, Highland 131

Cairnpapple Hill, Lothian & Borders.....................45

Caisteal Grugaig broch, Highland........................123

Calf of Eday chambered barrow, Eday, Orkney 182

Callanish standing stones, Lewis 118

Cambuskenneth Abbey, Central region 83

Cardoness Castle, Dumfries & Galloway 63

Carlungie earth house, Tayside...........................154

Carnasserie Castle, Argyll & Bute........................93

Carn Ban chambered tomb, Isle of Arran 105

Carn Liath broch, Highland 123

Carsluith Castle, Dumfries & Galloway 63

Castle Campbell, Central region 84

Castle Fraser, Grampian....................................137

Castle Girnigoe & Sinclair, Highland 125

Castle Kennedy, Dumfries & Galloway 69

Castlelaw hillfort, Lothian & Borders 52

Castle Menzies, Tayside 158

Castle of Park, Dumfries & Galloway 69

Castle of St John, Stranraer, Dumfries & Galloway.............69

Castle Stalker, Argyll & Bute 112

Castle Sween, Argyll & Bute................................94

Cawdor Castle, Highland 125

Chesters hillfort, Lothian & Borders 52

Clach an Trushal, Lewis 119

Clackmannan Tower, Central region 83

Clava cairns, Highland 124

Claypotts Castle, Tayside...................................159

Clickimin broch, Shetland 183

Click Mill, Dounby, Orkney 175

Cnoc Freiceadain long cairns, Highland...............131

Coille na Borgie chambered cairns, Highland 131

Coldingham Priory, Lothian & Borders..................59

Corgarff Castle, Grampian..................................137

Corrimony chambered cairn, Highland..................125

Craigievar Castle, Grampian...............................138

Craigmillar Castle, Lothian & Borders 46

Craignethan Castle, Glasgow region 73

Crathes Castle, Grampian 139

Crichton Castle, Lothian & Borders 47

Croft Moraig stone circle, Tayside 158

Crookston Castle, Glasgow region 78

Crosskirk church, Westside, Westray, Orkney 181

Crossraguel Abbey, Glasgow region 72

Cubby Roo's Castle, Wyre, Orkney 180

Cullerlie stone circle, Grampian 139

Culloden battlefield, Highland 133

Culross Palace and Abbey, Central region 91

Culsh earth house, Grampian..............................140

Culswick broch, Shetland 187

Culzean Castle, Glasgow region 78

Cuween Hill chambered cairn, Orkney..................171

Dean Castle, Kilmarnock, Glasgow region.............78

Deer Abbey, Grampian.......................................149

Delgatie Castle, Grampian..................................139

Dervaig standing stones, island of Mull 109

Dinvin motte, Glasgow region...............................78

Dirleton Castle, Lothian & Borders 48

Doonhill homestead, Lothian & Borders ....

Dounby Click Mill, Orkney 175

Doune Castle, Central region 85

Doune of Invernochty motte, Grampian 149

Dreva Craig hillfort, Lothian & Borders.................59

Druchtag motte, Dumfries & Galloway..................69

Drum Castle, Grampian 140

Drumcoltran Tower, Dumfries & Galloway 64

Drumlanrig Castle, Dumfries & Galloway 69

Drumtroddan cup and ring carvings, Dumfries & Galloway...69

Dryburgh Abbey, Lothian & Borders 48

Duart Castle, island of Mull...............................108

Duffus Castle, Grampian 141

Duffus St Peter's church, Grampian 141

Dumbarton Castle, Glasgow region 74

Dunadd, Argyll & Bute..96

INDEX OF PLACES

Dun Aisgain, island of Mull........................109

Dun an Sticir, North Uist 121

Dun Ardtreck, Skye 115

Dunbar Castle, Lothian & Borders 59

Dun Beag, Skye 116

Dunblane Cathedral, Central region 91

Dun Carloway broch, Lewis 119

Dunchragaig cairn, Kilmartin valley, Argyll & Bute 103

Dundonald Castle, Glasgow region 73

Dun Dornaigil broch, Highland 133

Dundrennan Abbey, Dumfries & Galloway 64

Dunfallandy Stone, Tayside 161

Dunfermline Abbey & Palace, Central region 86

Dunideer hillfort and castle remains, Grampian 149

Dunkeld Cathedral, Tayside.........................165

Dun Mor broch, Tiree 113

Dun Nosebridge fort, Islay 113

Dunnottar Castle, Grampian 142

Dunollie Castle, Argyll & Bute 97

Dun Ringill, Skye......................................116

Dunrobin Castle, Highland 133

Dun Scaich Castle, Skye 117

Dunstaffnage Castle, Argyll & Bute 97

Dun Telve, Highland..................................128

Dun Troddan, Highland 128

Duntulm Castle, Skye 117

Dunure Castle, Glasgow region 78

Dunvegan Castle, Skye 117

Dwarfie Stane, Hoy, Orkney 181

Dyce symbol stones, Grampian 143

Earl's Palace, Kirkwall, Orkney 169

Eassie sculpted stone, Tayside.......................161

Easter Aquhorthies stone circle, Grampian 151

Eday, Orkney 182

Edinburgh Castle, Lothian & Borders 50

Edin's Hall broch, Lothian & Borders 49

Edrom church, Lothian & Borders...................59

Edzell Castle, Tayside.................................159

Egilsay, Orkney..182

Eildon Hill hillfort, Lothian & Borders 52

Eileach an Naoimh, monastery remains............113

Eilean Donan Castle, Highland......................126

Elcho Castle, Tayside..................................160

Elgin Cathedral, Grampian 144

Eynhallow church, Eynhallow (off Rousay), Orkney............182

Falkland Palace, Central region 85

Fast Castle, Lothian & Borders.......................59

Fort Charlotte, Lerwick, Shetland...................187

Fort George, Highland 127

Fortrose Cathedral, Highland........................133

Foulden tithe barn, Lothian & Borders 59

Fowlis Wester sculpted stone, Tayside 161

Fyvie Castle, Grampian 145

Garrol Wood stone circle, Grampian 151

Glamis Castle, Tayside................................163

Glasgow Cathedral, Glasgow region 78

Glebe Cairn, Kilmartin valley, Argyll & Bute..........102

Glenbuchat Castle, Grampian 145

Glenelg (brochs of), Highland 128

Glenluce Abbey, Dumfries & Galloway...............65

Grain earth house, Orkney 171

Greenknowe Tower, Lothian & Borders 59

Grey Cairns of Camster, Highland...................130

Hackness Martello tower, Hoy, Orkney 181

Hailes Castle, Lothian & Borders 53

Harris, island of.......................................118

Hermitage Castle, Lothian & Borders 53

Hillforts of the Border region 52

Hill o' Many Stanes, Highland 131

Hoddom Castle, Dumfries & Galloway................69

Holm of Papa Westray chambered cairns, Orkney.............182

Holyrood Abbey & Palace, Edinburgh 51

Huntingtower, Tayside................................162

Huntly Castle, Grampian 146

Inchcolm Abbey, Lothian & Borders..................59

Inchkenneth chapel, island of Mull..................109

Inchmahome Priory, Central region..................87

Innischonnel Castle, Argyll & Bute..................113

Inverlochy Old Castle, Highland 126

Iona 110

Isbister chambered cairn, Orkney 171

Islay (island of) 113

Jarlshof, Shetland 183

Jedburgh Abbey, Lothian & Borders 54

Keills Chapel, Argyll & Bute................................112

Kelburn Castle, Glasgow region 78

Kellie Castle, Central region 87

Kelso Abbey, Lothian & Borders 54

Kilberry Sculpted stones, Argyll & Bute..................113

Kilchurn Castle, Argyll & Bute 98

Kildalton Cross, Islay...113

Kildonan dun, Argyll & Bute.................................98

Kildrummy Castle, Grampian 147

Kilmartin sculpted stones, Kilmartin, Argyll & Bute 103

Kilmartin valley, Argyll & Bute 100

Kilmichael Glassary rock carvings, Argyll & Bute 95

Kilmodan sculpted stones, Argyll & Bute 113

Kilmory Knap chapel and carved stones, Argyll & Bute 94

Kilpatrick 'dun', Isle of Arran 105

Kingarth St Blane's church, Isle of Bute 111

Kinneil fortlet, Antonine Wall, Glasgow region.............77

Kinneil House, Bo'ness, Central region 91

Kirkwall Earl's & Bishop's Palaces, Orkney 169

Kissimul Castle, Barra 117

Knap of Howar, Papa Westray, Orkney.....................182

Knock Castle, Skye 117

Knowe of Yarso chambered cairn, Rousay, Orkney.............179

Lennoxlove Castle, Lothian & Borders 55

Lewis, island of..118

Liddle Burnt Mound, Orkney 171

Linlithgow Palace, Lothian & Borders 55

Lismore (island of)..113

Loanhead of Daviot stone circle, Grampian 150

Lochbuie stone circle, island of Mull 109

Loch Doon Castle, Glasgow region 75

Lochleven Castle, Tayside 163

Lochmaben Castle, Dumfries & Galloway 65

Lochranza Castle, Isle of Arran 104

Machrie Moor stone circles, Isle of Arran 106

MacLellan's Castle, Dumfries & Galloway...................66

Maes Howe, Orkney 172

Maiden Stone, Grampian 143

Meigle sculpted stones, Tayside 161

Melrose Abbey, Lothian & Borders..........................56

Memsie cairn, Grampian......................................147

Midhowe broch, Rousay, Orkney 180

Midhowe chambered cairn, Rousay, Orkney................180

Mingary Castle, Ardnamurchan, Highland 133

Morton Castle, Dumfries & Galloway 66

Mote of Mark, Dumfries & Galloway 69

Motte of Urr, Dumfries & Galloway 69

Mousa broch, Shetland..184

Muir o'Fauld Roman watch-tower, Tayside 167

Mull (island of) 108

Muness Castle, Unst, Shetland...............................185

Neidpath Castle, Lothian & Borders 57

Ness of Burgi iron age fort, Shetland.......................185

Nether Largie Mid cairn, Kilmartin, Argyll & Bute..............102

Nether Largie North cairn, Kilmartin, Argyll & Bute 102

Nether Largie South cairn, Kilmartin, Argyll & Bute 102

Nether Largie standing stones, Kilmartin, Argyll & Bute 101

Newark Castle, Glasgow region 75

Noltland Castle, Westray, Orkney 181

Norman's Law hillfort, Central region 91

North Ronaldsay, Orkney 182

North Uist, island of...120

Old Keig stone circle, Grampian 151

Old Wick Castle, Highland 129

Orchardton Tower, Dumfries & Galloway 66

Oronsay Priory, island of Oronsay 113

Orphir: round church and 'Earl's bu', Orkney................175

Paisley Abbey, Glasgow region 78

Papa Westray, Orkney 182

Peel Ring of Lumphanan, Grampian 149

Picardy symbol stone, Grampian 143

Pierowall church, Westray, Orkney 181

Pineapple House (the), Central region 91

Poball an Finn stone circle, North Uist......................120

Quoyness chambered cairn, Sanday, Orkney 182

Ravenscraig Castle, Central region....................................88

Recumbent stone circles, Grampian 150

Rennibister earth house, Orkney...175

Repentance Tower, Dumfries & Galloway..........................69

Restenneth Priory, Tayside 164

Ri Cruin cairn, Kilmartin valley, Argyll & Bute 102

Ring of Brodgar, Orkney 173

Rispain Camp, Dumfries & Galloway 69

Rosslyn Chapel, Lothian & Borders 59

Rothesay Castle, Isle of Bute 111

Rough Castle fort, Antonine Wall, Glasgow region 77

Rousay, chambered tombs of, Orkney 179

Rubh' an Dunain chambered cairn, Skye 117

Ruthven barracks, Highland..129

Ruthwell Cross, Dumfries & Galloway 69

Saddell Abbey remains, Argyll & Bute 99

St Andrews Castle and Cathedral, Central region 89

St Blane's church, Kingarth, Isle of Bute 111

St Clement's church, Rodel, Harris 119

St Cormac's Chapel, Eilean Mor, Argyll & Bute 113

St Magnus church, Egilsay, Orkney 182

St Mary's Abbey, Iona...110

St Mary's Chapel, Rothesay, Isle of Bute.............................111

St Ninian's Isle, Shetland..187

St Orland's Stone, Tayside 161

St Peter's church, Duffus, Grampian 141

St Serf's church, Dunning, Tayside 165

St Vigeans sculpted stones, Tayside 161

Sanday, Orkney..182

Scalloway Castle, Shetland...186

Scone Palace, Tayside...165

Scotstarvit Tower, Central region 88

Scottish Crannog Centre, Tayside..164

Shapinsay, Orkney...182

Skara Brae neolithic village, Orkney 174

Skipness Castle, Argyll & Bute 99

Skye, island of...115

Smailholm Tower, Lothian & Borders 57

Souterrains in Angus...154

South Uist, island of..117

Spynie Palace, Grampian 148

Staneydale 'Temple', Shetland 186

Steinacleit, Lewis..119

Stirling Castle, Central region..90

Stirling Old Bridge, Central region..91

Stones of Stenness, Orkney...173

Strome Castle, Highland 129

Sueno's Stone, Grampian...143

Sunhoney stone circle, Grampian 151

Sweetheart Abbey, Dumfries & Galloway 67

Tantallon Castle, Lothian & Borders 58

Tarbert Castle, Argyll & Bute..113

Taversoe Tuick chambered cairn, Rousay, Orkney 179

Tealing earth house, Tayside 154

Teampull na Trionaid, North Uist..121

Temple Wood stone circles, Kilmartin, Argyll & Bute 101

Thirlestane Castle, Lothian & Borders 59

Threave Castle, Dumfries & Galloway...................................68

Tioram Castle, Moidart, Highland..133

Tiree (island of)..113

Tirefour broch, Lismore...113

Tolquhon Castle, Grampian...148

Tomb of the Eagles (Isbister chambered cairn), Orkney 171

Tomnaverie stone circle, Grampian..151

Torhouse stone circle, Dumfries & Galloway 67

Torphichen preceptory, Lothian & Borders...........................59

Torr a'Chaisteal dun, Isle of Arran 105

Torrylin chambered cairn, Isle of Arran 105

Traquair, Lothian & Borders...59

Trimontium (Roman museum), Lothian & Borders 59

Twelve Apostles stone circle, Dumfries & Galloway 69

Unstan chambered cairn, Orkney..175

Urquhart Castle, Highland 132

Vinquoy chambered barrow, Eday, Orkney 182

White Caterthun hillfort, Tayside 157

Whithorn Priory, Dumfries & Galloway 69

Wideford Hill chambered cairn, Orkney 175

Woden Law hillfort, Lothian & Borders.................................52

Yarrows archeological trail, Highland....................................131